FULL BATTLE RATTLE

FULL BATTLE RATTLE

MY STORY AS THE LONGEST-SERVING SPECIAL

FORCES A-TEAM SOLDIER IN AMERICAN HISTORY

CHANGIZ LAHIDJI

AND **RALPH PEZZULLO**

ST. MARTIN'S PRESS   ﹡   NEW YORK

FULL BATTLE RATTLE. Copyright © 2018 by Changiz Lahidji and Ralph Pezzullo. All rights reserved. Printed in the United States of America. For information, address St. Martin's Press, 175 Fifth Avenue, New York, N.Y. 10010.

www.stmartins.com

Designed by Omar Chapa

Library of Congress Cataloging-in-Publication Data

Names: Lahidji, Changiz, 1950– author. | Pezzullo, Ralph, author.
Title: Full battle rattle : my story as the longest-serving special forces
    A-Team soldier in American history / Changiz Lahidji and Ralph Pezzullo.
Other titles: My story as the longest-serving special forces A-Team soldier in
    American history
Description: First edition. | New York : St. Martin's Press, [2018]
Identifiers: LCCN 2017037543| ISBN 9781250121158 (hardcover) |
    ISBN 9781250121165 (ebook)
Subjects: LCSH: Lahidji, Changiz, 1950– | United States. Army. Special
    Forces—Officers—Biography. | United States. Army. Special Forces—
    History. | Special operations (Military science)—United States. | Iranian
    Americans—Biography. | Persian Gulf War, 1991—Personal narratives,
    American. | Afghan War, 2001—Personal narratives, American
Classification: LCC UA34.S64 L35 2018 | DDC 356/.16—dc23
LC record available at https://lccn.loc.gov/2017037543

Our books may be purchased in bulk for promotional, educational, or business use. Please contact your local bookseller or the Macmillan Corporate and Premium Sales Department at 1-800-221-7945, extension 5442, or by email at MacmillanSpecialMarkets@macmillan.com.

First Edition: February 2018

10 9 8 7 6 5 4 3 2 1

"The nation that makes a great distinction between its scholars and its warriors will have its thinking done by cowards and its fighting done by fools."
—Spartan king, quoted by Thucydides

To all the brave individuals who have ever served in the US Special Forces. De oppresso liber! (To free the oppressed)

CONTENTS

FULL
BATTLE
RATTLE

PROLOGUE

Friends, ex-presidents, generals, and other members of the US military know me simply as Changiz. My full name and rank is Master Sergeant Changiz Lahidji, and I have the distinction of having served on Special Forces A-teams longer than anyone in history—twenty-four years in total. The SF A-teams I served on include:

ODA 561	ODA 174	ODA 134	ODA 596	ODA 113
ODA 562	ODA 171	ODA 136	ODA 326	
ODA 564	ODA 176	ODA 595	ODA 324	

I also happen to be the first Muslim Green Beret.

Friends and colleagues tell me I'm some kind of legend in Special Forces because of my unique background, the number of top secret missions I deployed on, and my thirty-six years of service—twenty-four as a Green Beret and twelve as a private contractor, during which time I completed over a hundred combat missions in Afghanistan.

I tend to think that my outgoing personality has a lot to do with my notoriety. One thing that distinguishes me is my love of life and the fact that I never shy away from having a good time! I consider myself a friend to everyone who isn't trying to do me harm, which has happened many times. I've survived bullet wounds, parachute mishaps, helicopter crashes, broken bones, and other calamities too numerous to count.

The photo on the cover is of me on a combat mission in June 2008 near Firebase Wilderness in southeastern Afghanistan. Please note three things: One, the Black Hawk helicopter in the background is on its side, because twenty minutes before this picture was taken our chopper was hit by intense fire from the Taliban and crash-landed. Minutes after that, I kicked the side door open, helped the FBI officer and soldiers who were riding with me and the pilot get out, fired over 300 rounds from my M4 to drive the Taliban back, then radioed for help. Two of my teammates died in the crash.

Two, see the blood dripping down my face? That's real. During the crash, I sustained a deep cut to my forehead, which was later closed up with stitches. I also fractured my right leg and banged up my knee and arm. It took three doctors and four nurses to patch me back together.

Three, you might have also noticed that I'm smiling. Why? Because I was so damn happy to still be alive. The guys on the medevac team that flew us out thought I was crazy, because I laughed and trembled all the way back to base.

It's been my good fortune to serve my adopted country in every war and military engagement since Vietnam, starting with Operation Eagle Claw in 1980, when I entered Tehran on a one-man mission to spy on Iranian soldiers and Revolutionary Guards guarding the US Embassy where fifty-two US diplomats were being held hostage.

Friends have likened me to the military equivalent of Zelig—the Woody Allen character who had a knack for turning up at dramatic moments in history. In 1980, I trained mujahedeen in Pakistan and Afghanistan to fight against the Soviets. Three years later, I was in Beirut, Lebanon, when a suicide car bomb exploded in front of the US Embassy, killing sixty-three people and wounding hundreds. Weeks after that, I was on a night mission with Lebanese Christian militiamen when Hezbollah terrorists ambushed us and I was shot in the leg.

I was part of 5th Group Special Forces that made the initial assault during the invasion of Grenada. In 1991, I was deployed to Kuwait to participate in Operation Desert Storm. At one point during the war, I snuck into Baghdad dressed as a civilian and stayed there for four days collecting important intelligence.

I returned to Iraq twelve years later for Operation Iraqi Freedom, and led a convoy that was ambushed on its way to Fallujah. In 1991, I was assigned to work with the FBI Special Antiterrorism Unit in New York City and went undercover to gather evidence on Omar Abdel-Rahman (the "Blind Sheikh"), who helped plan the first World Trade Center bombing.

I was on the ground clearing houses in Mogadishu, Somalia, on October 3, 1993, when a US Black Hawk helicopter was shot down fifty feet away from me—an incident that inspired the book and film *Black Hawk Down*. In 2002, I dressed as a Pashtun farmer and snuck into a village high in the White Mountains of eastern Afghanistan and located Osama bin Laden for the CIA. In '04, while working in Darfur, Sudan, as a cease-fire monitor, I brokered an agreement with the non-Arab Justice and Equality Movement (JEM) rebels opposing the Sudanese government to stop attacking UN refugee camps.

Those are some of the missions I deployed on. Others took me to Pakistan, Senegal, Cambodia, Laos, Vietnam, the Philippines, Spain, Egypt, Okinawa, and Haiti.

Along the way, I've earned numerous commendations, including the Special Forces Legion of Merit, Purple Hearts, multiple US Army achievement and commendation medals, six Joint Service medals, and awards from the FBI, Department of State, DEA, African Union, NATO, Thailand, Haiti, Kuwait, and Sudan. Last year I was nominated for induction into the Military Intelligence Hall of Fame and cited as "the finest noncommissioned officer to ever serve in Special Forces" and someone who "exemplifies the American Dream."

I love the United States with all my heart, but can't say that making my way here as a twenty-four-old from Iran with Hollywood dreams in his head and very little English was easy. It wasn't.

Hopefully, I've learned a few things from my experience about determination and hard work. And time after time, across the globe, I've seen politics and religion drive people into conflict. I've come to realize that you can be a bad motherfucker when you serve in your unit, but underneath be a thoughtful, kind, fun-loving, and compassionate man. I've had the privilege to serve with dozens of them.

I've also seen firsthand how the greatest military power on the planet is losing the war on terrorism because we don't spend the time to learn local languages and customs. Instead of dropping bombs and making enemies, we should be educating people about our freedoms and way of life. And instead of relying on technology for collecting intelligence, we should be developing reliable local sources.

This is my story—warts, laughs, defeat, triumph, and all. I hope you enjoy it.

1

TEHRAN, 1980

On a cold Sunday afternoon in November 1979 I was walking through the day room at Special Forces 5th Group headquarters at Fort Bragg, North Carolina, when I saw a dozen of my teammates crowded around a TV set. One of them shouted, "Hey, Changiz, you raghead son of a bitch, come look at your brothers!"

"What brothers?" I asked.

On the television I saw footage of Iranian student radicals using ladders to climb over the walls of the US Embassy compound in Tehran. The TV announcer reported that rioters had taken control of the embassy and seized more than sixty American hostages.

Powerful emotions started to course through my body. "First, I'm not a raghead. I'm Persian. And secondly, these are not my fucking brothers!"

"Bullshit," one of my teammates replied.

On TV, a young bearded Iranian spokesman proclaimed

that they wouldn't free the hostages until the US turned over the exiled former Shah, Mohammad Reza Shah Pahlavi, who had fled Iran in July. US president Jimmy Carter had recently granted him permission to come to the United States to treat his advanced malignant lymphoma, thus unleashing a torrent of anti-American hatred from the young supporters of Ayatollah Ruhollah Khomeini.

My blood turned cold. I'd been watching the Iranian Revolution unfold over the last several months with mixed feelings and trepidation. While growing up in Iran, I'd seen the Shah develop into an increasingly unpopular, brutal, and arbitrary dictator. I knew then that his days in power were numbered. But I didn't trust the mullahs who were opposing him, either, and particularly Ayatollah Khomeini, a radical Islamic cleric who had been living in exile in France and had promised a break with the past and greater autonomy for the Iranian people.

I had fled Iran myself at the age of twenty-three to seek a better life in a country that protected individual freedom and kept church and state separate. I also understood why many young Iranians distrusted the United States. The US had been the Shah's closest ally and supporter for years, trading cheap oil for advanced military equipment and fighter jets.

My Special Forces teammates almost certainly didn't understand this complicated history as they started to hurl abuse my way.

"Changiz, those savages are your brothers."

Another said, "They touch a hair on any American's head, we should nuke all of Iran into dust."

"You belong with them, Changiz, not us!"

I responded with the only words I could think of: "Shut the fuck up!"

How could my teammates appreciate the depth and complexity of my feelings as I watched radical Islamic students chant anti-American slogans and burn the American flag? I'd grown up in Iran. My father, uncle, cousins, and two of my brothers still lived there. In fact, our house stood a mere half a mile away from the US Embassy. I'd visited the compound in 1974 to secure a visa that allowed me to travel to the United States. Five years later, I was a proud American citizen and a member of the Green Berets.

"Changiz, go back to Iran. We don't want you here!"

"Shut your mouth!"

"Go home, camel fucker, and be with your own kind!"

"This is my home!"

Before we came to blows, a couple of my friends escorted me out. But over the next several days of what became known as the Iranian Hostage Crisis, I was subjected to almost constant insults and abuse.

Sometimes I got so frustrated and angry I responded with my fists. One evening I got into a fight with four fellow Green Berets around the pool table in the team lounge. Another morning just after PT, five guys jumped me on the first-floor barracks. Having trained for years in self-defense and martial arts, I knew how to defend myself. A couple of my SF buddies came to my aid. The staff sergeant on duty heard the ruckus and broke it up, and reported it to our first sergeant.

The next morning, with two black eyes and a swollen lip, I stood in formation with eighty-four other Green Berets when I heard the first sergeant call my name.

"Corporal Lahidji, front and center!"

I stepped forward, shoulders back. "Yes, sir."

"At ease . . ." the first sergeant started. "Listen guys. . . . This guy's a fucking American, and he's a Green Beret, regardless of where he comes from. He works his ass off, and he's here to protect the American people. So I don't want you to fuck with him anymore. You understand?"

He repeated his statement three times, for which I was enormously grateful. Afterward, a couple SF soldiers who'd jumped me came over and apologized. I let it go, but internally continued to wrestle with the situation at the embassy in Iran. Knowing Tehran like the back of my hand and knowing that I could help free the hostages, I went to see First Sergeant David Huckson, who helped me compose a letter to President Carter.

It said: "Dear President Carter: My name is Sergeant Changiz Lahidji and I am an Iranian native serving in Special Forces at Fort Bragg, North Carolina. Please give me permission to choose an A-Team and deploy to Iran to free the American hostages. I know the area well, and used to play soccer at the stadium across the street from the US Embassy. With your approval and support, I am sure I can come up with a plan that will succeed. Please don't say no."

Two months later, I received a reply on White House stationery that said, "Thank you for your concern. We appreciate that you have volunteered for a rescue mission. Please stand by."

Around midnight on January 5, 1980—three months into the hostage crisis—I was sitting in my room on the third floor of the SF barracks, when I heard someone knock on the door. It was Sergeant Huckson. He said, "Get up, Changiz. Get up and get your shit together. You've got orders to leave immediately. Don't forget to bring your ID."

I threw my gear into a duffel and hurried outside. Two sergeants ordered me to get into a jeep and drove me to nearby Pope Air Force Base. In the bitter cold, I was instructed to line up with about two dozen other SF operators standing on the tarmac.

A captain said, "You're going to be screened, tested, and trained for a special mission. Don't ask any questions."

"Yes, sir!"

A military C-130 flew us to a base in Colorado where we deplaned in the freezing cold. From there we were bused to a hospital where I underwent a physical examination. At the end I was given the code name Hector.

The guys in my unit immediately started busting my balls about my name. "Hector? You must be a Chinese Mexican."

I secretly enjoyed it. It was better than being called a camel fucker or radical Islamist.

The next day all of us were up at 0630 for a PT test. Push-ups, sit-ups, a five-mile run. Three guys failed.

Five days later, they flew us to a camp that bordered Area 51 in the Nevada desert for a month of rigorous training that included endless hours at the shooting range, navigation tests, and running obstacles set up in underground tunnels that had previously housed nuclear missiles.

One afternoon they left me alone in the desert armed only with a radio beacon. Surrounded by sand dunes and with the sun beating down on me, I charged the beacon and waited for a plane to drop three bundles. The first contained a five-hundred-foot rope; the second, a balloon with a canister of helium; and the third, a special suit with a harness. I filled up the balloon and then put on the suit and tied one end of the rope to the balloon and the other end to the harness. Upon hearing a plane approach, I released the balloon, which pulled me into the sky.

A C-130 flew in low, snagged the rope, which cut the balloon free, and the load master and this assistant slowly reeled me in. The procedure, code-named Starlift and used by Special Forces to exfil forces from behind enemy lines, went smoothly, but the force of the plane pulling me messed up my back.

At the end of training, all two dozen of us had to complete a twenty-mile march through the desert with a rucksack and full combat gear in under five hours. Only fourteen passed.

The next day we were bused to Las Vegas and put up in a motel. Each man was handed a bag of a different color. Mine was black. The instructor said, "Go to Harrah's casino. Observe everything and take mental notes. Then find a good place for extraction. We'll have people watching you. Go to this pay phone and we'll call. If you miss it, go to the next one, and we'll call you."

A couple days later, we were back at the barracks outside Area 51. One by one we were led to a small hangar filled with random gear and equipment. Our task was to mentally record as many items as we could in a minute.

After two months of training, only ten of us remained in the group. We still hadn't been briefed on the mission. I was given a ticket back to Fort Bragg and dropped off at the Las Vegas airport wearing khaki pants, desert boots, and a long beard.

As I walked through the terminal looking for a place to

buy coffee, I was surrounded by five policemen, who led me into a room and started asking questions.

"Where are you from?"

"I'm an American."

"What kind of work do you do?"

"I'm in the US Special Forces." I handed them my ID card.

They looked confused. One of them said, "You have an accent."

"Yes, I do."

"How come?"

"Look, I'm with Fifth Group Special Forces. Call my superiors at Fort Bragg. They'll confirm that I am who I say I am." I gave them my commander's number.

They searched me and my duffel first. In one of my pockets, they found a map of Las Vegas.

One of them asked, "What are you doing with this map?"

"Guys, I have a plane to catch. If you have any questions, call my commanding officer."

After an hour of questioning they finally called Fort Bragg. I heard my commanding officer shout over the line, "You have no right to hold this man. Release him immediately!"

Sheepishly, one of the policemen looked at me and said, "Okay, you can go."

I was back at Fort Bragg a couple of weeks, when I was summoned to the base's JFK Center. An officer there asked, "Hector, do you still have your Iranian passport?"

"I do, sir, but it's no longer valid."

"We want you to go to the Pakistani Embassy in DC to have it renewed."

Since Iran and the US had broken off diplomatic relations,

the Iranian consulate was being run out of the Pakistani Embassy. The man who interviewed me there asked why I wanted to go back to Iran.

I lied and said, "I want to see my father."

Once I was in possession of a valid Iranian passport, I was briefed on my mission. I was to go into Tehran on my own to collect intel and prepare things on the ground for Operation Eagle Claw—a top secret mission to rescue the hostages. After the US Embassy takeover, practically all of the CIA's sources and assets in Iran had been arrested. They needed someone like me who knew the country well and could get around.

I was instructed not to tell anyone where I was going, not even my brother and mother living in California. I simply told my mother that I was being deployed to Florida for jungle training and would call her when I returned.

Part scared to death and part excited, I flew from Charlotte to New York City, then Kennedy Airport to Frankfurt, Germany. There, I was met by an intel officer, who gave me money, some of which I used to buy a ticket to Tehran.

In a matter of hours I was on a British Airways jet flying over Eastern Europe. I sat by the window dressed in civilian clothes—long-sleeved blue oxford shirt, chino pants, a short beard, and short hair. With my heart beating 200 times a minute, I breathed deeply to try to calm down. But the same fears kept popping into my head: *What happens if I end up in jail? No one's going to stop the Iranians from interrogating and torturing me, and putting me before a firing squad.*

Since I had told the consul in DC that I was going to visit my family, I made sure to carry souvenirs—polo shirts for my father and uncle wrapped in nice paper, blue and white, not red, because Muslims think the color red brings bad luck; blue jeans for my cousins; and boxes of See's chocolates for my female relatives.

We landed. Trembling from head to toe, I shouldered my black backpack and entered the terminal. The building looked the same as it had last time I'd seen it, seven years ago. But the people seemed different. No one was smiling. Women wore long skirts, and the men had long beards.

I retrieved my small suitcase from the baggage claim area and got in line for Customs. Five very serious-looking officials started looking me over. My heartbeat rose even higher.

"Open your suitcase and backpack," one of the guards barked.

I complied.

Guards started to rifle through them. One uniformed official asked, *"Suma as kuja amadi?"* (Where are you coming from?)

"The US," I responded in Farsi.

"Why?"

"To visit my father. He's sick."

"How long are you staying?"

"Two weeks. Maybe more."

"What do you do in the United States?"

"I work in my brother's gas station."

"What's your job at the gas station?"

"I pump gas."

The senior official studied my passport and said, "Lahidji. . . . Who is Yusef Lahidji to you?"

"You mean Colonel Lahidji?" I responded.

"Yes."

"He's my uncle."

The senior official's face creased into a smile. He patted me on the back and said, *"Kush amadi Changiz Khan."* (Welcome, Changiz.)

I was so relieved that I gave him a hug. *"Merci."*

"Did you bring us anything from the States?" he asked with a wry smile.

"Only my love of Iran."

He waved me through. Outside the terminal, I saw a well-dressed man in his midthirties holding a sign with my name on it. He introduced himself as Massoud. As we drove in his BMW 5 series, he explained that he used to work for the US Embassy, and asked what I had been doing in the United States.

I repeated the same answer from before. "I work in my brother's gas station."

He seemed well educated and socially polished. If he knew anything about my mission, he didn't let on. But he did say, "Don't worry about anything. I don't like the present regime either. I want to be free."

On the way to the hotel, I asked him to drive past the US Embassy. Outside, I saw sidewalks crowded with people, dressed in black or shades of gray. The women wore hijabs (head coverings). It appeared as though all the color and joy of life had been drained out of them. What remained were serious, dour expressions, dark-colored clothes, and beards. The names of streets had been changed to honor martyrs and mullahs.

At an early age I had learned to distrust holy men. They struck me as crooks and hypocrites who sold religion as a way to gain control over people. Now I watched them parade proudly down sidewalks in long robes and beards.

I also saw lots of shabbily dressed soldiers and policemen. As we drove up South Moffatteh Street and approached the Shahid Shiroudi Stadium, the large US Embassy compound with several buildings appeared to our left. A huge banner atop the eight-foot-high fence read DEATH TO AMERICA.

We'll see about that, I said to myself.

I asked Massoud to turn right on Taleqani Street and drive slowly past the main gate. Past it rose the large two-story, brick-and-stone chancellery where some of the hostages were being held. About a dozen civilian and military men dressed in ragtag uniforms stood guard with rifles and automatic weapons. I saw no tanks.

The security at the other four gates around the seventy-acre compound was equally unimpressive. Pedestrians passed freely on adjacent sidewalks as though unaware that fifty-two Americans were imprisoned inside.

I filed away these mental notes, then asked Massoud to stop at a café near the main bazaar so I could stretch my legs. I also wanted to talk to people and get a sense of what was going on.

I asked the stoop-shouldered waiter who served us, "How's business?"

"Pretty good," he answered.

"You happy?"

"Yes. Why do you ask?"

"I've been traveling out of the country the last several years and notice lots of changes."

He shook his head and said, "Yes, this place is a zoo

compared to before. Everything is more expensive, especially food."

I checked into a modest five-story hotel close to the downtown telecommunications center. After I showered and changed clothes, I went downstairs to enjoy a delicious dinner of *challow kabab,* stewed tomatoes, *adas polo* (lentil rice), baklava, and tea. Some things hadn't changed.

In the morning, I took the #111 bus and got off one stop past the embassy. I noted the guards at the front gates were changed every two hours. The guards in back rotated in four-hour shifts.

After a lunch of barbecued sheep's liver and nan, I went to the telecommunications center near my hotel and called a number I'd been given of a special operation center in Germany. Speaking in code, I said, "Hey, John. How are you doing? I've got the candy. Now I'm going out to buy bread."

It meant: I've arrived safely and am gathering intel. That night I drew a detailed map of the embassy compound noting the placement of guards and machine guns. The next morning I mailed it to someone at the German Embassy.

The next several days followed the same pattern—surveillance of the guards at the embassy compound day and night, noting numbers of guards, the times that shifts started and ended, and which direction the guards came from and went. I also listened to local television and scanned newspapers for news on what was going on inside the embassy and little details that revealed how the hostages were treated and where they were being held.

Because I knew that undercover soldiers patrolled the

streets looking for spies and dissidents, I did my best to blend in and check to see that I wasn't being followed. Every night, radical students gathered outside the gates to listen to speakers denounce the Great Satan. One day, I watched kids pour out of school buses and chant "Death to America" for the TV cameras. Another time, I saw guards beat several young men with clubs. Day five, as I circled the back of the embassy compound, someone struck the back of my head.

I turned abruptly to face my young assailant and said, *"Agha bebakhashan"* (excuse me), hoping he had mistaken me for someone else. Without saying a word, he continued throwing punches. I pushed him away, and hurried off. I wasn't sure if it had been a random strange event or an attempt by Iranian agents to try to engage me.

I communicated everything via telephone to my contacts in Germany or mail to the German Embassy. Meanwhile, inside the US Embassy compound, the hostages spent tedious hours isolated from one another. Some were interrogated. Some were placed in solitary confinement. Others were awoken at night, stripped naked, and lined up against a wall to face mock executions. Their biggest fear, some of them said later, was that the mobs that gathered outside the walls and were whipped into near hysteria by speakers would break into the compound and slaughter them.

I was frightened as well, and by the end of my first week in Tehran starting to feel lonely. I had to resist the impulse to contact my father, uncle, or other relatives. Merely talking to them on the phone would put us all at risk.

Feeling nostalgic, I wandered past my old high school on

Revolution Circle, passing shops and fruit stalls along the way. The gate was locked, but through the fence I saw boys playing basketball and soccer. I had participated in the same activities a decade ago. When I went to school, almost all of us were clean-shaven. Now the older boys wore full beards.

The second part of my mission involved hiring a bus to ferry US Delta and SF soldiers into Tehran from a staging area seventy-five miles south. The bus would also serve as backup transportation should US Navy helicopters be unable to land at the nearby soccer stadium to take the hostages out.

The plan for the Operation Eagle Claw was complex and involved multiple moving parts. It was scheduled to launch dawn April 24, when eight helicopters carrying 118 Delta Force soldiers would take off from the USS *Nimitz* aircraft carrier stationed off the coast of Iran and land at a site in the Iranian desert designated as Desert One, several hundred miles south-west of Tehran. USAF C-130s would rendezvous with the helicopters at Desert One, bringing with them 6,000 gallons of fuel. Eight RH-53D Sea Stallion helicopters would then refuel and fly 260 miles closer to Tehran and spend the night at a second staging area known as Desert Two.

The actual rescue operation would take place the following night. US special operators would travel into Tehran by bus and truck. Some would disable electrical power in the city. Others would deploy to the embassy compound. Once they rescued the hostages, Delta Force soldiers would escort them across the street to the Shahid Shiroudi Stadium. Meanwhile, AC-130 gunships would fly over Tehran to provide air cover. Additionally, Army Rangers would capture the Manzariyeh Air Base near Desert Two so that C-141 transport planes could land and carry off the rescue team and hostages.

My ninth day in Tehran, I hired a Mercedes coach bus and driver for a week from a local company named TBT. The driver was a simple man of forty-five with three children. I paid him well and had him drive Massoud and me to inspect Desert Two, which was in the middle of nowhere. We spent the night in the nearby holy city of Qom, then returned to Tehran and waited for instructions.

On the afternoon of the 23rd, Massoud called me at my hotel and said, "The guests are coming tomorrow night at 0100."

My anticipation skyrocketed. I telephoned the driver and told him to report with the bus in the evening.

That afternoon as I was trying to relax, Massoud called again and asked in an agitated voice, "Have you heard the news?"

"What news?" I asked back.

"There's a serious problem. The guests aren't coming."

I turned the TV on in my room. A man on State Television reported that several American airplanes had crashed in the desert and all the Zionists on them had been killed.

A cold tremor passed through my body. I asked Massoud, "What should I do now?"

"I don't know."

"How am I going to get home?"

"I don't know that, either."

I found out later that the mission had been canceled because of problems with the helicopters. Soon after they landed at Desert One on the 24th, one of them was forced down due to rotor failure. Another pilot was blinded in a sandstorm and returned to the *Nimitz*. One of the remaining six had to be scrapped because of partial hydraulic failure due to the blowing sand. Because the operation required at least six helicopters, President Carter aborted the mission.

Then tragedy struck. During refueling for the flight out, one of the Sea Stallion helicopters collided with an Air Force EC-130 transport plane. Both vehicles burst into flames, killing eight servicemen. Survivors quickly fled the scene leaving behind four helicopters, weapons, maps, and secret documents, and the bodies of the dead men in the burning wreckage.

I waited at the hotel and prayed, "God, please keep me safe. I'm doing this for a good cause." On the television news, I saw footage of Iranian radicals celebrating in the streets, chanting "Death to America" and "Death to Carter." I felt sick.

Officials at the German Embassy knew where I was staying but didn't contact me. So I called Massoud, who picked me up in his car and drove me to a safe house north of the city. There I waited another very anxiety-filled day with no additional news.

Clearly, the longer I remained in Tehran, the higher my chances of being arrested. Figuring that Iranian Revolutionary Guards and soldiers were closely watching the German and UK embassies, I abandoned the idea of seeking asylum there and decided to try to escape on my own.

Massoud drove me to the train station. As we passed through the city, the streets around the US Embassy were clogged by a massive demonstration.

I faced a choice: Either go west to Tabriz, which was near the border with Turkey, or travel south to Abadan, on the Persian Gulf. Tabriz was closer, but I wasn't familiar with the city and I'd never been to Turkey. So I chose the thirteen-hour ride to Abadan instead.

Abadan was very familiar to me because I'd spent my elementary school years there, when my father served as the city's chief of intelligence for the urban police. I returned to Abadan for the eleventh and twelfth grades and lived with my uncle, who was in charge of military transportation at the time.

I was a nervous wreck the entire bus trip, imagining I was going to be arrested by every man I saw in uniform. As I tried to sleep, horrible images of what would happen to me coursed through my head.

My plan was to go from Abadan to Kuwait, but I didn't have a Kuwaiti visa. Upon arriving in Abadan, I went to the docks to see if I could find someone to smuggle me across the Persian Gulf on a boat. As luck would have it, while I was talking to some fishermen, I spotted my old school buddies Mansour and Mustafa buying fish. They were big, rough guys and excellent boxers. They greeted me warmly and offered to take me home with them to see their family.

I ended up staying with them for two days. Not wanting to put Mansour, Mustafa, or any of their relatives in any kind of jeopardy, I repeated the same cover story I had told everyone else: I was in Iran visiting my father and worked at my brother's gas station in California.

Meanwhile, Mansour and Mustafa found a smuggler to take me to Kuwait on a redwood fishing boat for $150. The night I left, I said, "I love you guys, but I have to get back to work. Hopefully you can come visit me in the US sometime."

The crossing of the Gulf lasted a very tense nine hours. When I arrived in Kuwait, I showed the Customs official my US passport and handed him $40. He let me in despite the fact that I didn't have a visa.

I was hugely relieved and thanked God. From the dock, I took a taxi to the airport and bought an airline ticket for New York. At Kennedy Airport, I hopped a plane to Charlotte, North Carolina. From there, I hailed a cab that took me to Fort Bragg.

It was a beautiful spring day. As I emerged from the taxi with my full beard and backpack, guys in my unit looked at me with alarm. Then they slowly realized who it was.

"Holy shit, it's Changiz!" one of them shouted.

"Look! He's still alive!"

One of them ran off to tell our commander. Soon he and others were surrounding me, hugging me, and slapping me on the back.

"Changiz, you lucky bastard," I heard one of them say. "We're glad you're back."

My commander embraced me and said, "It's good to see you again, Corporal. We thought you were dead."

Then I heard one of my teammates say, "Changiz, you've proved you're one of us."

That comment struck to the center of my soul. I know the guy who said it meant it as a compliment. But after what I'd been through, his words were bittersweet.

2

CHILDHOOD, IRAN

I was born in Shapoor, Iran—a small town south of Tehran—in 1950 and named after Genghis Khan. My mother, a kind woman I've loved every day of my life, once told me that she and my father had discussed aborting me when she was pregnant because they already had three young boys and were going through difficult financial times.

My father—a strong-willed, ambitious man—was the hardworking mayor of the nearby town of Chambran and liked to drink and throw parties. He had little time for us children. Childrearing, preparing meals, and taking care of the home were my mother's responsibility. She did all those tasks gracefully and never complained.

Their marriage had been arranged by their respective fathers when my mother was a girl of fifteen and my dad was eighteen, and lasted until my father's death.

My oldest brother, Iradj, is seven years older than me, and my sister Mitra was born a year later. Five years separate me from my second brother, Torag; and there is only one year between me and my third brother, Jahanguir or Jon. My sister Lida is the youngest and was born ten years after me.

When I was a toddler, all seven of us lived in my grandmother's house south of Tehran close to the train station of Shapoor. It was a simple brick structure with no plumbing or air-conditioning and two bedrooms downstairs and three on the second floor. During the hot summer months all of us would sleep on mattresses on the flat roof, which was accessible by a ladder.

By all reports I was a restless child, because of persistent eye and stomach problems. My nose dripped constantly, which is why the neighborhood kids dubbed me "booger boy." I also had a belly button that stuck out like a big red apple. No exaggeration. To my mind, those two anomalies were the equivalent of being born with chips on both shoulders.

It might explain why I emerged from the womb ready to fight. If any kid so much as looked at me funny, I'd start throwing punches.

My grandmother, bless her heart, recognized my plight and tried to find a solution. Before I was old enough to walk, she placed a large coin over my belly button, covered the coin with a sash, and tied it to my back. I wore the coin and sash for two years with no improvement to my apple-sized protrusion.

Then a friend advised my grandmother to pray to the disciples of Mashhad—the city where she grew up. Together, she, my mother, and I went on a pilgrimage to Mashhad, also known as Farsi Ziarat. I remember watching my grandmother drop the coin I had been wearing into a sacred well, retrieve it, and replace it over my belly button. I also distinctly remember the dirty, smelly mullah praying by the well who asked my mother if she wanted to have sex with him.

I wanted to punch him in his ugly bearded face, but my grandmother held me back. The experience planted in my young mind a mistrust of all so-called holy men that continues to this day.

After a week of wearing the blessed coin, my belly button receded to normal size. Make of that what you will, but it's true, so help me God.

The belief that truth is the only way to wisdom was drilled into my head by my parents, who followed the teachings of the Prophet Zoroaster (or Zarathustra). Zoroastrianism espouses that the purpose of existence is to be among those who renew life and help the world progress to perfection. Among its main tenets are *Humata, Hukhta,* and *Huvarshta*—good thoughts, good words, and good deeds.

Despite what people think, a large percentage of Persians aren't Muslim zealots. My family, though nominally Muslim, never went to mosque. Like many Persians, my parents and grandparents advanced a set of values that were more in line with Zoroastrianism, which had been the most prominent religion in Persia before the Arab invasion in the seventh century.

When I was five years old, the Iranian government of Shah Mohammad Reza Pahlavi transferred my father to Abadan—the port city on the Persian Gulf. The Shah had assumed absolute control in 1953 after the CIA and British Secret Intelligence Service deposed Prime Minister Mohammad

Mossadegh. Mossadegh had made the mistake of nationalizing the British-controlled oil industry.

To the chagrin of many Iranians, out went the democratically elected Mossadegh and in came the autocratic Shah, who relied on SAVAK, the dreaded secret police, to suppress all forms of opposition. My father worked for the urban police, known as the Shahrbani.

When I grew up in Abadan during the late 1950s and early 1960s, it was a bustling city of 200,000 residents and the site of the world's largest oil refinery. In 1986, after being besieged by Iraqi forces led by Saddam Hussein during the Iran-Iraqi War, the population fled to the point that the official census for that year recorded a mere six people.

Luckily I lived there during a time of relative peace and prosperity, in a neighborhood that resembled a sleepy suburb of postwar Florida. It was a place where the Euphrates, Tigris, and Karun Rivers flowed together into the Persian Gulf, and where British order and discipline met with the rich peculiarities of Iran's multiethnic population. The people I met were warm, progressive, and athletic, which suited me perfectly. I was an energetic, active kid and spent as much time as I could in some kind of physical activity—swimming, wrestling, boxing, soccer.

By the time I reached ninth grade, my father's career took us back to Tehran. It was the mid-1960s and the pro-Western Shah had launched a massive program of modernization known as the White Revolution, whose object was to drag the country into the twentieth century. Women no longer had to cover themselves in chadors and were granted the right to vote.

Marriages were banned for people under the age of fifteen. Divorce was legalized. Free secondary school education was extended to all citizens, and new schools, colleges, and libraries were built.

The scenes I saw on the streets of downtown Tehran as a young teenager probably weren't much different from those of Washington, London, or Paris at the time. Young women wore miniskirts, tight pants, and modern fashions. Men sported mustaches, bell-bottom pants, and long hair. Ford Mustangs and other American-made cars cruised the wide boulevards.

But that modernity didn't extend past a few major cities: The rest of Iran remained undeveloped, and the majority of Iranians were illiterate. The contrast was dramatic, and when visiting the countryside I'd see camels, donkeys pulling carts, women covered from head to toe, and kids with no shoes.

As a young boy I dreamed of moving to the United States. Part of that had to do with the image of America I had gotten from watching Hollywood movies on the weekends in large movie theaters in downtown Tehran. Big John Wayne became my hero, especially in Westerns like *The Searchers* and *Rio Bravo*, and of course *The Green Berets*.

Also, my family had a strong connection to the States. My Uncle Alex, who also happened to be my godfather, moved there in 1956 and opened a gas station south of San Francisco. My oldest brother, Iradj, followed twelve years later, and two of my uncles joined Alex in '69. My ambition was to move to the US and become a pilot.

Soon after we moved back to Tehran, my oldest aunt and her husband asked my father if I could live with them in

Abadan and help look after their ten-year-old son. Since I had many good friends there, I jumped at the offer, and ended up spending the next two years in Abadan, through high school graduation.

I never became a great student, and was known more for my mischievous sense of humor and the trouble I caused than my academic achievements. I was a cocky kid with even features, light Mediterranean skin, and jet-black hair. When I received my high school diploma, I shook it in front of me and said, "It took me twelve years to get you, now you come with me!" Then I had it laminated, attached it to the back of my bike, and rode proudly (and with a big smirk on my face) down the streets of Abadan with the diploma flying behind me. That got a lot of laughs.

I was headstrong and always up for a good time. When my father came to visit for my high school graduation, I insisted that he take me to the American consulate to get a visa to go to the States so I could work in my Uncle Alex's gas station.

Me being a brash teenager and having learned a little English, I told the US consular officer that I wanted to be sent to Vietnam so I could kick the asses of the communists.

He said, "I'm sorry, Mr. Lahidji, but I can't approve that."

"Why not, sir?"

"Because to join the military you have to be a citizen or be in possession of a Green Card first."

I got pissed off. "What?" I asked. "To kill communists, you need to be a citizen?"

"At the very least you have to be a legal resident."

I walked away with a tourist visa, and the understanding that I had to serve in the Iranian military before I could get permission to leave the country. So at the age of eighteen, I was bused 1,500 miles south of Tehran with another 350 recruits to begin basic training for the Iranian military. Sixteen weeks later, I was sent to airborne school, and then qualified for ranger training.

As a member of the elite Iranian Special Forces, I was deployed to Shiraz near the ancient city of Persepolis, where the Shah was staging a massive festival in celebration of the 2,500th anniversary of the founding of the Persian Empire by Cyrus the Great. Spanning five days in October 1971, the festival was meant to remind the world of Iran's proud history and showcase the modern advances brought to the country by the Shah.

I considered it a massive waste of money. Hundreds of millions were spent building an elaborate tent city around the ruins of Persepolis, which had been looted and partially destroyed by Alexander the Great in 330 B.C., to house visiting dignitaries from around the world. Built in a star pattern with a central fountain and surrounded by thousands of specially planted trees, each luxury tent was equipped with direct phone and telex lines. The massive Banqueting Hall tent accommodated 600 guests, who were feted with a lavish five-and-a-half-hour banquet served on dinnerware created by Limoges and with wine and food provided by Maxim's of Paris.

Foreign dignitaries were shuttled back and forth to the airport in 250 identical red Mercedes-Benz limos and included Emperor Haile Selassie I of Ethiopia; the kings of Denmark,

Belgium, Jordan, Nepal, and Norway; the emirs of Bahrain, Qatar, and Kuwait; Prince Rainier III and Princess Grace of Monaco; twenty presidents; First Lady Imelda Marcos of the Philippines; and US vice president Spiro Agnew.

My unit trained six months for the festival in elaborate wool uniforms in the blazing heat and helped provide security. After the celebration, which was criticized for its excess in Iran and throughout the world, I was assigned to one of three special Shah units known as the Sepah-e Danash, Sepah-e Teb, and Sepah-e Qesha Barzi. While the Sepah-e Teb's mission was to provide medical assistance to poor villages, and Sepah-e Qesha Barzi's was to assist in agriculture, the role of the unit I joined, the Sepah-e Danash, was to spread literacy and basic education.

I received two months of training, and at the age of nineteen was shipped to northwestern Iran to work with Kurdish tribesmen in a village near Sufian. Unlike modern Tehran, this was an area untouched by the Shah's White Revolution and only reachable by a four-wheel-drive vehicle, horse, or camel.

I'd get up at six every morning, do PT with the kids and farmers, and then set off for a little mud schoolhouse. Since I was responsible for fifty students, ranging in ages from five to twelve, I split them between two classrooms and went back and forth between the two teaching reading, spelling, Farsi, and math. The other two Sepah-e Danash members with me taught the kids' parents how to read and write.

After a year and a half, I was transferred to a base in the same area to train Kurd militiamen who were trying to stop Iraqi soldiers from sneaking across the border to steal food and sheep and rape their women—which I found particularly detestable. During these eight months, I met and befriended the man who is the current president of Iraqi Kurdistan, Massoud Barzani. As two young guys patrolling the hills around Sufian at night looking for Iraqi raiders, we had no idea how history would unfold and how we would find ourselves on the same side of conflict several times in the future—first against the Iranian Revolution and later opposed to Saddam Hussein of Iraq.

Before leaving the Shah's army, I trained with US Special Forces units at a base outside Tehran, learning free-fall parachute jumps and counterinsurgency tactics. At the end of 1973, I was honorably discharged from the Iranian army and back in Tehran, living with my family, working in a record factory, and saving up money for a plane ticket to the States.

Despite Iran's economic growth throughout the early 1970s, the new social freedoms, and its standing in the international community, the gap between the urban rich and rural poor had continued to grow. Educated elites in Tehran and other major cities lobbied for social reforms and a voice in the government, while people in the countryside scrounged for food and regarded the excesses of the Shah and his family with disgust. The only thing that seemed to unite the two groups was abhorrence of the brutal tactics of the Shah dictatorship.

The situation reminded me of the opening lines from one of my favorites books, *A Tale of Two Cities* by Charles Dickens, when he described France before the revolution:

> It was the best of times, it was the worst of times, it was the age of wisdom, it was the age of foolishness, it was the epoch of belief, it was the epoch of incredulity,

it was the season of light, it was the season of dark-
ness, it was the spring of hope, it was the winter of
despair.

Most people I knew sensed that change was coming, and
I had a feeling it wasn't going to be good.

Finally, in January 1974, I boarded a flight from Tehran
to Frankfurt, Germany, then Frankfurt to New York, and
New York to San Francisco. My twenty-three-year-old head
was filled with fantasies. Believing that I had the darkly hand-
some looks of an Italian movie star, I expected beautiful
blondes to pick me up at the San Francisco airport and shower
me with kisses.

Instead, my uncle and brother met me with a beat-up
pickup truck. They drove me to Santa Clara and immediately
put me to work in their Mobil stations, making $2.50 an hour
pumping gas and washing windshields for as many as fifteen
hours a day. Iradj's station was located in Santa Clara and
Uncle Alex's in San Jose, so I'd bike from one to the other.

Gas at the time was 25 cents a gallon, and there was no
self-service. I spoke so little English that when customers said,
"Fill it up with high test," I didn't know what they meant. All
I understood was "regular" and "premium."

Because of my meager English and the high cost of flying
school, my dreams of becoming a pilot were immediately
crushed. Still determined to make a life for myself in the US, I
enrolled at San Jose City College and West Valley College and
earned credits at night.

To earn extra money and get closer to aviation, I took a

job cleaning Boeing 707s at San Jose Airport, working the graveyard shift and making $7.50 an hour. One night, as I was towing a Pan Am 707 that had just landed from Hawaii from the taxiway to the gate, the passenger door of a fuel truck swung open, and before I could stop, the door embedded itself in the nose of the jet. The plane's crew and over a hundred passengers waited an hour as repairmen separated the truck door from the nose. I was blamed for the incident and fired.

But it wasn't all bad, because a few months later my Uncle Alex helped me secure a Green Card, and also helped me get my own ARCO station in Palo Alto. In those days, gas companies would give them out for free to people with experience. All you had to do was pay for a truckload of gasoline. I had saved enough for two loads at $2,500 a pop.

I ran the station alone for six months, then hired a helper. I was netting around $2,000 a month, but still yearned to be a pilot.

After a year of owning the station, I came to the conclusion that running a business wasn't my calling, and sold the place for $10,000. A day later I walked into the Army-Navy-Marines recruitment office on Stevens Creek Boulevard in San Jose. A huge African American man in an Army uniform rose to greet me. He said his name was Sergeant Thompson.

"Can I help you?" he asked.

"Yes, sir. My name is Changiz and I was in the Iranian military. Now I want to be a Green Beret, or an Army Ranger."

"Are you sure?" he asked. "Ranger training is very difficult, and it's a dangerous job."

"I'm in shape. I'm ready."

"Okay. We have to do a background check on you first. You could go delayed entry. We have no openings for infantry now, but you could go in as a medic."

"Fine with me." It was November 1977, and I was psyched.

In January 1978 I went to Oakland for induction with fifty other recruits. A few days later we were flown to Fort Leonard Wood, Missouri, for nine weeks of basic training. We arrived in the middle of a cold spell with temperatures dropping to 20 below zero. I froze my ass off.

After completing basic, the Army sent me to Fort Sam Houston in Texas for three months of medical training. I had a bitch of a time, because my English still wasn't up to speed and I had difficulty learning the medical terms. Also, because of my accent, guys were constantly busting my balls.

I sucked it up, made it through, and was sent to Fort Benning, Georgia, for airborne school. Having already done static-line and free-fall jumps in the Iranian Special Forces and enjoying them, the training came easily. But during Tower Week, while practicing landings from 250 feet, I landed funny and sprained my ankle. No one except my jump buddy knew what had happened.

That night my ankle swelled up badly. Not wanting to be held back, I went to the PX, bought a load of elastic bandages, wrapped my ankle as tight as I could, and suffered through the last day of Tower Week. Then it was time to jump from an airplane. The first day I managed to get through two jumps from a C-130 at 1,250 feet and withstand the pain. Day Two, we jumped with a rucksack on our backs from a C-141. I landed fine, but my ankle hurt so bad I thought I was going to pass out.

The final day we did what was called a Hollywood jump, meaning we only had to wear a parachute and reserve, but no rucksack and no weapon. I figured: no problem, and landed smoothly. But when I got up I was limping badly and struggled over to the line to stand at attention.

The captain in charge of airborne school stopped in front of me and slammed a pair of brass wings into my chest. The pin stung like hell.

I shouted, "Airborne!"

I was an Army Ranger. A day later, a group of us were bused to Fort Bragg, North Carolina, for Special Forces training. I remember the excitement I felt as we stopped in front of the World War II–era buildings that housed our unit, called IMA (Institute for Military Assistance) and now called SWC, Special Warfare Center, for the start of Pre-Phase training.

Tall, square-shouldered First Sergeant Finney walked up to me and asked, "How do you pronounce your name?"

"La-heed-gee, sir."

"What kind of name is that?"

"I'm from Iran."

"Have you been in the military before?"

"Yes, sir. I served three and a half years in the Iranian Special Forces."

"Welcome," he said as he patted me on the shoulder.

Pre-Phase lasted six weeks and consisted mainly of classroom instruction that covered SF history, organization, patrol orders, and troop-leading procedures. It ended with 275 of us lined up on the 82nd Airborne's field for a PT test. I stood five-ten and 165 pounds amidst a row of much bigger, taller guys.

One of them turned to me and asked, "Hey, Changiz, you think you got a chance of making it?"

"We'll see," I answered.

I was one of 185 who passed and entered Phase One, the start of roughly a year of SF training. Phase One was run by a short, tough sergeant from Delta Force named Maxum, who loaded us into cattle trucks and drove us to nearby Camp Mackall on a steamy, hot day in August 1979. We were packed so tightly together we could barely breathe.

Once we arrived, the diminutive sergeant proceeded to smoke our asses. We bunked in barracks with no hot water, and were allotted one hot meal a day. The other two were cold sea rations. Sergeant Maxum would wake us at 3:30 A.M., line us up carrying fifty-pound rucksacks, and run us five miles through woods filled with chiggers.

When he returned, he'd close the gate, and anyone who hadn't kept up was locked outside. The guys who didn't make it would have to suffer through another rucksack march. The rest of us spent the rest of the day doing classroom work.

Land navigation was particularly difficult. Armed with a compass, we'd be dropped in the woods around Southern Pines, where we had to find three locations during the day and two at night with instructors watching us from behind trees.

Since I'd signed up to be a medic, I was sent to attend goat lab back at Fort Sam Houston. Each member of the class was assigned a goat, which was then shot with a .22 rifle. Our task was to keep the injured goat alive, which was nasty and stressful. What really screwed me up again was the classroom instruction and medical terms. My English still wasn't good enough.

Determined to become a Green Beret, I went to the first sergeant in charge and told him about the problems I was having and asked him to change my MOS (military occupational specialty) from medic to 11 Bravo, or infantry. He kindly agreed, and I was sent back to Bragg for weapons training.

It was at this point, Phase Two training, that I ran into a couple of instructors who didn't like the fact that I was from Iran and tried to get me kicked out. So far, all of the instructors had been great, but these two assholes deliberately messed with the elevation and traverse mechanisms when I was being tested on 60 and 81mm mortars. Knowing that I only had sixty seconds to set up each mortar and hit the target, and, therefore, no time to recalibrate the mechanisms, they figured out a sneaky way to get me to fail.

Angry and dejected, I went to see the sergeant major of 5th Group and told him what they'd done. He walked back with me to the range and said to the instructors, "Why are you fucking with this guy? He speaks Farsi and Arabic and we need him. He's been in the Special Forces in Iran. Don't do him any favors, but don't fuck with him, either."

Retested as the sergeant major watched, I passed and entered Phase Three. There we were taught guerrilla warfare, infiltration and exfiltration techniques, and covert operations. It included game playing with some guys as guerrillas and other guys trying to set them up in ambushes.

Out of 275 men who started SF training, only thirty-five of us graduated in September 1979. The pride I felt in reaching my goal of becoming a Green Beret—the first Iranian and Muslim Green Beret in history—was enormous. With the rank of Specialist 4 (or E-4, equivalent to a corporal in the regular

Army), I was assigned to 5th Group Special Forces, 2nd Battalion, ODA (Operational Detachment Alpha) 561—one of ten enlisted men, one lieutenant, and one captain that made up each SF A-team. My team sergeant was Phil Quinn, and the team leader was First Lieutenant Mike Repass.

Three months later, I was the only member of ODA 561 selected to train for the Tehran operation. It turned out to be my first mission.

3

PAKISTAN

None of my teammates on ODA 561 knew about my participation in Operation Eagle Claw, or the activities I had pursued in Tehran. But soon after I returned to Fort Bragg in early June 1980 following an absence of three months, word started to leak out about where I'd been, and guys started peppering me with questions. Their curiosity was natural. The presidential campaign that pitted President Jimmy Carter against former California governor Ronald Reagan was heating up, and because the US hostages were still held in captivity in Tehran, the failed rescue mission was a big topic of discussion.

A large majority of Americans couldn't understand why a group of radical religious students in Iran could be allowed to continue to hold and humiliate US diplomats and our government wouldn't do anything about it. I was one of them.

It was a time of huge frustration. Without question President Carter's prospects of reelection were badly damaged by his decision to abort the rescue mission. Meanwhile in Iran,

Supreme Leader Ayatollah Khomeini continued to denounce President Carter and the United States for admitting the deposed Shah into the country for cancer treatment. He credited the failure of Operation Eagle Claw to divine intervention. Much to the chagrin of my family and me, the Ayatollah's popularity within Iran skyrocketed.

Because I had been instructed not to discuss the role I played in Eagle Claw, I couldn't tell my teammates much besides the fact that I'd been in Tehran and was forced to get out on my own. And I had very mixed feelings about the result.

First, I was appalled by the political and religious repression in Iran under the new regime, and concerned about my father, uncles, and other relatives who remained there. And it pissed me off that the most powerful country on earth allowed itself to be embarrassed by a group of radical students in Iran, directed by hypocritical mullahs who preached reform and social tolerance out of one side of their mouths and incited violence and demanded vengeance out of the other.

Personally, the positive thing that came out of the experience was that my SF teammates treated me with a new level of respect. I wanted to be accepted. Through the JAG (Judge Advocate General) office at Fort Bragg I had already filled out my paperwork to become a citizen—a process I was told could take as long as a year.

My mother and younger sisters, Lida and Mitra, had already moved to the States and were living with my brother in California. I helped support them by sending two-thirds of my salary every month. With my board, most of my food, and medical paid for by the military, I didn't need much.

While I continued to worry about events in Iran, the outer reality of my life at Fort Bragg quickly returned to normal with daily training on PT and guerrilla warfare tactics and sessions at the firing range.

Because we were Special Forces and charged with unconventional warfare, reconnaissance, counterterrorism, and direct action, we held ourselves to higher standards of fitness, fighting skills, tactical training, and readiness. We considered ourselves badasses, wore mustaches, and carried ourselves with a certain swagger.

Our motto was *De oppresso liber* (Latin for "to free the oppressed") and our distinguished predecessors included American Revolutionary War hero Francis Marion (the Swamp Fox), the World War II OSS Jedburgh Teams that worked with the French Resistance, OSS Detachment 101, which fought behind Japanese enemy lines in Burma, and the Alamo Scouts—the US 6th Army Special Reconnaissance Unit best known for liberating American POWs from the Japanese camps in New Guinea and the Philippines.

Formed in June 1952 by the US Army Psychological Warfare Center, we were given the distinction to wear the green beret, awarded by President John F. Kennedy in 1962 with the following:

The green beret is a symbol of excellence, a badge of courage, a mark of distinction in the fight for freedom.

Today, Special Forces—which are part of the US Special Operations Command (SOCOM)—are organized into five active-duty Special Forces Groups (SFGs), each focused on a specific geographic area of responsibility (AOR):

1st Special Forces Group (Airborne)—Pacific
3rd Special Forces Group (Airborne)—sub-Sahara Africa
5th Special Forces Group—the Middle East, Persian Gulf, Central Asia, and Horn of Africa
7th Special Forces Group—Latin America, Central America, and the Caribbean
10th Special Forces Group (Airborne)—Europe

Each Special Forces Group consists of:

Headquarters and Headquarters Company (HHC)
Group Support Battalion—supports the Special Forces Group HHC and provides logistical, intelligence, medical, and signals support.

Four Special Forces Battalions (1st, 2nd, 3rd, 4th), are each made up of:

Operational Detachment-Charlie (ODC)
The Special Forces Operational Detachment Charlie (SFOD-C) is responsible for command and control of the Special Forces Battalion.

Three Special Forces Companies (A, B, C), comprising:

- **6 Operational Detachment-Alpha (ODA):** 12-man units, led by a captain, and the primary fighting force of Special Forces.
- **Operational Detachment-Bravo (ODB)**
- A SF Company usually contains one ODB, which

provides support to the SF Company's ODAs in training, intelligence, and counterintelligence.

Battalion Support Company

The Battalion Support Company consists of signalers, mechanics, riggers, cooks, intelligence, personnel services, chaplain, legal, and others, who support the Special Forces Battalion.

• The **Military Intelligence Detachment (MID)**—provides intelligence to the Special Forces Battalion. Typically consists of:

Analysis and Control Team

Counter Intelligence/HUMINT Section

Signals Intelligence/SIGINT Section

Commander's In-Extremis Force Company focused on Direct Action missions.

Back in 1980, I had the honor to serve in 5th Group Special Forces, 2nd Battalion, ODA 561. Anytime my commanders asked for a volunteer, I raised my hand.

One morning in July—two months after my return to Bragg—my team captain told me to go over to the JFK Special Operations Center on base and see the intel officer stationed there. I thought that maybe the officer wanted to ask me some follow-up questions.

Instead, the pale intelligence officer simply said, "We have another mission for you, Changiz, but you have to go to Washington, DC, first. Are you game?"

Eager to prove my worth to my newly adopted country and earn the further respect of SF officers and colleagues, I answered, "Yes, sir. I'm happy to help in any way I can."

He instructed me to take a commercial flight from Charlotte to National Airport (later renamed Reagan Airport), where I was met by a young man who identified himself as "Chandler from the Agency."

Chandler drove me to a hotel in nearby Crystal City. The next day he returned with an attractive middle-aged intelligence officer named Anne.

She immediately got down to business. "Specialist Lahidji," she said, "we've read your DD 214 [military personnel file] and know you were born and raised in Iran. We're here to ask you to do something for us."

"Yes, ma'am. How can I help?"

"You're probably aware that fundamentalist students have taken over our embassy in Tehran."

"Yes, I am."

She made no mention of the fact that I had recently returned from Tehran as part of Operation Eagle Claw, and I didn't say anything about it, either, because I figured she already knew.

She continued: "We also have a number of Americans who have been working in Tehran as civilians and are stuck there now. We'd like to get them out, but we need your help."

"Of course."

She and Chandler briefed me over the next day and a half. I learned that Texas billionaire Ross Perot owned a company called Electronic Data Systems (EDS) that had maintained a branch in Tehran since the mid-1970s. EDS had been hired by the Shah to set up a computerized social security database to keep track of Iranian citizens.

The two intel officers explained that in December 1978 as protests against the Shah escalated into violence in Tehran and other Iranian cities, two employees of EDS, Paul Chiapparone and Bill Gaylord, were arrested by the Shah's government and thrown into prison. Within four days of their arrest, Perot assembled a team of EDS employees with military experience, headed by retired US Army Special Forces Colonel Arthur D. "Bull" Simons, to plan and execute a commando raid on Gasr Prison to free his two employees.

According to Perot's version of events, recounted in the bestselling book *On Wings of Eagles* by British author Ken Follett (which later became a popular TV miniseries), Colonel Simons's team incited anti-Shah dissidents to storm Gasr Prison, and while the riot was under way entered the prison and spirited away the two EDS employees. But eyewitnesses and State Department officials reported a different story.

According to them, the EDS rescue team simply waited for the return of opposition leader Ayatollah Khomeini and the overthrow of the Shah's government during the first week of February 1979. When pro-Khomeini mobs opened the doors of Gasr Prison on February 11 as part of a coordinated assault on Shah government prisons and police headquarters, Chiapparone and Gaylord simply ran out with the rest of the 10,000 or more people being held there. The two Americans then went directly to the Hyatt Hotel, where they met Colonel Simons and his team, who engineered their escape through Turkey.

Whatever really happened, the fact was that a dozen of Perot's data service company employees had remained behind in Tehran. According to the intelligence officers who briefed me, these individuals were now holed up in EDS's downtown second-story office and were afraid to leave.

The Agency wanted me to return to Tehran and pay off local officials to secure the EDS employees' safe passage out of Iran.

"Are you willing to execute the mission?" Anne asked.

"Sure," I answered. "No problem."

Even as I agreed, fears and doubts played in my mind. *What if when I arrive in Tehran I run into the same Iranian Customs officials at the airport? How will I explain why I've returned to Tehran, and had slipped out of the country without being cleared by Customs four months ago? Where will I find a local Iranian official who'll be willing to help me? Will I be able to trust this person?*

I thought about my friend Massoud who had helped me last time I was in Tehran, and wondered how I could contact him.

The plan, which Anne and Chandler laid out the end of our second day together, called for me to fly to Tehran as I had months before. To my mind that seemed very unimaginative and way too risky. So I sat up that night and devised a scenario of my own, whereby I would fly to Turkey, then take a train to nearby Azerbaijan. From Azerbaijan, I would pass through Uzbekistan and Tajikistan before entering Afghanistan. From the western Afghan city of Herat, I would cross the border into Iran, and from the Iranian city of Mashhad board a bus to Tehran.

When I presented my idea to Anne and Chandler the next day at lunch, they seemed surprised. Anne asked, "How in the world did you come up with that?"

"I know the region and tried to design something that would be hard for the Iranian revolutionary government to trace."

"You certainly accomplished that," opined Chandler over burgers and fries in the hotel restaurant. "You think it will work?"

"I hope so. Once I'm in Tehran, I'll go downtown and visit the EDS employees, and then figure out a way to get them out of the country."

"Okay. We'll get back to you tonight."

I waited nervously, once again imagining my imprisonment in Iran and execution before a firing squad by angry Islamic extremists.

The two intel officers returned in the evening to announce that the mission to Tehran had been canceled.

"Really?" I asked, wondering whether I had heard correctly.

"Yes," Anne answered.

I was so relieved, I almost fainted, and was instructed to return to Bragg and report to their CIA colleague at the JFK Center. I later learned that the EDS employees had gotten up the nerve to leave their offices, drive to the airport, and depart the country without incident. Kind of like the movie *Argo,* but without the subterfuge and drama.

In 1980, at the start of my career, I had no idea that my time in SF and later as a military contractor would involve me in just about every major US conflict over the next thirty-five years.

Ironically, both my first deployment after Tehran and my final assignment involved the same country: Afghanistan. On the night of December 24, 1979, while I was at Fort Bragg fretting about the takeover of the US Embassy in Tehran, Soviet troops from the 40th Army were airlifted into the Afghan capital of Kabul, starting an occupation that would last nine years. Three nights later, as part of Operation Storm-333, 700 Soviet troops and KGB agents dressed in Afghan military uniforms staged an assault on Afghanistan's presidential palace that resulted in the death of President Hafizullah Amin and his replacement with pro-Soviet socialist Babrak Karmal.

As Western nations watched and wondered what Moscow would do next, the Soviet 40th Army under the command of Marshal Sergei Sokolov entered the country from the north and the 103rd Guards' Vitebsk Airborne Division 103rd landed at Kabul's Bagram Air Base. Within days, an estimated 1,800 Russian tanks, 80,000 soldiers, and 2,000 armored fighting vehicles had moved into Afghanistan.

With the arrival of the two additional divisions over subsequent weeks, the total Soviet force rose to over 100,000 military personnel. This wasn't just a show of support for the newly installed Afghan president, it was a full-blown invasion aimed at extending Soviet influence throughout the region and protecting their interests in Afghanistan from the West and the revolutionary regime in Iran.

The Soviets' bold move further embarrassed the Carter administration, which was reeling from the US Embassy takeover in Tehran. Worldwide condemnation of the occupation of Afghanistan was vehement, with the West, China, and thirty-four Islamic nations demanding an immediate and unconditional withdrawal of Soviet troops. In one of the most lopsided votes in its history, the UN Security Council by a margin of 104–18 passed a resolution against the Soviet intervention. President Carter upped the economic ante by placing a trade embargo on the Soviet Union and boycotting the 1980 Moscow Summer Olympics.

As had happened with other foreign occupiers of Afghanistan, including the British during the nineteenth century, things didn't go as easily as the Soviets expected. Even with the backing of the Russian army, new Afghan president Karmal was unable to muster much popular support. Soviet forces soon found themselves drawn into putting down urban uprisings, fighting tribal armies, and quelling mutinies of units of the Afghan army.

Whenever Soviet troops left strongholds in major cities, they were attacked by small units of insurgents and tribal groups—collectively known as mujahedeen—who viewed the Soviets as foreigners imposing their views and destroying local culture. Joining them were local and Arab jihadists who declared holy war against the atheist invaders they believed were bent on defiling Islam.

What became known as the Soviet-Afghan War developed into a stalemate, with the Soviets controlling major cities, and the mujahedeen moving with relative ease throughout the remaining 80 percent of the country.

Seeing an opportunity to punish the Soviets by bogging them down in an unwinnable war, the Carter administration launched a top secret CIA program known as Operation

Cyclone, which eventually funneled over $3 billion in weapons and training to the mujahedeen using Pakistan's intelligence service, the Inter-Services Intelligence (ISI), as an intermediary.

Together with similar programs by Saudi Arabia, British MI6, Egypt, Iran, and the People's Republic of China, the arms provided included Chinese and Soviet AK-47s and RPGs, and FIM-43 Redeye shoulder-fired antiaircraft weapons that were used to disable Soviet helicopters.

Despite the assertion from Pakistani General Mohammad Yousaf that "no American ever trained or had direct contact with the mujahedeen, and no American official ever went inside Afghanistan," I can tell you that's inaccurate.

In August 1980, my ODA 561 team sergeant informed me that I had been selected to go on a top secret mission to Pakistan and Afghanistan. The good news was that, since I would be traveling on an "official" red passport, which could only be issued to US citizens, my paperwork had been expedited and I would become a citizen immediately. I was thrilled. Also, I was to begin three months of language training in a special facility at Fort Bragg to help me transition from my native language, Farsi, to Dari, which is spoken in much of Afghanistan.

In November 1980, some of my ODA 561 teammates and I dressed in civilian clothes and boarded a commercial flight that took us to New York, London, and eventually Islamabad, Pakistan. There we joined members of another SF ODA team and bused to the city of Chaman, near the Afghan border.

Housed in a secret CIA-ISI compound in barren land outside Chaman, we spent the next two months training roughly 500 mujahedeen. All of them were Afghan tribesmen—hard dudes in good physical shape who had been fighting all their lives for basic survival. They seemed highly motivated to liberate their country.

We trained them in reconnaissance, patrol drills, linear and area ambushes, leapfrogging, shout-and-scout, and other small unit tactics. As the weapons man my job was to teach them how to fire and maintain Chinese-made AK-47s, mortars, RPGs, and the Russian-made DShK 1938 heavy machine gun. The mujahedeen picked up everything quickly.

Ranging in age from nineteen to fifty, they were divided between Pashtun tribesmen from southern Afghanistan and Tajiks from the center and north of the country. I spent most of my time with Tajiks because they spoke Dari, which was close to my native Farsi. Not only could I communicate with them easily, but with my dark features and black beard grown out I fit right in.

In nightly talks after dinner that usually included some variation of grilled lamb or goat, they expressed their appreciation for our help. Because the US wasn't able to resupply the mujahedeen from the air once they entered Afghanistan, we built and stocked arms caches inside the country.

We did this late at night, slipping across the border in trucks with the lights off. We'd either identify pre-existing caves or dig them near the tops of hills, at least 2,000 meters apart. Some caves had to be shored up with beams and boulders. We'd mark each cave on a map and indicate its location with stakes, a pile of rocks, or a felled tree tagged with camouflage paint 100 feet from the entrance so the mujahedeen could

find it. A night or so later, we'd return with a dozen mujahedeen to lug boxes of AKs, hand grenades, mortars, and ammo
from the road to the caves, while four of us SF guys kept watch
with M16s.

This was before NVGs—night vision goggles—or body
armor, and we were in enemy territory, so tensions ran high.
We stocked dozens of caves in southeastern Afghanistan during our stay at Chaman.

Halfway through our month at the CIA compound, our
team was given a few days off. I told the team captain that I
was using it to accompany some of the mujahedeen to recon
along the border.

"How long will you be gone?" he asked.

"A couple days. Maybe more. If I run into trouble, I'll
send word back with one of the locals."

"Be safe," was the captain's response.

I didn't tell him that I planned to recon as far north as
Kabul. I had noticed that the Tajik fighters in our group moved
with relative ease and frequency from our location near southeast Afghanistan to their compound and headquarters in the
rocky Panjshir Valley north of Kabul.

Being a curious type, I asked to accompany them on one
of their trips in early December. Dressed in a local knee-length
shirt (*perahon*) and baggy trousers (*tunban*) with a thick robe
(*pato*) over it and wearing a flat wool cap (*pakol*), I rode with
five mujahedeen divided between two pickups. One old guy
spoke decent Russian, enough he said to talk us through any
Soviet roadblock. I armed myself with an automatic pistol,
which I hid under the robe, just in case.

We drove through spectacular countryside and past mountains covered with snow, stopping at the occasional Taliban
roadblock. Even then, Taliban militants—Pashtun tribesmen
and Islamic fundamentalists armed and trained by Pakistan's
ISI—controlled much of southern Afghanistan.

The Pakistanis did this, officers in their intelligence service explained, because they wanted the Taliban to act as a
militia buffer should their longtime hated rival India attack
them through Afghanistan. And they still do, despite the fact
that Pakistan professes to be our ally in the fight against Islamic
terrorism.

As we proceeded north, I understood why Afghanistan
would never submit to foreign domination. Not only were the
people fiercely independent, they were tough as hell and lived
in conditions that could best be described as medieval. Their
distrust of outsiders, especially from the West, was strong.

Also, the terrain of much of the country was mountainous and difficult. Aside from a few roads that connected a
handful of major cities, the only way to get around—except
by air—was via dirt paths that were often only passable by
donkey or by foot.

Another thing that struck me was that, in general, all
Afghans looked alike. Men and women, young and old, poor
and rich, for the most part, dressed as humble farmers. With
no national system of documentation or database to speak of,
how was a foreign occupier supposed to separate a bus driver
from a mujahedeen?

Not well, I found out a day and a half later when we
stopped at a Russian checkpoint outside the capital city of

Kabul. As I waited nervously, my Russian-speaking travel-mate explained that we were peasants on our way to help a friend north of the city build a wall around his house.

The extent of the damage I saw when we entered Kabul shocked me. Piles of bricks and other rubble clogged many streets, bridges were badly damaged, many structures were completely uninhabitable, and I didn't see a building that wasn't pockmarked with bullet holes. We spotted grim-faced Russian soldiers standing guard at intersections and armored vehicles on patrol. The locals went about their business of shopping or walking from one place to another looking bedraggled and unhappy. I got the strong impression that the Soviet occupation wasn't going well.

As we drove past the US Embassy, I saw a sad, unattractive, yellowing building boarded up with sheets of plywood. The big brass US seal over the entrance was dirty, but intact.

We moved without interference, the mujahedeen showing no fear. I tried not to show mine as well, but was absolutely scared to death. After a day scouting the city and airport, we turned around and returned to Chaman. My captain stood waiting for me when we returned, arms crossed against his chest, looking pissed.

"You've been away five days. Where the hell have you been? We were worried."

"Sir, the mujahedeen offered to take me to Kabul."

"You went to Kabul? Are you crazy?"

"It's okay, Captain. I'm back and I got some good intel."

Fortunately, I wasn't disciplined. Since I had already

traveled into Afghanistan, the captain tasked me and five other SF operators to accompany a half-dozen Tajik mujahedeen to their camp in the Panjshir Valley directly north of Kabul. Again we passed through Taliban and Russian roadblocks without a problem, and after a day and a half of traversing difficult roads entered a large compound occupied by around 2,000 anti-Soviet fighters.

As we'd done in the south, my teammates and I spent a month running courses in reconnaissance, guerrilla tactics, and weapons training.

The mountainous terrain we patrolled daily was extremely tough, but the militiamen were used to it and scaled it like mountain goats. Upon hearing the roar of approaching Soviet Mi23 and Mi31 helicopters, they didn't panic, but quickly sought cover. Curiously, the Soviets never did engage us, or assault the compound—which was too big to conceal—while we were there.

The leader of the Tajiks, the legendary Ahmad Shah Massoud, affectionately known as the "Lion of the Panjshir," came and went during our stay. He was around thirty at the time and highly respected as a brilliant military strategist and humanist whose goal was an independent, progressive Afghanistan where women enjoyed equal rights to men.

A tough, charming man with tremendous magnetism, he dressed only slightly better than his men with a Western shirt, military jacket, and pakol cap. The first time I introduced myself to him as Changiz, he sat beside me and asked me to recite some poetry.

"I'm sorry, Shah. I don't know any poems," I responded

in Dari, addressing him as "Shah," meaning leader or king, to show respect.

"You're not the Urdu poet Muhammad Changiz Khan Tariqui?"

"No, Shah," I said. "My name is Changiz, and I'm Iranian by birth. Now I'm a member of US Special Forces. I've come to help train your men."

He stood and wrapped me in a warm hug. "Thank you, Changiz. Thank you for traveling here, and God bless America for its help."

Massoud went on to become a hero of anti-Soviet resistance and later fought against the Taliban regime that took power after the Soviets withdrew, objecting to their strict interpretation of Islam and treatment of women. On September 9, 2001, two days before Al Qaeda terrorists launched their attack on the Pentagon and World Trade Center, Massoud was assassinated by Al Qaeda operatives disguised as TV journalists. Today, he's considered a national hero.

I left Afghanistan in January 1981, sensing that the Soviets would fail. What I didn't anticipate was how the Soviet occupation of Afghanistan would contribute to the dissolution of the entire Soviet Union. Or how Afghanistan would occupy the world stage for the next thirty-five years, or how Afghanistan under the Soviets would develop into a breeding ground for foreign jihadists, who would go on to wreak havoc throughout the world.

One of them, a tall soft-spoken Saudi from a wealthy family named Osama bin Laden, helped funnel arms, money, and fighters from the Arab world into Afghanistan while I was there. He became so enamored with the concept of jihad (or war against the enemies of Islam) that he would later found the terrorist group Al Qaeda, whose goal was "to lift the word of Allah, and make his religion victorious."

Interestingly, our paths would cross again in, of all places, Afghanistan.

4

BEIRUT

As the threat of terrorism increased in the early 1970s, commander of Special Forces 5th Group Col. Robert A. Mountel was tasked by the Department of Defense (DOD) to create a specially designated hostage rescue team called Blue Light, or B500, that could deploy in a matter of hours. According to one of its founding members, those who qualified for the team "had to be so nasty that when released from duty you should be put in jail to be kept off the streets of America!"

I'm not sure I want to admit to fulfilling those requirements, but upon my return to Fort Bragg in January 1981, I volunteered for Blue Light Team and was selected. I like to think it was because of my language and combat skills, and the fact that I was highly motivated.

The formation of Blue Light followed the failure of Operation Eagle Claw, and happened during a period when the US government was reassessing its counterterrorist capabilities. In addition to Blue Light, several other new special quick-response units were created, including the Navy's SEAL Team Six, the 160th Special Operations Aviation Regiment (Airborne) (SOAR), also known as the Night Stalkers, and Delta Forces. And the Joint Special Operations Command (JSOC) was established to control and oversee joint training between the counterterrorist assets of the various branches of the US military.

At the start of 1981, 5th Group's Blue Light Team fulfilled the quick-response, antiterrorism role while the new units got up to speed. Housed at the Mott Lake compound fifteen miles from Fort Bragg that had been used during the Vietnam War and by FBI SWAT, we trained constantly and maintained a high state of readiness. Since our primary mission was hostage rescue, we spent a lot of time fast roping, rappelling, and practicing close quarters combat (CQC).

As part of Blue Light training, I attended HALO (High Altitude Low Opening) jump school, which was a blast until the third to last of the twenty-seven jumps needed to graduate, when I landed funny and broke my left leg. This was a whole higher echelon of pain than what I'd experienced when spraining my ankle during Ranger training. But again, being hardheaded, I wanted no part of being held back.

So I wrapped that baby tight with bandages, downed some aspirin, and sucked it up. We had two more jumps to complete from 12,500 feet with rucksack, weapons, and full combat gear. I managed to stick the second-to-last jump, but when I got to my feet I was limping badly.

I begged our instructor, Paul Ford, to let me stay and finish the course. Last jump, after prebreathing oxygen, he pushed me to the front of the line, and we jumped together. I opened my chute at 4,000 feet feeling free as a bird and shot a thumbs-up gesture to Ford. Everything was copacetic. At 200 meters (600 feet) I released my rucksack and controlled fine, landing on my good leg (my right). But when I tried to get up, my left couldn't support my weight.

Ford radioed for a deuce and a half (a 2.5 ton truck), and he and the other instructors loaded me in and placed my helmet under my left foot. Every bounce to Womack Hospital was like driving an ice pick into my spine. At Womack, the Army doc stuck a wad of gauze in my mouth, had two orderlies hold my hands, and then yanked my left foot to straighten the leg out. I screamed so loud people said they heard me on the other side of the hospital.

A few days later, I was back at Mott Lake struggling up and down three flights of stairs to my room in 5th Group barracks. Rehabilitation was greatly aided by a sweet brunette from the NCO club. Bless her heart. Soon after the cast came off, I was back training and doing PT.

Toward the end of '81, Delta became operational, and all of us on Blue Light were invited to join. I was one of the few men who accepted the invitation. On a cold morning in late October, Sergeant Jack Joplin—sergeant major of 5th Group—told me to report to the old MP Station off Riley Road for the Delta PT test. Having always taken pride in my fitness, and knowing I was in excellent shape, I expected to pass. But after waiting two hours, no one from Delta came to pick me up.

I figured it must have been an oversight. The next day, I went back, and waited two more hours with the same result.

The third day Sergeant Joplin took me directly to Delta headquarters and addressed the sergeant in charge.

"You see this guy," he said, pointing in my direction. "He speaks three languages, is highly trained, and as skilled and as tough as anyone I know. You need him. So why are you fucking with him?"

"Sergeant, it was a simple misunderstanding," the Delta sergeant responded. "We don't seem to have his paperwork."

"Bullshit. You do have his paperwork. It was sent three times!"

"I'm sorry, Sergeant. There must be some misunderstanding."

"No, I'm sorry," 5th Group Sergeant Joplin responded. "Fuck you guys! You've lost a good candidate."

Delta had a snotty attitude from the beginning. Fine with me. When Blue Light disbanded, I didn't hear the team mentioned again until 1990 and the movie *Die Hard 2*, when one of the characters was referred to as a former member of the "Blue Light counterterrorism unit."

From Blue Light, I went to ODA 562 and was immediately thrown in the water, so to speak. Combat driver's school involved three weeks pre-scuba training at Fort Bragg and then three grueling weeks in Key West. Up every morning at 0430, we jogged five miles, then ran another thirty minutes in the steamy heat with RB-15 boats over our heads, and did push-ups, crunches—all before breakfast at 0730. Then it was into the pool. Laps, crossover kicks, learning to tie a rope underwater. First week: 500 meters on the surface; 500 underwater.

By the third week we were doing that times six. The instructors took us 100 meters out into the ocean and told us to swim to shore underwater without coming up more than twice. I thought my lungs were going to explode, but I made it.

The night after graduation I was sitting in a bar on Duval Street relaxing and drinking beers with a couple of my SF teammates when I started chatting up a dark-haired Russian girl named Anya. One thing led to another, and she invited me to her apartment.

She led me into her bedroom, where a ceiling fan stirred the moist hot air, and she started to slip out of her dress. It wasn't the lacy black bra and panties she wore underneath that caught my attention. It was the chains, whips, clamps, handcuffs, and other S&M paraphernalia I saw hanging from the walls.

What the hell is this? I thought to myself. *Is she gonna torture me to death?*

Anya was so beautiful and sexy, and I was willing to take that chance. I figured, if she killed me, at least I'd go out with a smile on my face.

Thankfully, I survived her very skilled and passionate lovemaking. Afterward, the two of us were cooling off on her balcony when I heard two of my SF buddies walking up the street and singing off-key.

"Hey Frank. Hey Bob," I called.

"Changiz, what the hell you doing up there, buddy? And who's the babe with you?"

Anya invited them up, and after some shots of vodka, proceeded to get it on with the three of us at once. No shame, no inhibitions.

Having graduated SF scuba school, I was classified as Whiskey 9, which put me in the rare company of being Ranger, scuba, and HALO qualified. Due in part to my enhanced skill set, HQ transferred me from ODA 562 to ODA 564, which was a Green Light (HALO) team. My job was 11 Bravo—junior weapons man.

Each SF A-team boasted two officers, two medics, two commo guys, two intel, two engineers, and two weapons specialists. That way if one specialist went down in combat, the other could take his place. Or, if need be, the team could split into two units. Teams were structured to wage unconventional warfare and were capable of working independently in a decentralized manner.

In other words, we had a lot of flexibility and were given a high degree of responsibility and independence.

Green Light team's mission was to deploy behind enemy lines and destroy infrastructure and matériel. We were also designated a Special Atomic Demolition Munition (SADM) team, which meant that one man was chosen to carry an eighty-five-pound tactical nuclear weapon.

Guess who volunteered to carry it?

Our team sergeant, Bob Fleming, explained, "It's a dangerous job, Changiz. But you're perfect, because you've had extensive HALO training."

After passing DOD's personnel reliability program to make sure I was trustworthy and mentally stable, I was selected, but didn't really understand what I had signed up for.

During training, I learned that one strategic reality of the Cold War was that Soviet-aligned Warsaw Pact forces woefully outnumbered our US and NATO Pact counterparts in terms of manpower and armaments. The US had addressed this gap with the massive development of nuclear weapons. According to the doctrine of "massive retaliation" first expressed by President Dwight Eisenhower in the 1950s, any Soviet military aggression, especially in Europe, would be met with a nuclear onslaught of massive proportions.

Because it was a potentially suicidal strategy that could result in the death of millions of people, the US in its search for alternative options developed the concept of limited nuclear war. So, if Warsaw Pact forces launched a blitzkrieg on Western Europe, smaller "tactical" nuclear weapons could be used to delay the communist assault long enough for reinforcements to arrive.

The B-54 SADM (or backpack nuke) that I had been chosen to carry was one such weapon. It had entered the US arsenal in 1964, stood eighteen inches tall, and packed a maximum explosive power of under 1 kiloton—or the equivalent of 1,000 tons of TNT (roughly one-fifteenth the blast yield of the Little Boy bomb dropped on Hiroshima). It had a bullet-shaped cone on one end and a twelve-inch control panel behind a plate secured with a combination lock on the other. The lock had phosphorescent paint on it to help us unlock the bomb at night.

Our mission in Green Team was to parachute behind enemy lines at night and use the B-54 SADM to destroy enemy airfields, tank depots, antiaircraft installations, and transportation infrastructure. We conducted our initial HALO training with the bomb at the Sicily Drop Zone at Fort Bragg. Our team sergeant, lean Vietnam vet Bob Fleming, did the first jump from 13,500 feet with the bomb held in a rucksack strapped to his chest. I was one of four men who volunteered to jump with him.

I was curious to see how this would work. The five us were standing near the rear of a four-engine turboprop C-130 checking our equipment, when our company commander shouted "Stand by!" He tapped each of us out with the order "Go!" We jumped and started falling at twenty feet per second with the cold wind in our faces. I loved that sensation of falling and looking down at the green earth below.

We'd been instructed to land six feet apart, scurry to a predetermined rally point behind some trees, unseal the special bomb jump container (which looked like a metal garbage can), and inspect the bomb to make sure it was intact and not leaking radiation. Then we were supposed to slip the SADM into a rucksack, bury our chutes and the container, and carry the nuke to the detonation site, where an inspector would go through a dozen procedures to arm the bomb.

We trained with a dummy SADM that weighed and looked exactly the same as the real thing. During our first jump, Sergeant Fleming came down so fast that he lost consciousness at 4,000 feet, failed to open his chute, and started spinning. We screamed at him from above, "Bob! Bob, wake the fuck up!" to no avail.

"Sarge!" I screamed over and over until my lungs hurt. "SARGE!"

I thought Bob was a goner. But when his reserve chute opened automatically at 3,500 feet, it jolted him awake.

"Bob, you son of bitch. Look out!"

He was still disoriented. We called to him and helped guide him in safely. As soon as we touched down, the four of us ran over to Bob and found him in bad shape, woozy as hell, and his eyes completely red because the blood vessels had burst from the g-force of the jolt of his parachute—a medical condition known as subconjunctival hemorrhage.

The other three guys loaded Bob into a jeep and drove him to Womack Hospital, while I slipped the nuke into a rucksack and carried it to the detonation site. It took Bob forty-five days to recover.

A week later, it was my turn to do a static-line jump in full gear from 4,000 feet, holding an M-16 and with the dummy B-54 SADM in a rucksack strapped to my chest. Because my chute was attached to a line to the aircraft, it opened automatically. So that wasn't a problem. At 1,250, I pulled a cord that released the rucksack from my chest, causing it to tumble to my feet. That way, the container with the bomb could land first and wouldn't crush me.

But when I released the combined weight of the bomb and container—which amounted to more than ninety pounds—my body jerked back sharply and threw me off-balance. I steadied myself with the lines and used them to guide away from bushes and other obstacles. The bomb landed on the grassy field and I did a parachute landing fall (PLF) beside it—touching the ground balls of the feet first, then outer side of the calf, outer side of the upper leg, side of butt, and side of back.

Three of my teammates did PLFs nearby and helped me up.

"Good job, monkey," one of them said.

I wasn't insulted. The guy on the team who carried the warhead was affectionately known as "the monkey" because of the bent-over posture he had to assume when carrying it.

"Monkey this," I growled back.

My lower back barking like an angry dog, we buried the container and slipped the bomb into a rucksack, which they lifted onto my back. My teammates carried my food and ammo, while I broke into a trot with the nuke strapped to my back. Two teammates mirrored me on either side to keep me from falling, because the solid-metal nuke was awkward as hell to carry.

While I ran, I asked myself, *What the fuck were you thinking when you volunteered for this job?*

Military regulations required that no one individual service member had the ability to arm a nuclear weapon. So the code to unlock the B-54's cover plate had to be divided between two Green Light team members. Nor could we ever let something so lethal fall into enemy hands. For that purpose, one of our demolition guys carried the appropriate amount of explosives to destroy the bomb without triggering a nuclear explosion. Or so we were told.

Since the SADM had been built largely devoid of electrons to make it resistant to electromagnetic pulses, it relied on mechanical timers, which weren't very accurate. So we had to get close to the target.

Once we reached it, the code men would unlock the cover plate, remove it, and set the timer. Then they would reach into a small compartment at the top left of the control panel, pull out the hand-sized explosive charge used to trigger the bomb's nuclear chain reaction, place the charge in the armed position, and flip the switch. Now that the bomb was armed, we had roughly forty-five minutes to beat a retreat before it went off.

In a real war, our orders called for us to watch the device

from a distance to assure that it didn't fall into enemy hands. We knew that if we weren't vaporized by the nuclear blast, we'd almost certainly get scorched by the hot wind or exposed to serious radiation. Not a fun prospect either way.

The long and short of it was that if our Green Light team was ever called upon to deploy the SADM in combat, we would only have a general idea of when it would explode, which probably didn't matter, because it would almost certainly be a suicide mission. Even if we were fortunate enough to survive the bomb's detonation and radiation, we'd probably be trapped behind enemy lines with slim odds of slipping out without being captured or killed.

I did at least three HALO jumps with the dummy bomb each month. And once a week, I had to jog five miles with that heavy bastard strapped to my back.

One rainy night during a three-day exercise at Camp Mackall, I was carrying the B-54 SADM and its metal container strapped to my back and wearing a bulky chemical suit, gas mask, helmet, rain paints, rain jacket, and holding an M16. The rain came down hard so I couldn't see shit, and as I was running I fell into a four-feet-deep hole and smashed my face.

Stars spun in my head. When I tried to climb out, I slipped and slid in the muddy hole, and couldn't get any traction. My plight elicited peals of laughter from my teammates. Eventually they helped me out, and we continued on our way.

Before the night was over, we had to clear four checkpoints. After we reached the camp and handed over the SADM, we were showered with chemicals to wash away the radiation.

It reminded me of a scene out of my favorite James Bond movie, *Dr. No.*

I read somewhere recently that the US military had as many as 300 SADMs in its arsenal at the height of the Cold War. The last of them were declared obsolete and destroyed in 1988. At least one SADM parachute container survives and is currently displayed at the National Museum of Nuclear Science and History in Albuquerque, New Mexico.

If you ever get a chance to see it, picture yourself running with that thing for five miserable miles, and then imagine the damage it's done to my back!

While I was lugging the SADM around Camp Mackall, things were going from bad to worse in the Middle East. The new Iranian government of Ayatollah Khomeini finally freed the US hostages on January 20, 1981—the last day of President Carter's term in office. The radical change in Iran's relationship with the United States, from close friend to foe, encouraged Iraq's military strongman Saddam Hussein to invade Iran in a bid to annex the disputed oil-rich Khuzestan and achieve hegemony over the Persian Gulf.

Saddam Hussein's full-scale offensive with airpower and six divisions of ground troops and armor was met by strong Iranian resistance and quickly bogged down. The war between the two countries dragged on until August 1988, making it the longest conventional war of the twentieth century and inflicting massive human and financial damage on both sides—including at least a half million Iranian and Iraqi soldiers and an equivalent number of civilians.

But the conflict that seemed to get the most direct US attention wasn't the Iran-Iraqi War, it was the civil war in nearby Lebanon. After the dissolution of the Ottoman Empire at the end of World War I, France had assumed control over Lebanon and Syria under a mandate of the League of Nations and created Greater Lebanon as a safe haven for Maronite Christians. In 1943, Lebanon gained independence.

Maronite Christians controlled the presidency and much of the economy, and the large Sunni and Shiite Muslim populations were guaranteed a quota of seats in the parliament and certain positions in the government. This unsteady political balance lasted through the 1960s and early 1970s and allowed the country to prosper. Its capital, Beirut, became the commercial, intellectual, and banking center of the Middle East.

The influx of hundreds of thousands of Palestinians in Lebanon from what had once been the Palestinian territory, which started with the founding of the State of Israel in 1948 and continued through the expulsion of the Palestine Liberation Organization (PLO) from Jordan, slowly started to tip the political balance. In the mid-1970s the PLO, supported by Lebanese Sunni Muslims, established a stronghold in western Beirut and gained control of large swaths of southern Lebanon.

Fighting between militia groups representing the various political factions in Lebanon broke out in 1975 and quickly escalated. In January 1976 over 1,000 people were killed when Maronite militias overran the PLO-controlled East Beirut slum of Karantina. In reprisal, PLO units attacked the Maronite town of Damour.

As sectarian violence spiraled, Syrian president Hafez al-

Assad brokered a truce that essentially split the country in two, with Maronite Christian groups controlling northern Lebanon and Palestinian militias dominating the south. Beirut remained divided: fighting continued there between the PLO and Muslim-based militias in the west and between the PLO and Christians in East Beirut and Mount Lebanon. The demarcation between the two groups became known as the Green Line.

Meanwhile, PLO raids across the border into Israel and the PLO's attempted assassination of the Israeli ambassador to London caused Israel to retaliate with attacks on the PLO in south Lebanon and with bombing raids in West Beirut. With civilian casualties mounting in and around Beirut, the US brokered a truce in August 1982 that called for the withdrawal of PLO fighters and Israeli troops from Beirut and a multinational force of US Marines and French and Italian units to ensure the departure of the PLO and protect defenseless civilians.

But the country remained in chaos. In early 1983, I was selected with thirty other Green Berets from 3rd Battalion to deploy to a Lebanese army base in West Beirut. Our MTT (mobile training team) mission was to instruct Lebanese soldiers how to combat Iranian-backed Hezbollah rebels who occupied the Syrian-controlled Bekka Valley northeast of Beirut and were aggressively pushing into the eastern sector of the city, which had recently been abandoned by the PLO.

My job as the 11 Bravo weapons man was to teach SF patrol tactics—much as I had done with the mujahedeen in Afghanistan. I was selected in part because I spoke Farsi and some Arabic. We also had a Lebanese American SF guy in our group who was fluent in Arabic. About half of the Lebanese soldiers had some English and French. We overcame other language barriers with hand signals and hands-on instruction.

The atmosphere in and around the base and especially in the western part of the city was tense with daily battles between Hezbollah rebels and Maronite militia units. I got used to falling asleep at night to the sound of small arms and mortar fire. We also maintained a safe house in the city that we used when fighting around the Lebanese army base grew too intense.

I was about to climb into a 2.5 ton truck to run field drills with the Lebanese soldiers at around 1 P.M. on April 23, when a huge explosion ripped through the air and literally lifted me and the truck off the ground. My startled Lebanese American teammate turned to me and asked, "What the hell was that?"

"Don't know, but it wasn't good."

Minutes later we received word via emergency radio that the US Embassy had been attacked. Most of us in the MTT had received combat medical training, so we grabbed our medical kits, fired up the trucks and jeeps, and sped down pitted, potholed streets, past destroyed and damaged buildings, homes, and apartment towers two and a half miles to the embassy.

The scene we encountered there was horrifying. Black smoke and dust rose from the seven-story horseshoe-shaped building. When the smoke partially cleared I saw that the entire front bay and central facade had been destroyed. Layers of rubble and collapsed balconies clogged the blackened entrance. Nearby sat a crater and the charred, smoking chassis of the van that had carried 2,000 deadly pounds of explosives.

We had arrived approximately twenty minutes after detonation, but judging from the sights, sounds, and smells around
the embassy it seemed like it had just happened. Everywhere I
looked I saw death, pain, destruction, and chaos.

A handful of freaked-out Marines in full combat-readiness
guarded the gate as though they were expecting a new wave
of attacks. We had radioed ahead, so when they saw us, they
let us through and one of the Marines shouted at our backs,
"It's fucking hell. We're undermanned and totally vulnerable.
God help us."

The first order of business was to clear the road leading
up to the gate so emergency vehicles could get through. Then
half of us grabbed our M16s and secured a perimeter around
the embassy. The rest of us shouldered our medical kits and
got to work. There were so many embassy employees—both
locals and Americans, emerging from the damaged building,
some completely disoriented, others staggering and bleeding
from wounds to their heads, faces, and various parts of their
bodies—that we didn't know where to start. The white dust
that covered many of them made them look like ghosts.

We stepped over and around rubble, fragments of metal,
and shards of glass that covered a large swath. I set down my
kit and started wiping blood off of people's faces and out of
their eyes and then applying bandages. Most were in some
form of shock, and many of them were suffering from lacera-
tions.

Two of my teammates joined me and we worked together,
looking for the most seriously wounded and trying the best
we could to stop the bleeding and calm them down. We moved
from body to body. If they were dead, we'd turn them over.

Body parts we covered with abandoned clothing, paper, or anything we could find.

I was so hyped up on adrenaline, I didn't notice the passage of time. But I became aware that ambulances and fire trucks had arrived and emergency workers had set up a temporary triage area on the side of the embassy. We moved the wounded there, helped them onto stretchers, and loaded stretchers into ambulances.

People passed us cups of water.

We worked through the night. When the sun came up the next morning, I noticed that the dead and wounded had been cleared from the grounds. Now began the grim and dangerous task of clearing the damaged building.

Sometime during the afternoon of the 24th, we returned to our safe house for a few hours of rest. Then we returned to the embassy to help clear rubble and guard it against a follow-up attack.

Marine reinforcements arrived on the 25th. A Marine sergeant said to us, "Thanks for help. We're okay here now. Just make sure you watch your asses."

Sixty-three people died in the bombing, including seventeen Americans, thirty-two Lebanese employees, and fourteen visitors applying for visas to go to the States. Of the Americans killed, eight worked for the CIA. Among them was Station Chief Kenneth Haas and Near East Director Robert Ames, later the subject of the book *The Good Spy* by Kai Bird.

Investigators learned that the bombing had been carried out by the Hezbollah terrorist group and approved and financed by senior Iranian officials. It was one of the first major suicide attacks in the Middle East.

Sadly, many more would follow, including a much bigger and deadlier explosion at the US Marine Corps barracks in Beirut six months later that would kill 220 Marines from the 1st Battalion, eighteen sailors, and three soldiers—making it the largest single-day death toll of US Marines since the Battle of Iwo Jima in World War II.

The second bombing would also be the dirty work of the Iranian-backed Hezbollah terrorist group. I watched in trepidation as the Islamic fundamentalism I had seen in Iran spread its religious poison throughout the Middle East.

5

GRENADA

It was two weeks after the US Embassy bombing, and I was with nine of my SF colleagues on a night patrol with twenty members of the Lebanese army. The air was warm and a half-moon hung low in the sky and cast eerie shadows across the landscape. We walked down a street in formation on the western outskirts of Beirut that had been the scene of recent fighting. Lebanese army intel had identified a Hezbollah safe house in the area.

The street was paved and houses were scattered on either side. In the moonlight I saw the scars of bullet holes on many of them. Most looked like they'd been abandoned.

We proceeded in full combat gear, fingers on triggers, muzzles down. SF guys spread to the front, center, left, and right. I was the next to the last in line, scanning left and right.

I saw flashes of discharges from a house to my right, and shouted, "Enemy right! Two o'clock!"

Bullets whizzed past as I went to my belly and sought cover

behind one of the few cars parked on the street. Adrenaline slammed into my system. I took some quick deep breaths to remain calm. Tracers flew at us from the direction of the roof, which was flat and made of concrete.

"Enemy on the roof! Return fire!"

My mind quickly calculated that we faced four to six enemy fighters. They were shooting bursts from automatic rifles and single shots. No grenades or rockets, which was good because we wore no armor.

I got up from my belly to my knee, aimed my M16, and squeezed off a flurry of rounds that tore into the lip of the roof. As I went back down to change my mag, an enemy bullet ricocheted off the pavement in front of me and struck me in the knee. It felt like a bee sting.

I wasn't even sure it was a bullet wound at first. But when I reached down, I felt blood and called to our medic, Patrick, who was fifteen feet to my left. "Patrick, I'm hit!"

The big man scurried over and examined my knee in the moonlight as I cursed my bad luck.

"Calm down, Changiz," he said. "It's not bad."

I'd been trained just like he had to reassure a trauma victim to prevent panic. Hundreds of thoughts coursed through my head. *I'll never walk again. I'll have to leave the service.*

Patrick wrapped bandages tight over my knee without bothering to cut away my uniform. He said, "Wait here. We'll get you out of here soon."

I was so focused on the firing that I forgot the pain. I sat with my back against the side of the car with my M16 ready as Lebanese soldiers and guys in my rear kicked in the front door of the house the rounds had come from. As they climbed the steps to the roof, the firing stopped.

Minutes later, our guys returned, breathless. One of my buddies leaned over me.

"You okay, Changiz?"

"Got nicked in the knee. You find anyone?" I asked back.

"Lots of brass casings, that's all."

"No people? No blood?"

"Negative. We're gonna check the rest of the houses on the street. You okay to wait?" he asked.

"Yeah. No problem. Do what you gotta do."

I dragged myself over to the front of the house and leaned my back against it so I could get a better view of the street. It felt weird sitting there, thinking of my family in California and my father in Iran, wondering what they were doing while I bled onto some unnamed street in Lebanon.

I felt bad for the families who had once lived in the houses, and wondered where they were now.

War fucked up everything. The moon shone an ominous shade of yellow.

My teammates returned. The Lebanese driver backed our APC (armored personnel carrier) up to the house and Patrick and another colleague loaded me in. My knee throbbed, but the pain was bearable.

Back at the base, Patrick cleaned the wound, wrapped it, and gave me a couple shots of penicillin. He said, "It looks like a glancing wound. It's superficial. You want to see a doc?"

"No. I'll be fine."

"You sure, Changiz?"

"Fuck, yeah."

I spent the next two days at the safe house reading a Robert Ludlum thriller, playing solitaire, and resting. Patrick stopped by each night to check my knee and redress the bandages. He also brought lamb *sharwarna* sandwiches from a local vendor.

Day three, when he arrived, he found me on my feet doing chores around the house.

When Patrick saw me, he asked, "What the hell are you doing?"

"I'm good to go, man."

"You sure?" Patrick asked. "Don't you want to report the injury?"

"Report what?" I answered. "I'm fine."

By filing a report about the bullet wound I would have been eligible to receive a Purple Heart. Never one to be impressed with medals, ribbons, or ceremonies, I passed. A week later, I was back on night patrol with Lebanese soldiers in a different part of the city. The moon was fuller this time, and no one was shot.

Despite the horrific embassy bombing and getting injured in the knee, I generally enjoyed my time in Beirut and came to admire the joie de vivre of the Lebanese people. Nights when we didn't patrol, I accompanied friends I'd made among the soldiers and Christian militiamen to clubs and cafés on the western side of town. We were in a war-ravaged city with active fighting, so I expected to find only a few foolish souls out at night, and most of them drowning their sorrows.

What I discovered instead were clubs packed with young

men and beautiful women, laughing, dancing, singing, and clapping their hands in unison to the movement of belly dancers. The food and wine were delicious and abundant, and everyone seemed to be having a good time. I enthusiastically joined in.

No one mistook me for an American with my swarthy looks and beard, but I carried a concealed weapon just in case. It was never needed. And no one I encountered in the clubs ever asked if I was Christian or Muslim, Shiite or Sunni—religious distinctions that had inspired the fighting around us.

What did it really matter? Who cared if you considered yourself a Sunni and believed that the first four caliphs were the legitimate successors to the Prophet Muhammad or a Shiite who accepted only the fourth caliph, Ali, as your religious leader? Was this really a disagreement that warranted spilling blood?

And what was wrong with accepting Zarathustra, Jesus Christ, Muhammad, and others as prophets? Didn't they all preach about the sovereignty of one God and the values of honesty, charity, kindness, forgiveness, humility, and sacrifice?

In 1983, I was still a relatively young man and far from a scholar, but even then it struck me that religion divided people more than it united them.

June '83, I was back at Fort Bragg, following a familiar routine—up at 0500 hours, at 0600 report to Information for company head count, then an hour of PT. That usually involved crunches, pull-ups, push-ups, and a biweekly five-mile run with a rucksack through the woods. At 0730 we were back at the barracks to shower and dress, and then we humped to the mess for breakfast—scrambled eggs, hash browns, bacon, coffee. After breakfast we'd break into training sessions based on our MOS (military occupation specialty). I was a Bravo 11 weapons man, so mine could involve advanced weapons school both in the classroom and on the firing range.

Following a noon break for lunch, MOS training continued until 5 P.M. Generally after dinner was free time. I spent mine taking classes in American history, chemistry, and physics at Campbell University so I could earn my BA.

Weekends, I might go out to the movies with friends—*Return of the Jedi* and *Flashdance* were some favorites—or lounge at nearby Myrtle Beach, depending on the weather.

After six weeks of the old routine, I was itching to return to the field. The opportunity came in early August, in the worst of the summer heat, when my team, ODA 564, was selected to go to Egypt to participate in a joint US-Egyptian military exercise called Operation Bright Star.

Bright Star was an outgrowth of the historic Camp David Accords signed by Egyptian president Anwar el-Sadat and Israeli prime minister Menachem Begin after twelve days of secret negotiations organized and moderated by President Jimmy Carter. The accords set forth a political framework for the peaceful resolution to the Israeli-Palestinian issue and called for, among other things, the Israeli withdrawal from the Sinai Peninsula, the normalization of diplomatic relations between Israel and Egypt, and a commitment from the United States of several billions of dollars of subsidies to both governments, including money and training to help modernize the Egyptian military. All positive developments in my mind.

Operation Bright Star was conceived of as a biennial training mission to strengthen military ties between the US and Egypt, improve readiness, build key leader engagements, and foster cooperation. The first Bright Star had taken place in 1981.

On a hot afternoon in August our C-141 touched down at Cairo West Military Airport, which had been bombed by the Israelis during the 1967 Six-Day War, when the Israel Defense Forces (IDF) defeated the armed forces of Egypt, Jordan, and Syria and occupied the Sinai Peninsula, Gaza Strip, West Bank, Golan Heights, and East Jerusalem—thus tripling the area under Israel's control and building its military prestige.

Israel's opening air strike of the Six-Day War, known as Operation Moked, launched the morning of June 5, 1967, had crippled Egypt's air force, destroying eleven air bases and nearly 500 combat aircraft in a matter of hours. We could still see the devastation sixteen years later. The control tower, barracks, and hangars at Cairo West Military Airport lay in ruins.

With no standing buildings to speak of, we slept in bunkers that had been dug parallel to the main runway and lived on sea rations, bottled water, and reconstituted milk. Our mission was to train three squads of Egyptian rangers in the desert heat that generally rose into the mid-90s and sometimes hit the 100s. Joining us was the 2nd Ranger Battalion based at Fort Lewis, Washington, which included jovial Staff Sergeant Joe Campbell, who became my friend.

Our training group amounted to roughly sixty-five Egyptians and forty-five Americans. The Egyptian rangers were a sad-looking corps with plastic and foam helmets, old weapons, and no parachutes. Many of them lacked shoes. Our first order of business was to outfit them with new weapons and equipment and show them how to line up properly for inspection. From the basics we continued through our order of training that concluded with five HALO jumps in the desert.

While we Green Berets ran exercises on the ground, US Navy aircraft did air maneuvers with the Egyptian air force. Overhead passed a strange mélange of US F-4E Phantoms, F-16A Falcons, F-14A Tomcats, A-7D Corsairs, A-6E Intruders, French-made Mirage 5s, Russian MiG-21MF Fishbeds, and Chinese-built Shenyang F-6Cs. It was an impressive visual representation of multinational military cooperation.

Our training included patrols along Egypt's borders. We'd fly to the location via helicopters and C-130s. Most patrols passed without incident. But one night in late August, two other guys from ODA 564, a dozen 2nd Rangers, and I accompanied the Egyptians on a night patrol along the Libyan border.

As I walked, admiring the spectacular canopy of stars, wondering if one of the tens of thousands of them cast light on a planet that supported some kind of intelligent life-form like ours, I saw muzzle flashes to my left. The commander of the Rangers in front gave the order to take cover and fire back.

The Egyptians took this as an opportunity to empty their mags, and for several minutes an intricate array of tracers arced back and forth. The Ranger commander then gave the order to bound and cover, and we retreated 500 meters. At that point the firing stopped.

When we returned to Cairo West and reported the incident, the commander of 2nd Ranger Battalion was promptly relieved of his duties and sent home.

It struck me as a severe punishment, but no one asked for my opinion. Before we left, we were given two weeks of R&R and the opportunity to board buses to Cairo to take in the sights. Having admired the ancient Egyptian pyramids since I was a kid, I wanted to see everything and followed up my visit to Giza (built around 2,500 B.C.) with trips to multiple tourist destinations in and around Cairo. These included the ancient Khan el-Khalili *souq* bazaar—which featured everything from spices to gold jewelry to T-shirts and fake Nikes—the Citadel of Saladin, and the Egyptian Museum, where I marveled at the mummies of Hatshepsut, Tuthmosis II, Ramses II, and Seti I, which were more than 3,000 years old.

Aside from the incredible history, I was struck by the poverty I saw on the crowded narrow streets in the old walled sector of the city, where kids in rags, blind and emaciated beggars, bikes, pollution, dust, flies, chickens, goats, and camels all fought for space, and cows were slaughtered and sold out in the open.

Anyone who didn't appreciate the prosperity we enjoyed in the US needed to see this.

We left in September, but Operation Bright Star grew every year. At its height in October 1999, it involved 70,000 troops from eleven nations, including Kuwait, Germany, Pakistan,

UK, Italy, Greece, and France. It was suspended in 2011 because of the political crisis in Egypt.

I returned to Bragg twenty pounds lighter due to a stomach problem I developed in Cairo. We were given forty-eight hours downtime to clean our weapons and gear. Then each one of us had to file an after-action report, brief our commanders, and meet with the intel folks. Then it was back to our camp at Mott Lake and the shooting range.

In A-teams our year was broken into four three-month cycles. During green cycles we were on standby, ready to deploy on a moment's notice. In red light cycles things got more relaxed and our duties confined to more mundane tasks like driving trucks, doing guard duty, and supporting training.

The third cycle of 1984, two of us from ODA 564 were chosen to participate in Robin Sage—a nineteen-day exercise conducted four times a year over 4,500 miles of public and private land around Robbins, North Carolina. It was a grueling, unconventional warfare scenario used to evaluate the new class of SF candidates. Considered Phase IV of the Special Forces Qualification "Q" Course, Robin Sage was an opportunity for the candidates to apply the following lessons, which they had learned in previous phases of field and classroom training around ODA's seven doctrinal mission profiles:

Foreign Internal Defense (FID): Our bread and butter. It involves working with and through indigenous troops to conduct combat operations in war and train allied and friendly forces in times of peace.

Direct Action (DA): Short duration strike actions against enemy troops, sometimes conducted by ODAs unilaterally, but often carried out with indigenous soldiers.

Special Reconnaissance (SR): Strategic intelligence gathering, often carried out behind enemy lines.

Unconventional Warfare (UW): Infiltrating into hostile nations and linking with rebel guerrilla fighters to topple a rogue regime.

Counterterrorism (CT): Usually working with an indigenous combat unit.

Counter-Proliferation (CP): Preventing terrorist and criminal organizations from obtaining weapons of mass destruction.

Information Operations (IO): Communicating with local populations to let them know who we are and what we're doing in their environment.

In 1952 Colonel Aaron Bank, known as the father of Special Forces, created Robin Sage to put soldiers in "real-world" scenarios that would test their training in these doctrinal mission profiles and adaptability.

The scenario we participated in involved the training of a mock guerrilla force in a hostile environment overseas. I was chosen to play the guerrilla leader, Chief Bargini, in a fictitious Middle Eastern country. Other guys from 5th Group assumed the roles of members of the guerrilla force. We grew beards, wore jeans and jungle boots, and guarded our camp in the woods from "government" patrols. I spoke only Farsi and tied a bandanna over my head to look more authentic.

At the outset of the exercise, we established a camp deep in the woods. Soon, student ODAs approached us and offered to lend us training and support. They bore gifts of food and supplies and spoke to me through an interpreter. When I asked for money, they explained that they could help us in more important ways.

"How?" I asked.

"We want to help you in your fight against oppression. We can help you gather intelligence, and organize patrols and ambushes. We can assist the villages under your control."

"How are you going to do that?"

"How many schools do you have?" one of the trainees asked.

I held up six fingers.

"We can supply them with paper and pencils. We can build desks and chairs. Tell us what you need."

We invited them to sit around the campfire at night, dance with us, and tell stories. By fulfilling simple tasks in the camp, the students started to blend in and gain our trust.

Within a week the SF candidates and we guerrillas were patrolling together. We showed them how to stage different kinds of ambushes and even engaged "government" soldiers, firing blanks and encircling them and taking prisoners. All the time, observers were watching the individual candidates and grading their progress.

During the third week of October, two-thirds of the way through the exercise, I was suddenly pulled away and told to report to 5th Group HQ. There I was instructed to assemble my gear and prepare for immediate deployment with 3rd Battalion.

My gear included BDUs (battle dress uniform—heavyweight 60/40 cloth) with the "Elvis" collars, PASGT (personal armor system for ground troops) Kevlar helmet, PASGT body armor, mags, mag pouches, LC-1 pistol belt, 3-point LC-1 suspenders, first-aid pouch, M7 bayonet, M16A1 rifles, and M1911.

I reported to nearby Pope Air Force Base. Most of us believed this was simply another emergency deployment readiness exercise, even though we thought it odd that we were being called away in the middle of Robin Sage.

As we packed our rucksacks and checked our weapons, word started to filter through the barracks that we were going to a place called Grenada.

"Grenada? Where the hell is that?" I asked.

When we assembled at Pope a lieutenant colonel from 3rd Battalion briefed us, and we learned that Grenada was a small Caribbean island 1,500 miles southeast of Key West, Florida. It had a population of a little over 91,000 and covered a measly 220 square miles. The capital of Grenada, which happened to be the most southerly island in the Windward Island chain, was called St. George's and boasted an estimated population of 7,500.

Most of us were scratching our heads wondering why we were going to a place none of us had ever heard of before that was a third the size of Maui. The lieutenant colonel announced in a booming voice that we were deploying to Grenada along with elements of the US Navy and Air Force in something called Operation Urgent Fury, ordered by our commander-in-chief, President Ronald Reagan.

My heart started pumping faster.

We learned that Grenada had a leftist government aligned with the Soviet Union and Cuba ruled by the New JEWEL Movement (NJM), headed by a Marxist, Maurice Bishop. Though he cooperated with the Soviets and Cubans, Bishop had sought to keep Grenada nonaligned. Apparently hard-line communists in the NJM felt that he wasn't revolutionary enough and demanded he step down. Bishop refused, and on October 19, Prime Minister Bernard Coard and his wife, backed by the Grenadian military, deposed Bishop and placed him under arrest.

Pro-Bishop supporters weren't having any of that. They took to the streets and freed Bishop, who was recaptured by soldiers and executed before a firing squad. Grenada's new leader, Bernard Coard, imposed martial law.

Meanwhile, in Washington, Reagan administration officials were concerned about the safety of 140 US medical students at the True Blue campus of St. George's University. They also worried about the presence of 700 Cuban military personnel and construction workers who were building a new runway at the Point Salines International Airport—a runway that President Reagan and his advisors thought could be used by the Soviets to expand their regional influence and to ferry arms and supplies to Central American insurgents.

This was a time when the Sandinistas ruled Nicaragua, and leftist guerrillas were trying to overthrow the government of El Salvador.

It all seemed somewhat confusing to me. The long and

short of it was that at 0530 hours on October 25, A and B Companies of the 1st Battalion of the 75th Ranger Regiment began parachuting from C-130s onto Port Salines International Airport and Operation Urgent Fury was under way. The Rangers were greeted by Cuban and Grenadian military fire from Soviet ZU-23 antiaircraft guns and BTR-60 armored personnel carriers. They quickly knocked them out with the help of AC-130 gunships.

We landed that night after the Rangers had secured the airport and cleared Cuban jeeps and other vehicles that had been parked on the runway. Some were left conveniently with the keys inside. I remember numerous C-130s landing, lots of troops spilling out, klieg lights, sweat, generators growling, and officers shouting over them with megaphones. I overheard someone say, "One day I'm coming back here on vacation."

We were directed to hump a half-mile to the beach and to start putting up tents. The only things we heard as we worked were the sounds of breaking waves and cawing seagulls.

Within two days, the US landed over 7,000 troops and had gained military control of Grenada. There had been skirmishes at the governor's mansion, Richmond Hill Prison, the radio station, and outside the Cuban compound near the town of Calliste. Nineteen Americans died and over 600 Cubans were captured. My buddy, Ranger Staff Sergeant Joe Campbell, whom I had met in Egypt, was wounded in the leg while rescuing the US medical students from St. George's University.

My team conducted night patrols in the bluffs above

Port Salines Airport. With members of the 82nd Airborne, we camped on cots in a tent city set up on the beach near the airport and north of St. George's. We passed the time playing hearts and blackjack and generally talking shit. Guys boasted about the loveliness of their girls back home and balls were busted.

A Grenadian-born sergeant I got to know in 3rd Battalion spoke the local language, which was a strange hybrid of English, Spanish, and Creole. So I hung with him a lot, and he helped me communicate with the locals, who seemed happy we were there to establish order and eager to sell us mangos, papayas, bananas, and guavas.

The island struck me as a sleepy, primitive Caribbean paradise. Probably still is.

The only real danger we encountered was from the mosquitoes and the bad jokes. A couple guys on my team got sunburns. We left five days after we arrived without having fired a single shot. Upon our return to Fort Bragg, we all received medals.

My five-year enlistment was set to expire at the end of '84, which prompted Team Sergeant Fleming to get in my face. "We need you, Changiz," he said. "Besides, where else are you going to get to do anything as fun as A-teams?"

Sergeant Fleming had a point. Maybe I was unusual, but to my way of thinking, running a gas station wasn't nearly as exciting as jumping out of airplanes with a nuke strapped to my chest or deploying behind enemy lines. Even though I hadn't seen any action in Grenada, I was proud to serve my new country as part of one of the most elite military units on the planet.

So I re-upped for another five years, was promoted to E-6 (Staff Sergeant), and continued to send most of my pay to my mother and sisters in California.

Around the same time, word reached me that 1st Group Special Forces was being re-formed and they were choosing guys from 5th Group and 7th Group to fill the ranks. Founded in 1957, 1st Group's area of operations had been the Pacific theater. But in 1974, following the end of the Vietnam War, the group was deactivated. The decision had been made in DC to bring it back to life to support US strategic efforts in Asia and contingency operations throughout the world.

Intrigued by the prospect of deploying to East Asia, I was sent to see a Sergeant Major McCowsky, who was interviewing candidates for 1st Group.

Tall and dark, he looked at me and said, "Where are you from?"

I was thinking, *Here we go again*. I answered, "I was born in Iran, sir, but I'm a US citizen now."

"So you're an Arab."

"No, sir. I was born in Iran, which isn't an Arab country. People from Iran are Persians. But now I'm an American, sir, and very proud to be one."

He frowned and cleared his throat. "I see that you're a language specialist and speak Arabic and Farsi."

"Look at my two-one, sir. There's no mention of me being a language specialist in there." DA Form 2-1 was essentially a personnel record that listed all deployments, specialized training, and education. One glance at that and he would have seen that I was much more than a language specialist.

Despite what my 2-1 said, McCowsky denied my application. Before I had a chance to get angry, another sergeant in 1st Group put my name in the system.

But prior to receiving orders to report to Fort Lewis, Washington, and help train the new battalions for 1st Group, I was selected with fourteen other Green Berets to go to South Korea to teach the South Koreans how to survive if captured. I had some expertise in this area because I was SERE qualified—meaning that I had endured three weeks of Survival, Evasion, Resistance, and Escape training at Camp Mackall.

At the end of '84, I was sent on a commercial flight to Seoul and then bused with my colleagues to a four-star hotel. Since we were on TDY (in official parlance, a "temporary duty assignment"), all our meals and expenses were covered. That meant no living on sea rations or mess hall food.

Days were spent at the nearby Yongsan (or Dragon Mountain) Garrison—a former Imperial Japanese Army base that now served as HQ for the US Forces Korea. It sat smack in the middle of Seoul and looked like the suburb of a major US city and boasted elaborate barracks, PXs, dining halls, movie theaters, restaurants, and golf courses.

In a dark basement room of one of the command centers, we taught groups of US and South Korean soldiers how to resist the harsh and abusive techniques they might encounter in a hostile situation—including prolonged constraint, exposure to extremes of heat, cold, or moisture, deprivation of food or sleep, solitary confinement, threats of pain, deprivation of sensory stimuli, and the use of physical pressure procedures like waterboarding.

I had a blast. During the day I was mock-torturing South Korean soldiers and at night I was drinking and partying with the same South Koreans in the nightclub on the ground floor of our hotel.

6

THE FAR EAST

By the mid-1980s, things had gone from bad to worse inside Iran. Though casualties continued to mount from the war with Iraq, Iran's Supreme Leader, Ayatollah Khomeini, called the conflict "a gift from God." From his perspective that was true. Not only did the vicious fighting rally much of the country around his new Islamist regime, it also gave his supporters an opportunity to brutally suppress all internal opposition in the name of national security.

Through the early 1980s I heard reports of daily arrests, assassinations, disappearances, executions, and forced televised confessions throughout Iran. Meanwhile, the country went through a cultural revolution as the reforms of the Shah were turned back, opposition political parties banned, newspapers closed, and all universities shut down and reopened two years later after going through what was called an "Islamization."

What had begun as a popular movement to depose the Shah had turned into a power grab by the mullahs that yielded a strict and brutal Islamist government. Fortunately, by the mid-1980s most of my immediate family had fled Iran and were living in the States.

The only one who remained was my father. Despite his long service to the country and enduring national pride, he too obtained a Green Card and was planning to join my mother in San Jose, California.

In January 1985 I was at Fort Lewis, assigned to ODA 174 and tasked with training new members of 2nd Battalion Special Forces. At around 1 P.M. one afternoon, I had returned to the team room and was cleaning my weapons, when I got a call from the duty sergeant.

He said, "Sergeant Lahidji, you have a family emergency."

"What happened?" I asked as my blood pressure shot up.

"Come to the battalion day room and call your brother."

I hurried there and called Iradj.

His voice was heavy with grief, "Changiz, my brother, I have bad news. Our father is dead."

I felt the air go out of me. "Dead? How? What happened?"

"We don't know for sure, but from what we hear so far, he was killed."

"Killed? By who?"

Iradj had no answer. I was granted ten days leave and drove directly to my brother's house in San Jose. Gathered there in mourning were my mother, aunts, uncles, and my brothers and sisters.

My uncle Alex pulled me aside and told me that he learned that my father had been pushed out of a window of his fifth-floor apartment in Tehran. His naked body was discovered in an abandoned lot at the back of the building. According to my uncle Yusef, who had found it, it had been lying there for days.

Mad as hell, I called Uncle Yusef in Tehran. Yusef had made it a habit to visit my father twice a week. The last time he went to my father's apartment, he rang the bell, and no one answered. So he asked the building super to let him in.

Inside, he saw signs of struggle—a chair knocked over and a broken vase. When he went to the back bedroom and looked out the window, he spotted my father's naked body lying amongst rubble downstairs. A neighbor described four men visiting my father's apartment several nights earlier. He was almost certain that they were Revolutionary Guards from the people's army formed by Ayatollah Khomeini to defend his government from internal and external threats. They were religious zealots who took orders directly from the Ayatollah and his close advisors.

My mind understood why they might regard my father as a potential enemy, since he had worked for the prior regime. But my emotions told me to hunt them down and kill them.

When I asked my team sergeant for permission to return to Tehran to attend my father's funeral, my request was turned down. I understood that, as well.

My mother traveled there instead, held a ceremony in memory of my father, and made sure he was buried next to his mother.

It was a sad time for all of us. We loved America, but part of our hearts and many of our memories were in Iran.

My father's death hit me hard. Although he hadn't treated me well as a kid, I had forgiven him and grew to admire his mental toughness. I was the son who resembled him the most physically and personality-wise, which might have explained why he had been hard on me. We dislike in others what we fear in ourselves.

Even though he had passed, I often saw his face or heard his voice. He'd tell me what to do and how to behave the same way he had when he was alive. "Don't eat too fast, Changiz. Always leave something on your plate." He had instilled in me a love of people and public service, which I had brought with me to the US.

When I returned to Fort Lewis, I felt alone and isolated. It wasn't that my teammates weren't supportive. They were.

Three weeks later, when my team sergeant came to tell me that I was getting a PCS (permanent change of station) to go to Torii Station, Okinawa, and join ODA 134, I welcomed the news. I loved exploring new places and meeting new people, and needed a change. But I was concerned about my mother, who was living with Iradj and my two sisters in San Jose.

She was depressed about the death of my father and suffering from diabetes, and so I thought she might benefit from a change of scenery too. I requested permission to take her with me as a dependent, and it was quickly approved. But I hadn't asked her yet.

So two weeks before I was scheduled to leave for Okinawa, I drove down to San Jose in my VW van accompanied by an SF friend named Ricky—who was also being transferred to Okinawa—his wife, and their two young daughters.

There, I posed the question to my mother.

She was shocked at first, and asked, "What happens if I don't like it?"

"If you don't like Okinawa, I'll bring you home."

She decided to come. We left the summer of '85 on a charter flight to Okinawa—a 500-square-mile island at the southern tip of Japan, and the site of thirty US military bases including Torii Station, home to 1st Special Forces Group (Airborne). My mother and I were assigned a two-bedroom apartment a few miles outside of the base on Highway 58. Ricky and his family lived next door.

My mom liked it at first. The subtropical climate reminded her of Iran. But because of her diabetes she had to use a walker, which made it difficult for her to get around. Also, I had been assigned to ODA 134, which was a HALO-qualified hostage rescue team, led by Captain Barry Shapiro and team sergeant Larry Kramer.

Every month we traveled to Thailand, Singapore, Malaysia, or the Philippines, where we spent a month training local security forces and practicing free-fall HALO and HAHO (high-altitude, high-opening) and static-line LALO (low-altitude, low-opening) parachute jumps. It offered an amazing aerial tour of Asia with incredible sights, excellent food, beautiful women, and some danger. All good from my point of view, but difficult for Mom, who ended up spending most of her time alone.

My first mission with ODA 134 took me to Pattaya on the southern peninsula of Thailand. The locals were the gentlest, friendliest people I'd met so far. Even the fierce-looking Thai Special Forces we trained to be the personal security detail for the king always seemed chill and relaxed. Team Sergeant Larry

Kramer explained that they were polite and kept their cool in the most difficult circumstances, because of their belief in Buddhism. Buddhism, I learned, isn't a traditional religion in the sense that it doesn't preach a particular doctrine or worship of God, but instead sets out a path for enlightenment.

Maybe that explains why there have been very few wars fought in the name of Buddhism.

Our training program was called Cobalt Blue and included CQC, helo jumps, and medical training. Our medics could not only expertly treat battlefield injuries but also walk into any village and set up a fully functioning clinic in a matter of minutes. They performed physicals, diagnosed and treated exotic diseases, administered vaccinations, set broken bones, cleaned infections, filled cavities and pulled rotten teeth, and delivered babies. They were also trained vets.

In other words, they helped us built rapport with the local people—one of the central goals of Special Forces, which we called "winning hearts and minds." Wherever we went, we spent time in the local community hoping to make a positive contribution to their lives and villages and building goodwill.

At the end of the course, we did a couple of unloaded Hollywood jumps of our own. Then the Thais joined us for a full combat HALO jump from 18,500 feet. We let the Thai SF guys go first, because they tended to open their chutes quickly, which could pose a hazard to us since we liked to free-fall to about 4,000 feet.

Then the twelve of us in ODA 134 jumped next out of the back of a C-130, facing the tail and sit-flying on exit. I felt that lovely burst of adrenaline mixed with fear at the pit of my stomach and the wind in my face. Then a sensation of pure freedom and ecstasy. A patchwork of green fields stretched as far as the horizon. The sun warmed my back.

You couldn't ask for a clearer, more beautiful day. After a few hundred feet shy of 4,000, I looked around to make sure no one was nearby, then pulled my chute. It opened and jerked me to a gentle, controlled fall. All was good.

Then without warning something slammed into me from behind at 3,500. My first thought was *I'm dead!* But I remained conscious and became aware that someone was with me. I couldn't tell who it was because all I could see was the back of his head. His chute had collapsed and his riser was twisting around my neck.

Also, two cells of my seven-cell chute had collapsed, so we were falling fast. I was certain I was a goner.

His riser tightened around my neck. My first impulse was to cut his chute away, but if I did, he would fall and die. No question.

We were falling like stones, so I had to think fast.

Suddenly the man attached to me shouted desperately, "Changiz, don't cut away. Don't cut away, please!"

I recognized the voice of my teammate John Murphy—a commo guy, who always seemed to have bad luck on jumps.

His chute was in my face now. I pushed it away, and saw that we were maybe 1,500 feet from the ground.

Murphy shouted, "Changiz, don't do it!"

I opened my reserve instead. It wasn't strong enough to handle the weight of two men, but it slowed us down. I grabbed the toggles and tried to control our descent.

A light wind pulled us past the grassy medium between the two runways where we were supposed to land. I heard guys shouting at me, but had no time to maneuver. We came in hard.

"Watch out!"

Murphy was hanging a few feet below me, so he hit the cement runway first. He groaned as his right leg shattered. I landed about a meter in front of him on both feet, fell back hard, and landed on my left side.

I was in serious pain, but at least I was alive. SF guys, both Thai and US, crowded around us. Neither Murphy nor I could get up.

The two medics on our team started to examine me. I said, "Get Murphy first." He had taken the harder fall.

They placed us gingerly in the back of a truck and drove us over to the nearby medic's shack.

Guys were giving us encouragement. "Good work, Changiz."

"You'll be okay, Murphy."

"Changiz, you did good."

"We'll get you both patched up as good as before. Maybe even better."

It hurt like hell to breathe. Beside me, Murphy's face had turned white.

"Thanks, Changiz," he moaned.

"No problem," I whispered back. "You would have done the same for me."

"Maybe not," he replied.

I held back a laugh. Murphy hadn't lost his sense of humor. The medics shot us up with morphine. Since there was no X-ray machine at the Thai SF base, there wasn't much more they could do. We waited five hours for a C-130 to arrive and fly us to Clark Air Force Base in the Philippines. It was a miserable eight-hour flight.

Twin ambulances waited for us on the Clark tarmac and rushed us to the ER. The military doctors discovered I had three broken ribs. They couldn't do anything for me and released me after three days. Pain shot through my chest every time I took a breath.

Still, Murphy had it worse. He remained in traction for three weeks, and then had to hobble around on a hard cast and crutches for three months. I cut back my PT to jogging and swimming for about a month, then hopped a military jet back to Okinawa.

When I returned to our team room, I was smiling.

"You had a good time, didn't you?" Sergeant Kramer asked.

I was happy to be back at Torii Station, but my mother was miserable. She missed our family in California and wanted me to take her back, which I did.

Thankfully, both Murphy and I were alive and healthy when ODA 134 returned to Thailand six months later. That two-week training mission ended with a big celebration at the base hosted by a Thai two-star general. Included was an enormous feast with all the trimmings—mussels; blue crabs; grilled shrimp; blood cockles; grilled fish with lime juice, garlic, and chili; pad thai; and coconut rice.

The general kept my glass filled with Mekong whiskey

and Coke. Then the lights dimmed and Thai singers and dancers in local costumes entertained us.

I was feeling no pain. The entertainment continued with nude dancing women. All of them were incredibly lovely. The Thai officers and soldiers clapped to the rhythm of the music.

When one of the young women stopped in front of me and shook her breasts in my face, I couldn't resist pulling her into my lap and kissing her breasts and neck. She giggled and the Thai soldiers laughed and chanted my name, "Changiz! Changiz! Changiz!"

If part of our mission was to build goodwill with the Thais, we had succeeded. A great time was had by all!

The late 1980s were a time of relative peace. Aside from some horrible terrorist airplane bombings, continued violence in Israel and the Palestinian territories, and several regional conflicts, there wasn't much need for Special Forces to deploy in a combat role. I spent most of my time with 1st Group assigned to Okinawa and traveling to other Asian countries on rotational training.

The pace and physical toll of A-teams were incredible—nonstop traveling, jumping, and training. I loved it. According to customary practice, most guys were transferred from A-teams to support jobs after three or four years of service. Whenever it became time for me to be reassigned to a less physically challenging job, I'd go to the company sergeant major and say, "Cut me a break, man. You know my English isn't good. Besides I love being on A-teams, and that's what I signed up to do."

"Come on, Changiz," he'd say, "you know the drill."

Every time it came up, I managed to get my wish, in part because of my unique qualifications. I also tried to make myself as valuable as possible. As an operations sergeant, I did the scheduling for the sergeant major, which meant that I had to keep track of what every member of the five A-teams in the company was doing at all time.

We deployed constantly. One of my favorite places to go on assignment was the Philippines, which turned out to be a good thing because we went at least three times a year. While training Filipino rangers we'd do three jumps a day for two weeks. We spent most of our time at Clark AFB—a huge 156,204-acre facility fifty miles north of Manila on the main and largest Philippine island, Luzon, one of the more than 7,000 islands that make up the country.

Clark sat on a lush plateau framed by the Zambales Mountains and Mount Pinatubo volcano. The base was originally built by the US Army Cavalry in 1902 and called Fort Stotsenburg and selected for its abundant grass, which was used to feed the horses. Eventually the cavalry left and the Air Force took over.

Within the twenty-six-mile perimeter sat approximately 3,500 buildings and military structures, 1,600 houses, dormitories, barracks, restaurants, schools, stores, playgrounds, a golf course, cinemas, riding stables, a zoo, and other facilities. The base had a turbulent history—overrun by the Japanese in 1942, witness to the famed Bataan Death March a month later, when 70,000 Allied prisoners were force-marched past the main gate, recaptured by the US after fierce combat in 1945, and a key logistics hub during the Vietnam War. At its peak in the late 1980s, it had a permanent population of 15,000 and was our largest military base overseas.

Immediately adjacent to the base was a barrio called Angeles City with a population of something like 200,000. Among its major industries were the barmaids, hostesses, and g-string-clad dancers who kept US servicemen entertained. It was also the site of a San Miguel brewery distribution center that supplied the base and hundreds of go-go bars with good beer.

Other products of Angeles consisted of wood carvings, wicker furniture, and the capiz shell lamps that decorated many officers' homes. It was a slum by US standards with narrow dirt streets clogged with human-powered pedicabs, bicycles, the occasional water buffalo, and colorful, chrome-splayed vehicles of all sizes known as jeepneys. But fascinating to me. I spent my downtime there.

It wasn't like we had a lot to do otherwise. During our assignments to Clark, our twelve-man team did daily HAHO jumps from as high as 36,500 feet. We'd open at 31,000 and try to land within five feet of one another—which we often did. When the wind was blowing north we'd jump at 26,000 feet over Manila, and our lead man would use a compass to guide us all the way to Clark. Our chosen impact point was a huge circular antenna that rose from the center of the base. We'd follow in at staggered distances and hit the target within a few feet.

Nights at Clark, we'd parachute from 18,500 with chemlite sticks and full gear, then go to the bars in Angeles to party.

Favorite haunts included the Crow's Nest, Honey Ko's, and the Golden Nile, where you could get a cold glass of San Miguel for 50 cents. The same beer purchased for one of the bar girls or hostesses cost eight times that.

Jumps usually ended at 2100 and started up again 1000 the next morning. I loved them, and the scenery, and the Filipino people, who were mostly warm, and friendly, and trying to make a life for themselves under very difficult circumstances.

Every night I went out, I'd always stop and buy orchids, gardenias, and paper daisies from the preteen girl vendors on the streets outside the bars. As soon as they'd spot me, they'd run over and shout, "Changiz. Changiz! You buy beautiful flower. One dollar. Make your girlfriend smile."

"Yeah. Yeah. Of course."

One time, late into the night after my teammates had gone off in search of carnal pleasure, I staggered out of the Crow's Nest alone and inebriated to the point that I passed out on the street. Usually that meant you were relieved of your wallet and valuables by one of the toughs or billy boys (transvestites) who frequented the neighborhood. In my drunken state, I heard the street girls screaming at several of the billy boys to stay away from me. One of the girls said, "Leave him alone. He's my cousin!"

Four of the girls managed to pull me to my feet and walk me several blocks to Gate Four of the base. Under a sign that warned, SLOW DOWN AND LIVE, I heard them arguing with the Filipino guards to let me in. One of the guards demanded to see my military ID. One of the girls fished my wallet out of my pocket. The guards not only granted me access, they also hailed a cab that drove me the half mile into the base to my barracks.

I thanked the guards later and took them out for drinks. Next time I saw the flower girls, I handed each of them a twenty. From then on whenever I went barhopping, the girls would escort me from place to place.

Another late night on the town some weeks later, I was somewhat tipsy again and in need of change for a hundred-dollar bill. I went over to a money exchange window and kept my eyes on the rough-looking dudes behind me as the money changer counted out what I thought were five twenties.

Later that night when I went to pay the cab driver who returned me to the barracks, I noticed that what I really had been given were one twenty and four dollar bills. *Stupid me,* I thought. *No more going out at night and getting wasted.* Out of curiosity, I reported the incident the next day at the Filipino police station on base.

I didn't expect any follow-up. To my surprise a young police officer I had become friendly with went with me into town that night and asked me to point out the money changer. The officer grabbed the guy by the neck and took him to Gate One.

At Gate One he was confronted by other local security guards I knew. One of them got in the money changer's face and shouted, "What the fuck are you doing robbing this guy? This man is our friend."

The money changer removed a wad of money from his wallet, counted out five twenties, and handed them to me.

Another night, I invited three of the Filipino security men to go out with me for drinks. As we walked along Perimeter Road, some guy reached into my pocket and tried to steal my wallet. I reacted by grabbing his wrist and throwing him to the ground. Within seconds, three dozen angry local toughs surrounded me. I expected to be pummeled.

But before the first punch was thrown, one of the guards I was with drew his pistol and fired in the air. The toughs scattered. A distress call was made and more armed guards arrived from Gate One. Their message was clear: Don't fuck with this guy. From then on, I was left alone.

It helps to make friends.

I love jumping from planes almost as much as sex, and tried to do both as often as possible. A-teams certainly satisfied my appetite for the former. But with anything that's so much fun as jumping from high altitudes comes danger and possible complications.

Once, while at Clark, my A-team and another traveled to a CQC compound to train Philippine Army Special Forces. The Filipino commandos weren't yet jump-qualified, so we arranged to do a demonstration with full combat gear. The plan was to jump from 18,500, land near their shooting range, and start firing and hitting targets.

We carried large MC-5 chutes with rucksacks underneath, Kevlar helmets with parachutist foam impact pads and retention straps that wrapped forward and back around the chinstrap and under the buckles, and black jungle boots. The chute system alone weighed around forty pounds. Our rucksacks, first-aid kits, radios, weapons, and mags added another eighty or ninety.

Visibility was good, and with a light SW wind I jumped from the C-130, did a quick skill roll, and fell chest-first, arms out for almost a minute. I checked the gauge on the altimeter on my wrist and opened at 4,000 feet. My canopy then opened without a problem. At 500, I pulled the tab to lower my rucksack, then pulled my knees up into prepare-to-land position. But I brought my toggle down and let it up too fast, and at 100 feet saw that I was heading straight for a big boulder and had no room to maneuver.

I hit it and the pain from my legs was so massive that I immediately went into shock. Our team medic, Bernie O'Rourke, rushed over to me, saw a piece of my right femur poking through my uniform above the opening of my boot, and undid my chute.

He administered two shots of morphine and wrapped a bandage over the top of my uniform. Our team sergeant summoned a truck to drive me to Clark.

Bernie said to him, "Are you crazy? It's a five-hour drive."

Bernie called for medevac instead, which arrived forty-five minutes later. As he and another team member were carrying me on a stretcher to the back of the Chinook helicopter, Bernie slipped and dropped his end of the stretcher, which hit the tailgate.

"Changiz, I'm so sorry," he said.

"What the fuck, Bernie," I replied smiling, totally numb from the morphine.

Waiting on the Clark AFB tarmac was an ambulance that

rushed me to the hospital. I spent five and a half hours in surgery and didn't feel a thing.

I woke up the next day with my leg in traction and my ankle held on with plates fixed to either side with a dozen screws. A month later, I was medevaced to Okinawa, where I spent another three months hobbling around with a hard cast and crutches.

Six months after the accident, I went to the naval hospital in Okinawa to finally get the screws removed. The doctor said, "This is only a minor surgical procedure. You want anesthesia to put you out?"

"No thanks, Doc," I answered. "I'll be okay."

The nurses placed a wad of gauze in my mouth, and the doctor made a small incision to access the screws. As I lay on the table bleeding, he realized he didn't have the right screwdriver.

He yelled to the nurse, "Run downstairs and get a smaller screwdriver."

I said, "Please hurry, Doc, I'm losing all my blood."

By the time she returned, the sheet under my leg was soaked red. The doc patched me up and put me in a walking cast that I wore for another three months. From accident to full healing lasted a frustrating fifteen months.

December 1989, I was in Guam as a member of ODA 136 practicing CQC and hostage rescue as an E7 (Sergeant First Class) when we got an urgent message to report back to Okinawa for immediate deployment. Back at our SF base at Torii Station, the twelve of us packed our black deployment bags with radios, goggles, knee pads, extra mags, etc. Then we reported to the team room for a briefing.

An SF colonel told us we were flying that night to Clark to help put down a military coup against democratically elected President Corazon Aquino. I knew little about President Aquino at the time, except what I had heard on the news. During a briefing I learned that she had been a quiet housewife raising five children while her husband was elected senator and rose to political prominence as a leading critic of the government of longtime strongman President Ferdinand Marcos. When Marcos declared martial law and abolished the constitution in September 1972, because it forbade him from running for a third term, her husband was arrested and sentenced to death. Corazon Aquino thrust herself into Filipino politics to campaign on her husband's behalf.

And when he was assassinated in 1983 upon his return to the Philippines after receiving medical treatment in the US, she assumed her husband's mantle as figurehead of the anti-Marcos political opposition. When Marcos made a surprise announcement that he would hold presidential elections in 1986, his opposition clamored for Corazon to run against him and she reluctantly agreed.

The presidential election of February 1986 was marred by massive fraud, violence, and intimidation. Marcos's ruling political party declared him the winner. But millions of Filipinos took to the streets in support of Aquino, the US and other countries condemned the election, and military officers led by defense ministers announced their defection from the Marcos government and declared Aquino the real winner.

After three days of peaceful protests throughout the Philippines, in what became known as the People Power Revolution, Aquino was sworn in as president. She immediately enacted a series of reforms and proposed a new constitution that put strong emphasis on civil liberties, human rights, and social justice. She also ordered that our military vacate our naval base at Subic Bay, as well as Clark Air Base.

In an interesting bit of irony, we landed at Clark on the morning of December 2 to help support the Aquino presidency against a military coup launched by soldiers loyal to former President Marcos the previous day. Apparently 3,000 of them had shut down the international airport—named after President Aquino's late husband—seized several military air bases, and even tried to take over the presidential palace.

President Aquino had requested US military assistance, and we launched Operation Classic Resolve. US Air Force Phantom II fighters took off from Clark with clearance to buzz rebel planes at their bases, fire in front of them if they attempted to take off, and shoot them down if they did.

We stayed in a hangar at Clark with two US Navy SEAL teams on full military alert waiting to be called into action. Our mission was to rescue President Aquino from the presidential palace and take her to Clark AFB, should the palace come under siege. We spent the next ten days working out and playing cards.

Some of the SEALs were standoffish. Some were cool. After the ten days, we were recalled to Okinawa.

My last stay at Clark was one year later, in May 1991, when volcanic ash from nearby Mount Pinatubo started to rain over the base and seismographs recorded hundreds of minor earthquakes that geologists believed were precursors to a major eruption. Because of the falling ash and dangerous levels of sulfur, all combat aircraft and nonessential personnel were being evacuated. We left the day before the volcano erupted on the 15th of June, producing the second largest terrestrial eruption of the twentieth century.

The entire base was shut down and subsequently turned over to the Philippine government, which reopened it as a commercial airport in 1993.

7

FIRST GULF WAR

During my time with ODA 136, we traveled frequently to Guam—a US territory in the Pacific Ocean and the largest island in Micronesia with 210 square feet and a population of roughly 150,000 people. On December 7, 1941, it had been captured by the Japanese army hours before the attack on Pearl Harbor. It was liberated by the US in July 1944 and had since been home to several large US military bases, including Andersen Air Force Base and US Naval Base Guam.

During a stay there in 1990, my teammates and I decided to try to break the world HALO team jump record. Our plan was to go up in a B-52 bomber and jump from 40,000 feet. It would have been awesome. But when we submitted our request to SOCOM, they turned it down.

So we settled for a C-130 instead and were going to be joined by three US Marines, two Air Force officers, and six AF crewmen. The day before the jump, we packed and repacked our chutes—like we always do—checked our equipment, and practiced switching from the pure oxygen we would breathe on the plane to the mixed oxygen bottle that would be attached to our stomachs as we descended.

Jumping from 40,000 feet isn't something you take casually, and involves serious health hazards, like hypoxia and decompression sickness. To compensate for a lack of oxygen in the air, heart and breathing rates increase. We knew that hypoxia or oxygen deprivation could result in dizziness, euphoria, blurred or tunnel vision, poor muscle coordination, and slow reaction time—things we didn't want to experience when we were falling to earth at up to 128 mph. You forget to open your chute and for some reason your reserve doesn't open, and you're a goner. Pigeon feed.

Decompression sickness (DCS), or the bends, occurs when nitrogen bubbles form in the tissues and blood due to a rapid reduction in pressure. It manifests as joint pain and can cause paralysis and death.

The higher the altitude, the higher the risk of developing DCS. So before we took off, we spent an hour and a half on the ground breathing pure oxygen to purge nitrogen from our systems. Then we ascended to 40,000 feet—roughly 11,000 feet higher than Mount Everest. Since we weren't in a pressurized cabin, we continued to breathe O_2 from a console on the plane. That didn't prevent the two Air Force officers from developing air embolisms—gas bubbles that entered the bloodstream due to trauma to the lungs caused by the lack of pressure and our rapid descent.

The symptoms were similar to decompression sickness—

in the case of the Air Force officers, tremors, numbness, and loss of consciousness. Not good at all when you needed to be alert.

So we descended to 37,200 feet to lessen the strain on our bodies. The Air Force guys felt better. But when we tried to open the back gate of the C-130, the wind speed outside was so strong that we couldn't lower it. We had to open the side doors instead.

The temperature inside the plane was a bone-chilling -10 degrees Fahrenheit, and it promised to be even colder given the windchill factor outside. It wouldn't be out of the question if it dipped to -40. All of us wore long underwear under our jumpsuits, sock and glove liners, and hoods over our necks and ears. The cold was a critical factor, because we needed a few minutes of manual dexterity to properly adjust our equipment before exiting the aircraft and time to maneuver our parachutes immediately after exiting.

The racket from the plane made speech impossible, so our team leader raised his hand to signal the two-minute warning. We unhooked our breathing masks from the C-130's console, attached them to our individual oxygen bottles, then checked each other's eyes to make sure no one was suffering from hypoxia. We were all good so far.

We quickly double- and triple-checked our equipment, connections, and bottle pressure. Then the jump light shifted from red to green. I took a deep breath, and three seconds behind our team sergeant starting falling at 140 mph. The feeling was indescribable. We were so high above the clouds we couldn't see the ground. I knew that if I opened my chute at this height, it would explode into shreds. But I had no interest in ending the exhilarating fall.

As I dropped like a stone, air pushed against my arms and chest. The closer I got to earth, the denser the pressure grew, until the force of it threatened to rip my mask and helmet off my head. The temperature grew warmer, too, as I sank through layers of clouds and saw the beautiful green earth spread below.

After falling for four and a half minutes, I reached 4,000 feet and opened my chute.

Our landing site was the runway of the international airport, but the wind was strong and pulled us west. I watched the sergeant ahead of me drift past the runway. I came down in a field of sugarcane. The guys behind me landed even farther away, as far as a Kmart parking lot.

Aside from our team sergeant, who suffered frostbite to his face, the remainder of us came through unscathed. What an experience. The icing on the cake was when we learned we broke the world record and made the news locally and in the US.

Upon my return to Okinawa, I heard that Iraqi strongman Saddam Hussein had invaded Kuwait and was placing troops on the border of Saudi Arabia. It sounded ominous as hell, knowing as I did that Iraq possessed the world's fourth largest army and had developed a stockpile of biological and chemical weapons and that its leader, Saddam, was an aggressive SOB who wanted to dominate the Persian Gulf.

Saddam's war against Iran—which ended in 1988—had left his country highly indebted to Saudi Arabia and Kuwait.

With his economy in shambles and his countrymen disheartened, Saddam asked the Arab countries to relieve the debts. They had refused.

Adding to Saddam's displeasure with Kuwait was a long-standing dispute over territory and the fact that Kuwait had been exceeding its OPEC quotas for oil production. When Kuwait refused to yield to Iraqi diplomatic efforts and threats, Saddam launched an invasion on August 2, 1990.

Iraq's million-man standing army quickly overwhelmed Kuwait's tiny military, the Kuwaiti royal family fled the country, and within twelve hours Iraq gained control of most of oil-rich Kuwait.

The rest of the world responded with shock and outrage. US president George H. W. Bush joined the United Nations Security Council and the Arab League in condemning the invasion and calling for the immediate withdraw of Iraqi troops from Kuwait. Through the remainder of 1990, a diplomatic tug-of-war ensued as Saddam tried to wangle concessions from Saudi Arabia, the US, and other countries, and they demanded that he leave Kuwait.

Also of serious concern were Saddam's mounting verbal attacks on Saudi Arabia. With large elements of the Iraqi army now within easy striking distance of Saudi oil fields, the world feared Saddam would extend his ambitions even further. The Saudi oil fields, along with Kuwaiti and Iraqi reserves, would give him control of the majority of the world's oil reserves.

For obvious reasons, this was an unacceptable scenario to the US and many other countries. On August 7, President Bush announced an immediate buildup of US troops in Saudi Arabia at the request of its leader, King Fahd, to protect its border with Iraq. Under the code name Operation Desert Shield, the US quickly deployed more than 200,000 military personnel to Saudi Arabia, including thirty-six F-15s from the 36th Tactical Fighter Wing based in Bitburg, Germany, and forty-eight F-15s from the 1st Fighter Wing from Langley Air Force Base, Virginia. Additionally, the aircraft carriers USS *Dwight D. Eisenhower* and *Independence* and their battle group and the battleships *Missouri* and *Wisconsin* stationed themselves in the Persian Gulf.

As soon as I heard about the buildup of forces in the area leading to what looked like a showdown with Iraq, I wanted to be included.

So I marched into the Special Forces administrative office in Okinawa and asked the sergeant major on duty to be deployed immediately. I said, "Sir, I speak Arabic and Farsi and know I can be useful. I request that you send me to be part of Operation Desert Shield."

He seemed surprised by my request and reminded me that I was assigned to 1st Group Special Forces, which wasn't being called and was slated to remain in Okinawa to continue its rotational training.

"With all respect, sir," I replied, "I'm not complaining. All I'm saying is that I think I can be of more use in the Middle East. I speak the local languages. I know the region. I can help in whatever capacity I'm needed."

"Sergeant," he shot back, "you're assigned to First Group, and as far as I know that's not going to change. So return to your unit."

It was typical by-the-books bureaucracy. Not to be deterred,

I went to see 1st Group Sergeant Major McGuire and SF Major Ronnie Strand, who happened to be visiting the base, and made the same request to them.

The two saw the value I could bring to the operation and told me they would send me to Fort Campbell, Tennessee, to join 5th Group, which had already deployed to the Middle East. My former SF group was no longer headquartered at Bragg and had moved to Campbell.

"Why can't you just send me to Saudi Arabia to join Fifth Group there?" I asked.

"Sorry, Sergeant, it doesn't work that way," Major McGuire explained. "You have to be processed out of First Group first and file a PCS [permanent change of station] before you can go to Fifth."

"Thank you, sir."

I flew to California in late December 1990 and spent a couple of days with my family, making sure not to tell them that I was deploying to the Middle East. The looming conflict with Iraq was the lead story on the news every night.

In late November, the UN Security Council had passed Resolution 678, which gave the Iraqis a deadline of January 15, 1991, to withdraw from Kuwait. It also authorized the use of force should Iraq fail to comply. Meanwhile, the Pentagon determined that the 200,000 men it already had in Saudi Arabia weren't enough to drive the heavily armed, well-entrenched Iraqis out of Kuwait. So President Bush, with Saudi approval, deployed an additional 140,000 US soldiers, including the 3rd Armored Division and its Abrams M1A tanks. Concurrently, he and his representatives started to assemble a coalition of forces to oppose Iraq that eventually included thirty-four countries—among them the UK, Argentina, Canada, Egypt, Italy, Pakistan, Senegal, France, and Syria.

Germany and Japan didn't commit troops but made financial contributions that totaled over $16 billion. Even the Soviet Union supported the US-led coalition. As I watched and waited, 956,600 coalition forces arrived in the Persian Gulf under the command of US Army General Norman Schwarzkopf, Jr.

I was at Fort Campbell, where I spent a very frustrating month being processed and taking gas mask and advanced weapons training.

On January 15 the UN deadline for Iraqi withdrawal from Kuwait came and went, and the following morning Coalition forces launched Operation Desert Storm, which began with a powerful bombing campaign aimed at destroying Iraqi border radar stations and key elements of their antiaircraft network. Targets expanded over the next several days to include Iraqi command and communications facilities, weapons research facilities, and naval forces.

The initial air attacks gave our military an opportunity to see how our new weapons performed in combat conditions. We quickly found out that ground-fired M1A1 Abrams and MIM-104 Patriot missiles gave the Iraq military little time to defend themselves. And the groundbreaking new Global Positioning System (GPS) helped to pinpoint hits by the Tomahawk missile and other weapons and allowed troops to find their way in the desert without the use of maps.

Iraq responded to Coalition air strikes by launching Scud

missiles at Saudi Arabia and Israel, which did some damage, but were relatively ineffective. Then on January 29, Iraq attacked and occupied the Saudi city of Khafji, which was retaken by elements of the Saudi National Guard backed up by US Marines two days later.

Meanwhile, the Coalition took complete control of the skies over Iraq and Kuwait and continued a brutal day-and-night air assault, which averaged 2,555 sorties every twenty-four hours. US F-15s, AH-64 Apache helicopters, B-52 Stratofortress bombers, and F-117A Stealth fighters inflicted devastating damage to Saddam Hussein's vaulted Republican Guard.

I saw this with my own eyes when I finally arrived in Saudi Arabia the third week of February attached to ODA 596. Our top secret mission was to sneak into Iraq at night and ID targets. Covered with face paint, night cammos, and body armor, we deployed in four-man teams—sometimes all four of us in a Humvee with a .50 caliber machine gun mounted in back, and on other occasions two guys each riding four-wheel dirt bikes.

We got our orders directly from the J2s (military intel guys) at Coalition headquarters with specific quadrants to search. Our rules of engagement (ROE) required that we avoid detection but allowed us to return fire should we be engaged by Iraqi forces.

Going across the border at night into enemy territory was extremely tense, especially when we knew the enemy was in a high state of alert. We carried AN/TVS-5 night observation scopes with a range of over one kilometer and GPS markers.

We used them to identify and mark targets such as Iraqi bunkers, tanks, and hard sites for future F-15 strikes.

I participated in a dozen such missions. Training for them was one thing, but actually venturing into enemy territory and avoiding land mines, snipers, and ambushes was different. All my senses were on high alert. We knew that, if captured, the Iraqis would likely torture us. It wouldn't be the game playing we had participated in at SERE school. It would be the real thing with real pain and real degradation.

I squelched my fears and focused on the mission. The landscape was a desert with a few low hills. Stars spread bright overhead as though they were watching. Our ears strained to hear over the muffled engines. Our eyes scanned the horizon for shadows, movement, and flickers of light.

Third time out, four of us were on two dune buggies, bouncing over mounds of dirt. I stopped our buggy on a bluff, cut the engine, and surveyed the land in front of us through Steiner night binos. Nothing to the left or in the middle, but 200 meters away and to the right I saw a group of five soldiers standing outside a fence that encircled two one-story cement structures. They were huddled together. I couldn't tell if they were actively guarding the compound or drinking tea.

The Iraqis heard an echo from a buggy behind us, shouldered their AK-47s, and opened fire. We shot back, causing them to scurry inside the compound and seek cover.

"Cowards," one of my colleagues muttered.

"Let's get the fuck out of here before they send out a patrol," I said back.

We quickly noted the GPS coordinates of the compound, radioed them to base, and set out looking for new targets. Two nights later when we passed through that sector, the buildings had been reduced to piles of charred rubble.

Poor fools, I thought to myself. *Blindly following the ambitions of a megalomaniac.*

Another time, we were sent out to inspect a suspected WMD (weapons of mass destruction) site about twenty miles inside Iraq. Late at night, we passed through a sandstorm and found what looked from a distance like an empty compound—no lights, no sign of movement. Fingers on the triggers of our M16s, we moved all the way up to the fence. As my colleagues kept watch, I cut through the lock at the gate. Then while two guys kept guard, myself and another colleague donned chemical suits and went inside.

We found two low, abandoned buildings and some old barrels and rusted cylinders. I wasn't a chemical weapons expert, but it looked like a whole lot of nothing.

Nevertheless, we called in the coordinates to an F-15 pilot overhead, then cleared out and watched from a safe distance as the jet swooped in and obliterated the compound. The spectacle from a half mile away was incredible, and the destructive power of one F-15 was awe-inspiring.

Now I understood why the resolve of the Iraqi forces wasn't strong. We witnessed that phenomenon over and over in the three or four firefights we engaged in. As soon as we directed fire at Iraqi soldiers they generally fled right away, even though we were operating in their territory at night and almost certainly outnumbered.

So it wasn't a surprise to me that when the Coalition ground assault launched at the end of February, it met little resistance. The liberation of Kuwait took four days. With the exception of a few intense tank battles, most Iraqi units surrendered quickly. They left behind looted homes and businesses, land mines, and over 700 burning oil wells.

The US-led Coalition juggernaut didn't stop at the liberation of Kuwait but proceeded into Iraq and punished Saddam's Republican Guard. US Army VII Corps led by the 2nd Armored Cavalry Regiment rolled into southern Iraq from western Kuwait. Simultaneously, the US XVIII Airborne Corps spearheaded by the 3rd Armored Cavalry Regiment and the 24th Infantry Division attacked across Iraq's undefended southern desert. They were joined by UK's 1st Armoured Division and France's 6th Light Armoured Division Daguet.

This time some Iraqi Republican Guards fought back fiercely from dug-in positions and with tanks. But they were outmaneuvered, flanked, and eventually trapped between the two large forces and pounded. After taking heavy casualties, they turned and ran—troops, tanks, and vehicles—in a massive retreat northwest up the six-lane Iraq-Kuwait Highway (Highway 80). Coalition air forces pounded retreating Guard units with rockets, machine guns, and bombs, turning the road into what became known as the Highway of Death. Meanwhile, Coalition forces pursued Iraqi soldiers to within 150 miles of Baghdad, before they withdrew to Iraq's eastern border.

One hundred hours after the Coalition ground assault

started, it had achieved its goals. And on February 28, President Bush declared a cease-fire.

An estimated 20,000 to 26,000 Iraqi soldiers and military personnel died in the conflict, while the Coalition suffered 348 casualties. One hundred and forty-eight of them were Americans.

The humiliating defeat suffered by Saddam Hussein's army inspired uprisings among Shiite Muslims and demoralized soldiers in the southern city of Basra and among Kurdish nationalists in northern Iraq. Saddam loyalists responded to both attacks without mercy.

It was during this time, in the second week of March 1991, that US intelligence officers were looking for volunteers to infiltrate into Iraq and report on the internal violence. Like always, I raised my hand, and due to my background and language skills, I was selected by the two S2 military intel guys who were directing the mission.

Our five-man team included a big African American E5 in Special Forces named Leonard, who claimed he spoke Arabic, which turned out to be a big exaggeration, a tall Lebanese American SF medic named Yusef, and two young Kuwaiti military intel guys, Abdullah and Majeed.

The S2 officers who briefed us included this warning: "This isn't going to be an easy job. Don't do anything to call attention to yourselves. Constantly monitor your own behavior. Take mental notes of everything you see, but don't write anything down."

"Can we carry weapons?" Leonard asked.

"That's up to you. If you do bring a weapon, make sure

it's a Russian- or Chinese-made pistol and keep it hidden, and keep in mind that you're doing so at your own risk. You're on your own. If you're caught, don't expect us to help you."

The mission brought back memories of going into Tehran a decade earlier. Except Iraq wasn't familiar to me. All we knew was that if we were found out to be Americans, we were certainly going to suffer.

In consultation with the J2 guys, we came up with a cover. We were going to be Iraqis who had been working for an oil company in Kuwait and were returning to Iraq to find our boss and see what we could do to help our families.

When it was time to select a name for my fake Iraqi ID card, I chose that of one of my heroes, former heavyweight boxing champ Muhammad Ali. One of the Kuwaitis bought us clothes in a local market, short-sleeved cotton shirts, loose pants, and inexpensive leather shoes. I grew my beard out and wrapped my head in a turban.

The five of us crossed into Iraq from Kuwait in a beat-up Toyota 4Runner. Yusef drove at moderate speed so as not to attract attention. Traffic on Highway 80 was extremely light, and we immediately saw why it had been dubbed the Highway of Death. Lining both sides of the road at macabre angles was a shocking array of destroyed civilian and military vehicles— particularly Soviet-built T-72 tanks and BMP-1s and Chinese Type 63 armored personnel carriers. Sections of the highway had been torn up by US bombs. Others had been completely obliterated, leaving huge craters and forcing us to leave the road and drive around them.

Upon reaching the outskirts of Basra, we stopped at a local

coffee shop to take the pulse of the dozen or so men gathered there, smoking, sipping coffee, and exchanging gossip. They were suspicious and asked who we were, and where we were from. Yusef did most of the talking, because I had a slight Persian accent.

Our cover story seemed to put them at ease.

The men told us that people in the city were in desperate need of food and water. The uprising started, they said, when a tank returning from Kuwait had fired at a large portrait of Saddam Hussein hanging in the town square. Other soldiers fired their guns in the air and cheered.

The rebelling soldiers inspired masses of Shiite civilians to take to the streets shouting antigovernment slogans, looting Sunni-owned stores, and staging protests outside government buildings, especially offices of the security forces. Gun battles eventually broke out, and besieged security forces called for reinforcements. The response by army units loyal to Saddam Hussein was swift and brutal. Thousands of civilians were killed, and hundreds of Shiite leaders and clerics thrown in jail.

The men at the coffee shop warned us that the situation in the city was still extremely tense. And as we approached downtown Basra, we heard sporadic gunfire. The center of the city was clogged with groups of men standing around and being watched by grim-looking soldiers in military gear with tanks and armored vehicles. It felt as though violence between them could ignite again any second.

We saw signs of recent fighting everywhere, on pockmarked buildings, burned-out cars and trucks, and shattered storefronts. We moved cautiously, took copious mental notes of street names and numbers of civilians and soldiers, and moved on.

That night we stayed with a family friend of the Kuwaiti officer Abdullah. They were nice people, but very frightened. They told us they couldn't say anything before for fear of being arrested, but now complained openly about Saddam Hussein and how he was destroying the country. They struck me as the type of normal, decent family you'd find in any country—a high school teacher father, housewife mother, and kids going to school. Their distress moved me. They said they had no beef with Kuwait, Iran, or Saudi Arabia, and just wanted to live in peace.

I barely slept that night and was startled awake every twenty minutes or so by an explosion or a peal of automatic arms fire. At 0430 hours the next morning we were back on Highway 80 headed north to Baghdad. Again we saw a staggering number of destroyed and abandoned military vehicles along the road as we passed.

Traffic was light, and we proceeded without being stopped until we reached an Iraqi military checkpoint about 100 miles outside of Baghdad. There, soldiers in full battle gear waved at us to stop. Behind them stood trucks with mounted machine guns and gunners. The soldiers didn't look happy.

As Yusef slowed our 4Runner to a stop, we debated whether we should offer them money or not.

"Don't do it," one of the Kuwaitis warned in Arabic. "They'll want everything we have. They'll take our vehicle."

"I don't agree," the other Kuwaiti said, while Leonard seemed to be praying quietly from the backseat.

A very tired and grim-looking young soldier approached the driver's side window and pointed an AK at Yusef's chest.

"Papers," he grunted.

We handed him our fake documents and he scanned them quickly as more soldiers gathered around and started peering in the windows, not really at us, but at what we had. We had hidden our pistols under the seats.

"Where are you going?" the young soldier asked.

"Baghdad," answered Yusef.

"Why?"

"We work for an oil company in Kuwait. Everything is shut down there. It's very bad. We're going into Baghdad to talk to our boss and ask him what he wants us to do."

"Who's your boss?"

"Ahmed."

"Ahmed what?"

"Ahmed Hassani."

Both were common Iraqi names. The young soldier handed back our ID papers and said, "It's very bad here, too. We're all starving. You have any food?"

We had brought dates and hard cookies with us from Kuwait, which we shared with the half-dozen soldiers. More hurried over when they saw we had food.

A couple of cars had stopped behind us and were waiting. As the soldiers devoured the dates and cookies, smiles returned to some of their faces.

"Thank you, brothers," the young soldier said.

This moved Yusef to reach into his pocket and hand him two US twenty-dollar bills. I tensed for a second, but the soldier immediately expressed his appreciation.

"May God bless, you, my brother," he said.

"Use the money to buy some food and drink for you and your friends," Yusef said.

The soldiers waved us through, and we relaxed.

"This is fucked," Leonard groaned from the back, expressing what all of us were feeling.

We continued into Baghdad, past torn and defaced pictures of Saddam Hussein and walls splashed with angry graffiti in Arabic, which read, FUCK YOU SADDAM AND FUCK YOUR MOTHER! SADDAM IS THE DEVIL. SADDAM, WE HATE YOU!

Interestingly, none of the graffiti was directed at the US or the Coalition. My heart beating hard and fast, we drove past the huge unfinished Umm al-Qura (Mother of all Cities) mosque, which Saddam later used to commemorate his "victory" in the Gulf War.

Baghdad had once been a thriving city, but now the streets were filled with people begging for food and money—women, children without shoes, and grown men in tears. We handed out the spare dollars and dinars we had and moved on, trying to avoid the military roadblocks we saw every fifty yards.

As we had in Basra, we saw lots of destruction. But this time it wasn't at the hands of rebels and rioters, but the result of Coalition air strikes. Many government buildings had been destroyed, and we saw workers clearing rubble from some of the streets. No one was attending to the piles of garbage we saw on practically every street corner.

Weeks after the end of the war, Baghdad was still without running water and electricity. We slept that night at the house of Yusef's cousin, who was a Christian and lived in one of the suburbs. The next two days, we drove around the city collecting intel and talking to people in tea shops. Then we turned around and headed back to Kuwait.

8

FBI SPECIAL ASSIGNMENT

I returned to Fort Campbell from Kuwait in April 1991, where all of us in 5th Group were ordered to put on our dress uniforms and march with the legendary "Screaming Eagles" 101st Airborne. Then we lined up to receive battle patches as part of a big celebration for the success of Desert Storm.

Again, as with Grenada, I felt embarrassed, because much of what I had contributed came after the Iraqi surrender. To my mind, what we had achieved in Iraq was worthwhile, but nothing to beat our chests about. We had organized an international coalition to thwart the ambitions of a madman and drive him out of Kuwait. But he was still in power, and his country remained in shambles.

While military officers and civilian dignitaries stood behind a podium talking about our great victory, I had a nagging feeling that we hadn't heard the last from Saddam Hussein, the Iranian mullahs, or other disgruntled groups in the Persian Gulf.

One night several weeks later, I was in a neighborhood bar unwinding with my SF buddy Steve, when I noticed this pretty blond woman stealing looks in my direction. Doubting that she could be interested in me because I wasn't tall, nor did I fit the usual American standard of masculine good looks, I pointed her out to Steve.

Steve sized up the situation and said, "Yeah, she's definitely giving you the eye. You should go for it."

"Really? You think so?"

"Hell, yeah, Changiz, you ol' horndog."

"All right. Wish me luck."

I walked over and asked her to dance. To my surprise she accepted, and before I knew it we were in each other's arms dancing to "Start Me Up" by the Rolling Stones.

It seemed fitting.

Her name was Bonnie. She was divorced with two kids and worked in a mattress store near the base. We hit it off immediately and started dating. After several weeks, she introduced me to her family.

For the past ten years, I had thought of myself as a rough soldier who loved the company of women but had no time or inclination to settle down. Now suddenly my head was filled with domestic matters—moving in with Bonnie and her children and making a nest together. We were even talking about getting married.

Just as things started getting serious, my company commander called me into his office and asked me to volunteer to accept a transfer to New York City on special assignment to the FBI. The commander was vague about the nature of the work I would be doing, except that the FBI was in critical need of Farsi and Arabic speakers and it would be top secret.

As I always did when asked to volunteer, I agreed, even though this time I had strong misgivings. I didn't want to leave Bonnie and her children, and she wasn't happy, either. I explained to her that by becoming a member of SF I had dedicated myself to defending the principles of freedom that form the bedrock of our country and way of life. And since I was being called on a special mission, I had to go.

Bonnie didn't agree. On an overcast morning in early June, I kissed her and her kids good-bye and boarded a commercial flight for JFK Airport. I had been told to wear my uniform so that the FBI agent meeting me in New York could identify me easily. Entering the arrival area I saw a pretty young blonde holding up a sign with my name on it.

She introduced herself as FBI Special Agent Leslie Sanders (not her real name), and drove me directly to One Federal Plaza in downtown New York City—a tall, black, glass-covered skyscraper that housed FBI headquarters. I accompanied Leslie up to the twenty-second floor, where FBI staff took my photo and handed me an ID card. Leslie informed me that I was being assigned to the IT-2 FBI Special Anti-terrorism Unit.

Next followed a briefing by the leader of the unit, John—an FBI special agent in his early fifties who had previously served in the military. The first part of my job, he explained, was to listen to surveillance tapes that dated back as far as ten years and hadn't been transcribed because of a lack of people who understood Farsi and Arabic. Also, I was to visit mosques in Brooklyn and Queens and listen to the anti-American propaganda that was being spewed by some mullahs.

Other members of our top secret unit were restricted to only listening to the tapes. They included several retired US Marines, a couple of guys from the Army, a tall Iranian American contractor who had served as a translator for Delta during Operation Eagle Claw and had been aboard the USAF EC-130 when it was hit by a RH-53 helicopter in the Iranian desert staging area—which led to the mission being canceled.

Seated two cubicles away from me in the language unit was a very attractive young Iranian woman. Several days into my assignment, I introduced myself.

Hearing my name, she did a double-take and asked, "What's your last name again?"

"Lahidji," I answered.

She covered her mouth in surprise and said, "You're not going to believe this, but we're related."

"Really? How?"

Her name was Azita and she explained that her aunt was married to my father's oldest brother, who had been a colonel in the Shah's army. He had died about ten years earlier of brain cancer. Now she lived in a nice condo overlooking the New York harbor.

My living quarters were more spartan—a room in the BAQ (basic allowance quarters) at Fort Hamilton Army Base in Brooklyn. But I wasn't complaining, because my room was free and I was receiving TDY to cover my meals, travel, and other living expenses, so I didn't have to spend a penny. So half of my E7 salary went to my mother in California, and I stashed the rest in my savings account.

I adjusted to my new routine quickly. Mornings, I'd get up at 0430, do some PT, shower and dress, then hoof it over to 77th Street subway station, where I'd catch the R train to City Hall. During the two-block walk to One Federal Plaza, I would stop at one of the sidewalk vendors to buy a cup of coffee and two bagels with cream cheese.

Work would start at 0700 and sometimes I'd continue late into the night. Some evenings after translating surveillance tapes all day, I'd attend evening prayer at mosques the FBI wanted me to infiltrate in Brooklyn and Queens. In the Shiite mosques I had gone to occasionally in Iran, I was taught to pray with my arms at my sides. Now I had to adjust to praying like a Sunni with my arms stretched in front.

It was while attending Al Farooq Mosque located in a converted factory on Atlantic Avenue in Brooklyn that I first heard Sheikh Omar Abdel-Rahman, the Blind Sheikh. The ground floor of the six-story building housed the Al-Kifah Refugee Center. A decade earlier it had been used to recruit Arab immigrants to become mujahedeen and fight the Soviets in Afghanistan.

There I listened to fiery sermons by Rahman and others and heard them talk about how Zionists had duped the American people, and blood and martyrdom were the only ways to build an Arab society. Sometimes I'd play dumb and ask the guys around me what the speakers were saying.

When I reported on these sermons to the FBI, I was surprised to learn that they were well aware of the Blind Sheikh's influence and radical Islamism. I learned that he had been born in Egypt and had lost his eyesight due to a childhood illness. He was jailed for three years in Egypt during the late 1970s because of his radical activities. After his release, he was expelled from his native country and traveled to Afghanistan to join the mujahedeen. While in Afghanistan, he developed a strong bond with Osama bin Laden, who had assumed control of the international jihadist arm of Maktab al-Khidamat (MAK), charged with raising funds and recruiting foreign mujahedeen for the war against the Soviets. As the Soviet-Afghan War wound down, MAK morphed into Al Qaeda. That the Blind Sheikh was allowed to preach anti-US and anti-Zionist hate from a mosque in Brooklyn in 1991 surprised me.

My FBI supervisors asked me to try to identify the faces and record the names of Sheikh Rahman's followers. "If you can get a phone number," one of the agents said, "that would be gold." This was before cell phones, so I did the best I could.

My reports caused the FBI to keep a closer eye on the Blind Sheikh and his circle of followers. Roughly a year and a half later, on February 26, 1993, a 1,336-pound car bomb went off in the underground parking lot of the North Tower of the World Trade Center, killing six people and injuring hundreds more. It was intended to topple the North Tower and send it crashing into the South Tower.

On June 24, 1993, Rahman and nine of his lieutenants were arrested for the role they played in planning the bombing. A year later he was convicted of seditious conspiracy. He died on February 18, 2017, while serving a life sentence at the Butner Federal Medical Center in North Carolina.

CNN correspondent and journalist Peter Bergen called Rahman "the ideological architect or the spiritual guide of 9/11." At a meeting of bin Laden and his lieutenants in 1998, Rahman's sons passed out laminated cards with a fatwa (Islamic religious ruling) from their father that read, "To all Muslims everywhere: Destroy their countries. Tear them to pieces. Destroy their economies, burn their corporations, destroy their businesses, sink their ships, and bring down their airplanes. Kill them in the sea, on land, and in the air."

It was signed, "Your brother Abdel Rahman, from inside American prisons."

During my FBI assignment, I was also sent to record the comings and goings from an Iranian government safe house several blocks from UN headquarters on First Avenue. Most of what I heard had to go with the arrival of various Iranian government officials and what they were going to say at the UN.

I wasn't an expert, but the results of the Iranian surveillance seemed mundane compared to the hatred that was being spewed at the Sunni mosques in Queens and Brooklyn. The latter struck me as alarming.

When the FBI assignment ended in April 1993, I returned to Fort Campbell, Tennessee, and was quickly dispatched to Somalia as a member of ODA 596. Accompanying us were two additional ODAs from 3rd Battalion 5th Group. Our mission was to help secure the US Embassy and provide security to humanitarian groups (known as NGOs—nongovernmental organizations) who were delivering food to starving civilians caught in the country's civil war.

Somalia, a country of 10 million on the Horn of Africa, had been slipping toward anarchy since the overthrow of dictator Mohammed Siad Barre in January 1991, who ruled since 1969. Adopting the name Comrade Siad, he instituted a form of scientific socialism based on the Quran and the writings of Karl Marx. But his oppressive style of rule, which pitted one clan against the other, and his harsh treatment of political opponents eroded his support.

By the late 1980s, armed opposition groups started to challenge the Siad Barre dictatorship. Prominent among them was the paramilitary United Somali Congress (USC) made of up Hawiye clansmen from southern and central Somalia, which included the capital, Mogadishu.

Following Siad Barre's ouster at the end of 1991, the USC also disintegrated into two major factions. One, led by warlord Ali Mahdi Mohammed, controlled the northern part of Mogadishu and parts of central Somalia. The second, commanded by Mohammed Farah Aidid, ruled the rest of the capital city and most of southern Somalia. Their factions were the most prominent of at least sixteen other warlords vying for power.

The *Army Times* of December 14, 1992, listed the major warlords and their organizations:

Somali National Movement—Abdul Rahman Tur
Somali Salvation Democratic Front—Colonel Tusuf
United Somali Congress—General Mohammed Farah Aidid faction
United Somali Congress—Ali Mahdi Mohammed faction

Somali National Front—General Mohamed Said Hersi Morgan

Somali Patriotic Movement—Colonel Omar Jess

Fierce fighting among these armed groups and others destroyed much of Somalia's agriculture. As famine spread, hijacked food provided by international relief organizations under a United Nations program known as UNOSOM (United Nations Operation in Somalia) became a means of power and a weapon used by warlords to win the allegiance of clan and subclan leaders. According to one estimate, 80 percent of internationally provided relief food to Somalia was being stolen by the end of 1992.

Relief agencies estimated that as many as half a million Somalis were in danger of dying from starvation. In response to the growing humanitarian disaster, the UN Security Council unanimously adopted Resolution 794 on December 3, 1992, which authorized the use of "all necessary means to establish as soon as possible a secure environment for humanitarian relief operations in Somalia." The result was the creation of a US-led, UN-sanctioned Unified Task Force (known as UNI-TAF). President George H. W. Bush launched what was dubbed Operation Restore Hope, and the first US Marines landed in Somalia one week later.

Over subsequent weeks and months, an international coalition similar in composition to the one used in Desert Storm arrived in the northeast African country. Though the US provided the bulk of UNITAF's total force (25,000 out of 37,000), other countries, including Australia, Canada,

Egypt, France, Germany, Tunisia, and Zimbabwe, also committed troops.

The operation was under way and, in the assessment of UN secretary general Boutros Boutros-Ghali, was having "a positive effect on the security situation in Somalia and the effective delivery of humanitarian assistance" when I arrived with ODA 596 in Mogadishu in early April 1993. We joined around 300 Rangers and bunked in a huge US compound that had been built on the beach, three miles from the city center and near the international airport, secured with barbed-wire fences, concrete barriers, and guard towers.

Teal-blue waters of the Indian Ocean sparkled to the east. Heat waves rose from the desert due west. In the constant heat, with sporadic fighting in and around the city, our job was to escort convoys of food and medicine from the port to various refugee centers outside the city. We traveled in desert cammos with five Humvees, our weapons fully loaded. Early in the morning, we'd drive northeast up London Road to the port, which was guarded by Rangers.

There we'd join a convoy of four to ten trucks carrying relief supplies from UNICEF, USAID, CARE, the Red Cross, Catholic Relief Services, or one of the other NGOs and form an escort, two Humvees armed with .50 calibers in front, one in the middle, and two in the rear. The rides were tense as we weaved through streets filled with garbage and rubble and passed through checkpoints manned by armed clansmen.

The refugee centers were sprawling tent cities with primitive sanitation, populated almost exclusively with women and children, with a sprinkling of old people. Throngs of kids greeted us with big smiles on their faces. I kept the pockets of my fatigues packed with hard candy to hand out to the kids.

From a distance, the ancient port of Mogadishu with its Spanish tile roofs and white-towered mosques promised sleepy postcolonial charm. But once we entered, that expectation quickly disappeared and was replaced with deep sadness and alarm as we confronted a catastrophic picture of the complete degradation of political order. It was *Mad Max* without the imaginative production design. Gritty, ugly, rat-infested, and disturbingly bleak.

Most of the auburn-hued buildings had huge holes ripped into them or were no longer standing. Those still intact were pockmarked with bullet holes. Stores, businesses, hotels, and banks had been completely looted down to the doorknobs and bathroom fixtures. Statues in public spaces had been torn down, leaving stone platforms covered with graffiti. The few governmental and university buildings still standing were populated with refugees and armed clansmen, most of whom were wild-eyed high on qaat (or khat), a leafy plant that, when chewed, induces euphoria and excitement like that of a mild amphetamine.

Side effects include mouth disease, tooth loss, psychosis, and depression. Signs of these were everywhere we looked, from the wired, jumpy armed clansmen who cruised the dirt streets in technicals—Toyota pickups with .50 caliber machine guns mounted in their beds—and who were supplied with khat by their leaders, to the stained teeth of women, to toothless, withered old men who wandered the alleys looking lost. Most women chose to chew the bark instead of the leaves, because they believed that the bark made their teeth clean and strong.

Mog, as we called Mogadishu, had been without electricity and running water for months. At night, campfires built in the streets, and sometimes fueled by animal dung, gave the place a weird, eerie glow. The smell these fires gave off wasn't pleasant.

Throughout the spring and most of the summer, Coalition soldiers seemed to suffer more from the wilting heat, bad water, and insect-borne illnesses than the trigger-happy gun-slingers. Our leaders warned us that Somalia was home to more than fifty-eight varieties of viruses carried by the ever-present mosquitoes and flies. Other major disease threats included malaria, which is transmitted by mosquitoes, sandfly fever, and leishmaniasis. The last two were spread by the tiny black sandflies that came out at night.

Despite these dangers, the relief mission proceeded throughout the spring and early summer with few incidents of violence. Meanwhile, we observed that life in and around Mogadishu started to assume a measure of normalcy. Markets reopened, more people ventured out into the streets, and there was even some talk of re-forming a Somali national police force.

Life in ODA 596 settled into a routine: PT and patrols during the day; card games, reading, and bullshit sessions at night. For safety reasons, we tried to avoid the city after dark. On those occasions when we ventured far away and couldn't return to our camp before dusk, we'd stay at the house of an older local man named Sheikh Abdullah who worked for the UN and lived near the football stadium.

Carefully written UNITAF rules of engagement reminded us that this wasn't a wartime environment, that all persons were to be treated with dignity and respect, and that only the minimum force necessary for the mission was authorized.

From my standpoint, it was hardly needed. Militiamen generally watched us warily and left us alone. Most men seemed to lounge in front of their tin shacks in plastic sandals, chewing khat and doing nothing. The women, dressed in brightly colored robes and head scarves, did all the work, usually with a baby strapped to their back as they carried water or other supplies in baskets. As we passed, the kids waved and smiled, and some women grinned revealing mouths filled with gold teeth. Others were afraid to engage us.

The locals spoke a strange dialect of Arabic, which I found hard to adjust to at first. But soon I was communicating with people and making friends.

Given the improved environment in Somalia by mid-May 1993, the new administration of President Bill Clinton started to press the UN to assume leadership of the relief effort, allowing the US to draw down its forces and handle only limited aspects of security and logistics. Concurrently, a number of UN diplomats lobbied the international organization to assume a more active military role to include confiscating weapons and forcing major warlords to accept some kind of political settlement as part of a long-term solution to the situation.

UN Resolution 814 authorized military intervention under

Chapter VII of the UN Charter, and UNOSOM slowly morphed into UNOSOM II with Turkish Lieutenant General Cevik Bir in command and US Army Major General Thomas M. Montgomery as his deputy. Retired Admiral Jonathan Howe assumed the critical role of UN envoy to Somalia. UN diplomats quickly identified warlord Mohammed Aidid as the biggest impediment to a political settlement.

Because Aidid controlled Mogadishu with his heavily armed militia, our mission in ODA 596 shifted in late May 1993 to include more frequent patrols in the city and house-to-house searches for explosives and weapons. Because I was the only one in my unit who spoke Arabic, I did most of the talking.

I'd greet the residents of every tin-roofed hovel we entered with *Allah Akbar*. Then I would quickly establish control and start giving orders, "Hold your hands over your head. Put the basket down. Stand away from the door!"

In between orders, I'd explain: "We have to do a search for weapons. We don't mean any disrespect, but we have to be careful."

Control and cooperation. Usually the response from the locals was *Mafi muchahka* (No problem).

Sometimes they would ask, "Why are you coming to kill us? We're just poor people trying to survive. You're making a bad situation worse."

I always carried cookies and candies to hand out to the kids, and extra MREs for the adults. On a few occasions our patrols took fire from militiamen hidden on rooftops and in alleys, and we'd call for helicopter support. Minutes later a very intimidating MH-60 Black Hawk helicopter would swoop down with its M134 miniguns and M230 chain guns blazing, and the locals would scatter.

The more aggressive UN military posture didn't sit well with warlord General Mohammed Farah Aidid of the United Somali Congress. On June 5, his forces ambushed and killed twenty-four Pakistani soldiers assigned to UNOSOM II and wounded forty-four more.

Aidid's message was clear: I control this city. If you try to wrest power from me, you'll pay a high price.

Tension and violence in and around Mogadishu mounted throughout the summer. I noticed the changed reaction we got from the locals. Before, as we passed on foot or in Humvee, they had responded with smiles, waves, and benign nods of their heads. Now men and women scowled, shook their fists at us, and shouted curses, and teenagers threw rocks.

Previously all the fighting had been between rival gangs vying for control of different neighborhoods. Increasingly UNOSOM II forces became the militiamen's targets. Coalition forces struck back with AC-130 attacks on militia weapons-storage facilities and Aidid's propaganda station Radio Mogadishu.

In mid-June Admiral Howe issued a warrant for Mohammed Aidid's arrest and authorized a $25,000 reward for his capture. As a consequence, we were ordered to step up our patrols and be more aggressive. Aidid ratcheted up the violence, which included a mine attack on the US Military Police (MP) vehicle on Jialle-Siaad Street that killed four Americans MPs.

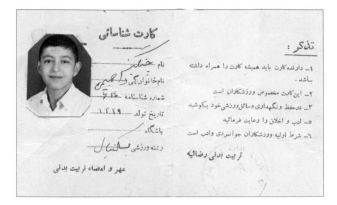

Me as an eager young gym student in Iran, 1967.

Standing guard during the Shah's massive festival celebrating the 2,500th anniversary of the founding of the Persian Empire, October 1971.

Teaching in a Kurdish village as a member of the Sepah-e Danash, a special unit of the Iranian Special Forces, 1971.

Working the pumps at my brother's gas station, Santa Clara, California, 1974.

My very dear mother and niece, taken at my brother's house in Santa Clara, 1979.

Studying martial arts in San Jose, California, 1974, in preparation for joining the US Army.

Receiving my black belt, 1975.

Returning to San Jose after graduating into the US Special Forces, 1979.

That's me in the center about to be pulled into the air by an aerial balloon while training for a secret mission to Tehran, January 1980.

Minutes later. I'm the dot hanging from the rope behind the C-130 that is about to pull me in during training in the Nevada, 1980.

As a member of an SF A-Team, we trained constantly. That's me at Ft. Bragg, North Carolina, 1979.

Me in the center breathing oxygen before a record-breaking 37,200-foot HALO jump in Guam, 1987.

Minutes later, jumping from 37,200 feet. What a thrill!

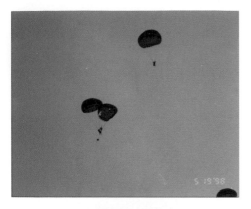

That's me in the center, entangled with another jumper during parachute training in the Philippines, 1986. Not a great position to be in, but I survived.

I'm on the right carrying a rucksack and training with my team sergeant, Ft. Bragg, 1979.

Doing PT in the Egyptian desert during Operation Bright Star, 1983.

With a good friend from SF Fifth Group as he and his lovely wife renewed their vows, Okinawa, Japan, 1985.

Sniper training, Okinawa, Japan, 1986.

Training with a .203 machine gun, the Philippines, 1986.

Standing with my brother John on a New York City subway platform, during my special assignment to the FBI, 1991.

Confiscating weapons in Haiti as a member of ODA 326 during Operation Uphold Democracy, 1994.

On special assignment for the DEA in Spain, working with members of the Spanish FBI, 1996.

Close quarter battle training with members of Delta Force, Thailand, 1986.

A rare look at me in my formal uniform, 1997.

With President Jimmy Carter in Darfur, Sudan, 2006.

Teaching self-defense in Senegal, 1996.

Demining in Cambodia, 1995.

Standing with friends I made while distributing food in Haiti, 1994.

Training President Karzai's security detail, Kabul, Afghanistan, 2002.

Minutes after the Black Hawk helicopter I was riding in was shot down near Firebase Wilderness, Afghanistan, 2008. I'm smiling, because I'm still alive. The pilot and another man died.

Riding a camel to meet rebel leaders as a peacekeeping monitor in Darfur, Sudan, 2007.

Discovering a Taliban arms cache near the border of Afghanistan and Pakistan, 2009.

On August 22, newly appointed secretary of defense Les Aspin ordered the deployment of a Joint Special Operations Task Force (JSOTF, also known as Task Force Ranger) to Somalia. Its mission, code-named Operation Gothic Serpent, was to capture Aidid and his key lieutenants and turn them over to UNOSOM II. Our unit became part of Task Force Ranger, which consisted of 160 elite operators, including Rangers, Delta, Navy SEALS, and 160th SOAR helicopter pilots, commonly known as Night Stalkers.

The Night Stalkers were considered the best chopper pilots in the world and had been formed after the failed hostage rescue mission in Iran. They favored three varieties of helicopter—the troop-carrying Black Hawk MH-60, the Black Hawk AH-60 attack version, and smaller AH/MH-60 Little Birds.

Delta was a tier-one, high-speed team that fast roped in, seized or destroyed their targets, and exfilled quickly. Suddenly we were working with the best of the best, usually securing areas of operation and providing support while Delta swooped in and eliminated or captured targets.

During August and September, Task Force Ranger launched six such missions in Mogadishu, all of which were moderately successful. A raid near Digfer Hospital on September 21 yielded Osman Ali Atto, Aidid's chief financial aide. But for the first time, we received massive RPG and automatic weapons fire from Somali militiamen.

Then at 0200 on September 25, as rain fell on the city, Black Hawk helicopter COURAGE 53 took off on a night surveillance mission to investigate the source of mortar fire near the city's port area. As pilot Chief Warrant Officer Dale Shrader buzzed the Black Hawk low over rooftops at 100 knots per hour, an RPG round smashed into the right side of the aircraft and exploded. The blast and resulting fire knocked out copilot Chief Warrant Officer Perry Alliman and melted the sleeve of Shrader's flightsuit onto his arm.

Still, he had the presence of mind to slow the careening craft and guide it past buildings. As it spun closer to the ground, COURAGE 53 grazed the top of a building, which shredded the rotor blades, then ricocheted onto a dirt street and slid a hundred yards before it came to rest against an embankment.

The three US soldiers aboard—twenty-one-year-old PFC Matthew Anderson and Sergeant Eugene Williams of the 101st Aviation Regiment and Sergeant Ferdinan Richardson of 10th Mountain, 25th Aviation—died in the explosion.

In the orange glow of the burning helicopter, a semiconscious Alliman turned to Shrader and mumbled, "Dale . . . I'm burned. I'm burned real bad."

"Stay with me, Perry," pilot Shrader moaned back. "We're going to make it."

Despite the fact that his arm was broken, Shrader managed to pull Alliman out of the burning wreckage and set him down in a dark corner of an alley. But when he went back to retrieve the other three crewmen, the craft was engulfed in flames.

Shrader hurried back to Alliman in the alley. As he leaned over him, he heard the click of an automatic weapon behind him and turned to see two Somali men with AK-47s running toward them. He raised his pistol, aimed, and counted his last breaths.

When they were within fifty feet, the Somalis turned into a side alley and disappeared. Shrader had no sooner breathed a sigh of relief when one of the Somalis returned running toward him holding a grenade. Shrader fired as the burning helo exploded behind him.

Stunned for several seconds by the blast, he opened his eyes to see the grenade lying two feet away. Shrader jumped back and muttered a quick prayer, thinking his life was over. But the grenade failed to detonate. He turned to see Perry slumped against the wall behind him, trying to load his pistol, and, because his hands were so badly burned, dropping the bullets.

As Shrader knelt beside his copilot to help him, a young Somali man ran into the alley from the opposite direction as the ones before, waving a flashlight. The man locked eyes with Shrader, shouted, "American boys!" and pointed to a street to the left.

Shrader wasn't sure he could trust him. But absent of any better choice, he pulled Perry to his feet and helped him to the street, where he saw an armored personnel carrier manned with soldiers from the United Arab Emirates. The UAE soldiers, who spoke no English, helped the two Americans into the APC and drove them to a field hospital. Both men survived.

A half dozen blocks away, Sergeant Christopher Reid of C Company, a soft-spoken Jamaican immigrant and member of

2nd Battalion, 10th Mountain Division, had been sent as part of a QRF (quick reaction force) to help rescue the men from the burning Black Hawk.

As Reid and members of his unit carried the bodies of Anderson, Williams, and Richardson from the smoldering helo to their APC, they came under heavy fire from Somali militiamen who spilled out of nearby streets and alleys. Reid was laying down cover fire when he took a direct hit from an RPG that severed his right hand at the wrist, blew off his right leg above the knee, severely burned his left hand, ruptured his eardrums, and blinded him temporarily. Still he managed to survive.

When news of the attack and US deaths reached us back at base, we were shocked, saddened, and pissed off. We had come to Somalia to help save the people from starvation. Now some of them were turning against us.

What was particularly unnerving was the fact that one of our Black Hawks—the most visible symbol of our technological and military superiority—had been shot down. To my mind what had seemed unthinkable a few days ago was only going to embolden Aidid's ragtag gang of thugs.

I'd find out later that the downing of COURAGE 53 hadn't been a lucky accident. Aidid and his men were getting money and training from bin Laden and other members of Al Qaeda. Specifically, veterans of the war against the Soviets in Afghanistan like Yusef al-Ayeri and Saif al-Adel were teaching them how to replace the detonators on their RPGs with timing devices, so instead of blowing up on impact they could detonate in midair. They also taught them to aim at the Black Hawk's tail rotor, which was its most vulnerable spot.

By the end of September 1993 a showdown was looming in Mogadishu, and Aidid and most of his aides were still at large.

9

BLACK HAWK DOWN

One week after the downing of COURAGE 53, the incident continued to haunt us members of Task Force Ranger. As I did PT, trained, or passed idle hours playing gin rummy, hearts, or blackjack in the hangar by the beach that served as our barracks or endured nightly mortar attacks, I wondered how we had quickly gone from heroes to villains in the eyes of the residents of Mogadishu and if the diplomats and generals who were guiding our mission really had a grip on what was going down in war-torn Somalia.

Most of the guys I talked to had as much interest in going into the city as entering the white-shark-infested ocean to our east. If the Somalis didn't want us here, what the fuck were we doing?

The place was hot, uncomfortable, dirty, smelly, and swarming with disease-bearing bugs, rats, and mosquitoes; the water was undrinkable; the food sucked; and the militants who controlled the city were trying to kill us. In no way, shape, or form was it a friendly environment. What were we trying to accomplish? Keep them from killing one another, when they seemed to be directing most of their hatred at us?

As soldiers we weren't privy to the strategic thinking of UN envoy Admiral Howe or other decision makers in Washington. So we sucked it up and tried to make the best of what was an increasingly dangerous situation.

Sunday morning, October 3, I ran into my old buddy Master Sergeant Tim "Griz" Martin, who was with Delta. He'd arrived in August and, like many of us, was counting the days until he got orders to return to the States.

"Hey, Changiz. How's it going?" Tim asked. "What's the word from home?"

Tim was an easygoing guy from Indiana with a good sense of humor and a seen-it-all, dealt with-everything attitude. We'd met in Okinawa in 1990 when we were both assigned to 1st Group Special Forces. Tim, who had previously been in Delta and wanted to be promoted from E8 (First Sergeant) to E9 (Command Sergeant Major), took a year-and-a-half assignment in ODA 116, while I was with ODA 113. After getting his E9, he transferred back to the Dreaded D (Delta).

Friday nights at Okinawa, he and I chowed together with a group of guys at the base cafeteria, where Tim would talk about his wife and three daughters and plans for retirement. He'd been in the Army since graduating from high school in '74. There was a lot of wear on his military tires.

But they didn't show that Sunday morning outside the hangar. He looked as affable and confident as ever as he stood smiling and waiting for me to respond.

"All good, Tim," I answered. "I've got thirteen years in, another seven at least to go. How about with you?"

"My girls miss me, and I miss them. This coming June I'll hit twenty years active service. Probably pack it in and start a business." While at Okinawa, Tim and I had trained at the firing range together. He'd taught me some advanced pistol-shooting techniques, which had come in handy since.

"Sounds good, Tim. Hopefully we'll be out of this hellhole soon."

"Your words to God's ears, Changiz."

"Yeah, life's good."

Several hours later, while cleaning my gear, I was summoned with my teammates to a nearby two-story whitewashed structure that served as Task Force Ranger HQ. There, in the downstairs briefing room, a major from S-2 told us that they had received recent intel that located several of General Aidid's top aides at a meeting in a building across the street from the Olympic Hotel in downtown Mogadishu. The plan, approved by TFR commander General William Garrison, called for Special Forces and Ranger teams to establish a perimeter around the area so that Delta could fast rope into the street from MH-6 Little Bird helicopters, secure the building, and seize the targets—Aidid's foreign minister, Omar Salad Elmi, and his top political advisor, Mohammed Hassan Awale.

Meanwhile, another Delta and Ranger recovery column would drive to the site in nine armored Humvees and three five-ton trucks to take the assault team and its prisoners out. The entire mission was to be in and out in thirty minutes.

The major reviewed call signs and orders of battle and

answered questions that mostly had to do with timing and air support. Someone asked why we weren't going in under cover of night.

"Because the targets are there now," he snapped back. He went on to assure us that this was a high-priority mission and all available assets including Black Hawks would be aloft and ready. The code word for launch was Irene.

Our role in ODA 596 was to help secure Chalk 2—a perimeter several blocks north and east of the target. I knew the area well. It was not only one of the most upscale sections of the city and had two- and three-story stone houses with inner courtyards instead of tin-roofed huts but also an Aidid stronghold that offered a perfect urban fighting environment with lots of tight streets, alleys, and passageways, as well as flat roofs. Not a place you wanted to engage the enemy. Only a few wide streets ran through the area and were capable of accommodating the twelve-vehicle recovery convoy that was a key component of the plan.

I pushed whatever fears and doubts I had out of my head, said a quick prayer, and hurried back to the hangar to grab my gear and weapons. ODA 596, like the other Special Forces and Ranger units, was lightly armed with M16 assault rifles and small-caliber M60 and SAW M249 machine guns. Our Humvees mounted with .50 cals would be parked 500 meters away from the perimeter so we could get out of there fast. Our lack of heavy armor was deliberate so we could move quickly in and out.

For heavy support, should we be attacked, we'd have to count on the miniguns and .50 cal machine guns on the Black

Hawks and Little Birds overhead. Air command would be controlled by a Delta official circling in another Black Hawk and a US Navy P-3C would provide overhead surveillance. The powerful AC-130 Spectre gunships previously available had been recalled from Mogadishu due to their propensity to cause collateral damage.

At 1350, TFR intel received confirmation that Omar Salad Elmi and Mohammed Hassan Awale had arrived at the building downtown. Ten minutes later, we got the order Irene, triple-checked all our gear—in my case an M16, thirteen mags of thirty rounds each in my vest and pouch and another five in my pockets, a 9mm pistol, grenades, body armor, helmet, goggles, gloves, and knee pads—and hurried to our Humvees. There we were joined by six Green Berets from another A-team. The eighteen of us packed into four vehicles and started to deploy single file north toward the port. Our instructions were not to shoot unless the enemy shot first.

From the port, we hung a left and proceeded up dirt-packed Hawlwadag Street. I stood in the back of the lead Humvee manning the .50 cal, goggles shielding my eyes from the thick clouds of yellow dust that rose from our tires. I chewed on a wad of gum to keep my mouth from turning dry.

By all appearances, it looked like a typical hot, sleepy Sunday afternoon with very few people on the streets. As I sweated under my Kevlar helmet, desert boots, and cammos, I waved at an old woman lugging produce from the market and young boys kicking a soccer ball that had been made out of rags. A few curious men poked their heads out of their tin-roofed huts to see what was going on.

We were the first team in and our team leader, Chris, kept in constant contact with Delta commander Lieutenant Colonel Gary Harrell in the command Black Hawk overhead. Their chatter echoed through the earpiece I had taped to the inside of my helmet.

"Six-Four, this is Tiger Six-Two. Two minutes to Chalk Two. No hostile activity encountered so far. Over."

"Tiger, Six-Four. We've got eyeballs on you from up here. Proceed with caution. Over."

"Will do, Six-Four. Over and out."

Our destination was the intersection of Marehan Road, National, and several alleys, a few blocks east and north of the target site. I kept looking left and right, keeping an eye on rooftops and alleys. All good. No militants in sight.

We parked about 500 meters south of the intersection and left a driver and one soldier to guard each vehicle. The remaining ten of us continued up Hawlwadag in staggered formation, fingers on triggers, scanning left and right, up and down, then right on National, and left of Shalalawi, which ran parallel to Hawlwadag. There, roughly two blocks east and three blocks north of the target, streets and alleys ran together to form a rough circle.

Like much of downtown Mog, the intersection was littered with garbage, burned carcasses of vehicles, and other detritus of war. The buildings around it were ghostly, pockmarked shells, covered with brown dust. Like a scene from an apocalypse film.

Dust had found its way into my boots and under my uniform. I wanted to get this over quickly.

Chris gave the signal, and five of us peeled away to inspect the three-story apartment building on the southeast corner. The makeshift tin door that covered the entrance was held together with a piece of wire. I pushed it open, entered, cleared the hallway, then hand-signaled to my teammates to move quickly into the rooms on the first floor. We cleared them one by one, just as we'd practiced hundreds of times in CQC.

The place stank of feces and garbage. While my unit searched the first building, Chris and the rest of the team entered a dust-covered two-story building farther south. We (Alpha) kept in constant radio contact with Chris's group (Tiger), the guys back at the truck (Beta), and one another.

"Tiger Six-Two, first floor clear."

"Roger, Alpha One. Continue up to deck two."

"Roger that."

We stepped around the bent rim of a bike tire on the stairs. The guys ahead of me heard something moving on two. One of them used hand signals to indicate the direction and that we should proceed with caution.

While we cleared buildings to the south and east of the circle, a team of Rangers fast roped from a Black Hawk into the intersection and started clearing streets and alleys to our left (west).

Meanwhile, the heavily armed twelve-vehicle Delta/Ranger recovery convoy, which included my buddy Tim Martin, proceeded up Hawlwadag Street from the port, following the same route we had taken.

All the windows of the apartment building we inspected were missing and the floors were covered with rubble, garbage, and dirt. I spotted a purple and orange head scarf peeking out from a pile of bricks, mortar, and garbage in the corner on two. Huddled there was a woman with her arms around two young children. I held my left finger to my mouth, and whispered in Arabic to be quiet and not to panic, we weren't going to harm her. She and her kids looked scared and emaciated. I asked, "Is there anyone in the rooms behind you?"

She shook her head.

My teammates confirmed that seconds later. Then as two guys kept watch, the rest of us cleared the third floor, which was empty, then hauled ass to the roof. We saw Black Hawks and Little Birds swooping in from the south and east. Three of the bigger helos hovered over the other three Chalk sites south, west, and southwest of us and Rangers started to fast rope down and secure their spots on the perimeter. Todd Blackburn, a young PFC in Chalk 4, missed the rope and fell seventy feet to the street. As a medic and another guy in his unit ran over to help him, they started to take fire.

I heard chatter through my headset.

"Man hit. Need immediate medevac, Chalk Four."

Then I watched four bubble-front MH-6 Little Birds pass to my left carrying Delta C Squadron. As the first two helos landed they kicked up an enormous cloud of dust that obscured my view. On the street below, I saw several Somali men in loose pants running toward the target site and shouting.

Four blocks from us, on the street in front of the target site, Delta C Squadron, wearing hockey-style helmets, hurried out of the Little Birds and into the target building, setting off flash grenades, ordering people inside to drop to the floor.

Simultaneously, our team leader, Chris, and Group Tiger started to engage in a firefight with armed men in the building to our right. It ended quickly as the militiamen retreated and ran.

Before I left the roof I heard sporadic small-arms fire to my left, in the direction of the Bakaara Market and the approximate location of Chalk 4. Through the swirling yellow dust I spotted the first of many columns of black smoke. They came from tires that had been set on fire signaling to militiamen where to gather and that the fight was on.

What I couldn't see were the thousands of armed militiamen who were streaming into the area and assembling to our north, west, east, and south. Nor could I hear the militiamen who were running through the streets and alleys shouting through megaphones, "Come out and defend your homes!"

Four blocks south, the operators in Delta C Squadron had found and identified Omar Salad Elmi, Mohammed Hassan Awale, and had even bagged another Aidid lieutenant, Abdi Yusef Herse. It was 1550 hours and the three men lay prone and flex-cuffed in the courtyard as other operators spread through the target building looking for more suspects.

Meanwhile, my friend Tim Martin was waiting in front of the target building with the rest of the twelve-vehicle extraction convoy. Tim, who was sitting in the rear seat of the third Humvee, jumped out to check on a Navy SEAL seated beside him who been shot in the right hip a few blocks before they reached their destination. Tim tore open the SEAL's pants and discovered that the round had hit the blade of his knife, shattering the blade and deflecting the bullet.

"You're a lucky man," Tim said as he pulled several fragments of the blade out of the SEAL's hip and bandaged the wound. That's when the convoy started taking fire from rooftops and alleys to the north and west.

My teammates and I were back on the street, arms ready, waiting for the signal to exfil, and expecting it any second. Through my headset I heard one of the Rangers in the Humvee taking PFC Blackburn back to base say that they were encountering groups of armed militants. Cracks of gunfire echoed from the alleys to our left.

The intersection and Chalk 2 remained clear and calm. I felt my heart pounding in my chest. The teammate to my right growled, "What the fuck are we waiting for?"

"Beats the shit out of me."

What I didn't know was that there had been a slight mix-up at the target site. Delta Squadron C remained inside the building waiting for a signal from the recovery convoy, while the convoy waited for Delta C and its prisoners to come out. Finally, thirty-seven minutes after Delta C had launched, they started to load their prisoners into the convoy's trucks and pull out. A Black Hawk passed low to our left, positioning itself to support the convoy.

I breathed a sigh of relief. The mission was almost over.

I turned right and spit the spent gum out of my mouth and, as I did, heard a loud explosion to my left. I looked up to see where it had come from. Two seconds later, I heard people shouting through my headset.

It was so frantic, I didn't register what they were saying at first. Then I made out distinctly, "Holy shit! Black Hawk hit! Black Hawk on fire!"

Other voices overlapped the first. "It's losing control!"

"Fuck! It's going down!"

"Black Hawk down!"

"Black Hawk . . . fuck!"

I spotted the injured bird in my left periphery. Black smoke rose from the rear rotor and the chopper started to go into a spin. As it neared the ground the helo spun faster. I made out the silhouette of the pilot and copilot in the cockpit, and several operators through the open door, holding on and bracing themselves for a crash landing.

It seemed unbelievable. Guys around me were shouting and taking cover. The big injured bird careened toward us.

"Oh Jesus!" someone beside me gasped.

"Oh, fuck!"

"Watch out!"

I took cover behind a four-foot-high wall.

Chief Warrant Officer Cliff "Elvis" Wolcott, pilot of the Black Hawk Super 6-1, and copilot CWO Donovan Lee "Bull" Briley, both of SOAR 160, had practiced for an emergency like this and knew to pull back on the power control levers, which cut the engines. That's what caused the bird to spin counter to the direction of the rotors.

Understanding that he had no control of the chopper, CWO Wolcott said calmly over the radio, "Six-One going down."

As the helo screamed closer, I dove behind a pillar and made myself small. Next I heard a horrible screech of metal as the rotor hit the ground and flew free, followed by the violent smash of the 6-1 slamming to the ground 200 meters to my left, throwing up sparks and a huge cloud of dust.

Chris shouted the whole time, "Take cover! Stay down!"

"Holy fucking shit!"

The impact was so violent that I was sure that everyone inside 6-1 was dead. My first thought was: We have to recover the bodies before the Somalis get ahold of 'em.

But I couldn't see shit or breathe because of the dust. And as soon as it started to clear, I heard vehicles hurrying toward the intersection and bursts of automatic gunfire. In a matter of seconds militiamen converged on the intersection from all directions like locusts. They were running on foot and they were arriving in Toyota pickups painted camouflage green and brown.

Several of us were already on our feet and moving in the direction of the downed helo, which we couldn't see because the empty three-story apartment on the corner to the left of us blocked our view.

Chris screamed, "Down! Get down! Watch behind you!"

Before I knew what was happening, bullets were whizzing over my head from several directions and slamming into the building and the ground. I knelt behind a low wall in front of the building, leveled my M16, and starting firing. We had to hold back the Somalis who wanted at the downed helo and the people inside.

A huge wave of adrenaline slammed my system. My body was pumped to the max and my arms and legs were shaking. I had to will myself to calm down, and pick out targets. The Somalis, on the other hand, were fucking crazed, firing wildly in all directions and running into the open with no regard to the danger they were exposing themselves to. I took down dozens of them, and they kept coming. When I could I did a double tap—a shot to the torso, followed by a second to the head. I hit a young guy in the head; a man with a gray beard directly in the heart.

There was no time to think, and they were too close to use grenades. It was just, point, aim, shoot, and search for a new target, which wasn't hard. They were pouring into the intersection from several directions, probably high on khat and seemingly with little regard for their lives. I saw women and a few boys mixed in the wild onslaught of men.

Bodies started to pile up, dotting the dirt with dark blotches of blood. I prayed for the whole fucking nightmare to end.

What I didn't realize was that all the 100 or so men in the TFR who had deployed on this mission were trapped in the heart of Mogadishu and surrounded by thousands of crazed militiamen, and we were in the fight of our lives.

Angrily I shouted, "Motherfuckers! You motherfuckers! Go away!"

A teammate to the right of me growled, "Changiz, calm down!"

"Fuck that. I'm going to kill all those motherfuckers!"

It was total hell. The noise alone was incredible. Overlapping bursts of automatic weapons fire, the whoosh, whine, and explosion of RPGs, men shouting, others screaming in pain, women howling. I was so focused on firing at targets that I couldn't discern the chatter coming through my headset.

Fire came at us in all directions.

Chris shouted, "Three-sixty. Form up three-sixty!"

The twelve us made a rough circle and inched closer to the downed chopper as we covered for one another. I faced northeast. The downed helo came into view in my left periphery, lying on its side like a beached whale.

It looked big and sad without its rotor and tail. The windshield was shattered and the side door wide open. Some of the operators inside were still alive, returning fire and trying to get out. *Very brave men*, I thought.

A Toyota pickup flew into the intersection, kicking up clouds of dust. A masked man in its bed shouted as he directed a stream of .50 cal rounds at the wrecked Black Hawk. We took cover as heavy bullets tore into the ground and concrete around us. When I peeked up to fire back, a rocket fired by another SF team on the opposite side of the intersection lit up the Toyota. The explosion flipped the truck in the air like a toy, and it careened out of view. As it crashed to the ground it sent up an arch of flames and sparks.

While we ducked, moved, covered, and fired, the Somalis kept coming in waves. Sometimes they used frightened-looking women as shields. The dust and cordite clogging the air made it hard to breathe. There was no time for even a sip of water.

Even though sweat poured off me, I didn't even think of my thirst, or anything else because I was so focused on defending the helo and holding back the clansmen. They popped up everywhere—doorways, windows, alleys, on roofs. We controlled our shots, conscious of running out of ammo. Forty minutes into the battle, I had gone through ten mags. There were two more in my vest, five in my pockets.

Another SF A-team took up positions on the NW corner and there were Rangers to our left, on the other side of the downed helo.

Chris was on the radio, screaming for air support again. "Chalk Two, under intense fire! Need backup! Support . . . now!"

What I didn't know at the time and learned later was that Lieutenant Colonel Gary Harrell in the command Black Hawk had ordered the Delta convoy to alter its route. Instead of returning to base, it had been directed to help rescue the downed pilot and crew of Super 6-1. This turned out to be hugely problematic, because the convoy increasingly ran into roadblocks and clusters of militiamen who shredded their vehicles with rocket and automatic weapons fire at every intersection. Additionally, the men directing the convoy hadn't prepared for this diversion and had gotten lost in the warren of streets and alleys around Chalk 2.

In fact, the twelve-vehicle convoy had done a complete circle around the crash site and was back where it had started on a street behind the target house. They'd already taken a number of casualties. Now, as they turned south, an RPG tore through the steel skin of the third Humvee and exploded, blowing the three men in the backseat onto the street. All of them were severely wounded. Private Adalberto Rodriguez had the back of one of his thighs torn off. As he struggled to his feet, the fourth vehicle, a truck bearing the Somali prisoners, rolled over him.

My buddy, Tim Martin, the third man in the backseat,

had absorbed the brunt of the blast. Although he was still conscious, the explosion had ripped off the lower half of his body.

All three men were loaded into a five-ton truck and the convoy proceeded and continued to take fire from rooftops, buildings, alleys.

While the convoy made its way south, another Black Hawk, call sign Super 6-4—which had inserted the team at Chalk 1—also took an RPG hit. Pilot CWO Mike Durant described it as like hitting a speed bump. He didn't know the extent of the damage or the location until the aircraft started to spin due to an inoperable tail rotor, which was unable to counter the torque of the engine.

A helo pilot for ten years, Durant's priority now was to save his life and the lives of his crew. As he attempted to guide the helo to a clearing, he shouted into his radio. "Six-Four hit! Going down."

Someone in the command Black Hawk radioed back, "Six-Four, you okay?"

"Going in hard," Durant responded. "Going down!"

Militants who saw black smoke coming from the tail of the stricken bird cheered and fired into the air in celebration. Filled with new confidence, hundreds of them converged on the crash site.

Pilot Durant managed to land Super 6-4 upright in a less urban area a mile and a half southwest of Chalk 2. But there were two problems. First, the low huts around it and rising black smoke made it easy to find. And, two, all US rescue forces were focused on getting to Chalk 2 and Super 6-1.

General Garrison back at base HQ hastily assembled a convoy comprised of mostly support personnel, including some cooks. But almost immediately after entering the city, the convoy ran into roadblocks and rebel ambushes that seriously hindered its progress.

With two Black Hawks down and the majority of the 150-man RTF pinned down in downtown Somalia, things were going from bad to worse. And the officers directing the operation were running out of options.

At the Super 6-4 crash site, pilot Durant, his copilot CWO Ray Frank, and the two crew chiefs had survived, but were badly injured. In an act of remarkable bravery, two Delta operators, Sergeant First Class Randy Shughart and Master Sergeant Gary Gordon, volunteered to jump from another Black Hawk to defend the wounded on Super 6-4 until the rescue team arrived. But sadly the two highly skilled operators were no match for the scores of frenzied militiamen who rushed to the crash site, firing AK-47s and RPGs.

Shughart and Gordon fought bravely until they ran out of ammo and were killed along with copilot Frank and the 6-4 crew chiefs. The Somalis plundered their possessions, stripped their bodies, and dragged them through the streets. Pilot Mike Durant was beaten and captured alive.

At Chalk 2, the Rangers to the left of us and the A-team on the north side of the intersection provided cover as we fought to within twenty yards of downed Super 6-1. That's when three helos swooped in—two MH Little Birds (Killer Eggs we called them) and one Black Hawk—their miniguns and .50 cals blazing. They unleashed a lethal torrent of high-caliber rounds and rockets on the militiamen to our north and west, causing them to pull back. It was an awesome display of US firepower and gave us a few minutes to reload and catch our breath.

Chris called out, "Status."

We responded one by one. Some guys on the team had sustained minor injuries, but miraculously we were all alive. I was so jacked on adrenaline, I had to check my legs and torso before I answered, "All good. Fucking A."

With the intersection finally clear of militants, a rescue Black Hawk swooped in and disgorged a team of PJs (Air Force Pararescue) and medics, who stepped over Somali bodies and quickly went to work extracting and patching up the wounded men from Super 6-1. In a matter of minutes they got everyone out, except for pilot Wolcott, whose body was pinned in the wreckage.

Incredibly, the battle dragged on until hours after dark, when a two-mile-long column of more than 100 armored vehicles that included Pakistani tanks and Malaysian APCs finally arrived. Rescue workers freed Wolcott's body from the 6-1, piled the dead and wounded into their vehicles, and started back to base. Mentally and physically exhausted, the twelve of us humped back to our Humvees.

I drove the lead Humvee with Chris seated next to me. All of us were stunned and quiet. Back at base, I heard the horrible news. Task Force Ranger had sustained nineteen casualties, including my friend Tim Martin, who had hung on bravely but died while being medevaced to Germany. Another seventy-three were wounded.

Somali officials estimated that 800 to 1,000 militiamen died in the battle with as many as 4,000 wounded.

For bravely volunteering to defend Super 6-4, Delta Force operators MSG Gordon and SFC Shughart were both post-humously awarded the Medal of Honor, the first bestowed since the Vietnam War. Tim Martin received a Silver Star.

10

HAITI

For many days after the battle, a sad, dark pall hung over all of us who had survived Operation Gothic Serpent. At the hangar on the beach, we mourned our dead colleagues and questioned the policies and tactics that had resulted in the terrible debacle.

I heard one Ranger ask, "With command helicopters overhead viewing the whole scene, how did we manage to get trapped in downtown Mogadishu?"

"Hell if I know," I answered.

Another Ranger chimed in, "Why didn't the Delta C Squadron assault team simply exfil by helicopter after they had seized the targets?"

"Beats the shit out of me."

"If Delta was going to leave with the prisoners by road, why weren't they given tanks and APCs so they could blast their way out?"

"Good question."

Terrifying images haunted us all. At night, I heard guys calling for their dead friends in their sleep. I had trouble sleeping as well and often woke up trembling and covered with sweat. In my nightmares I'd see my buddy Tim holding his intestines and begging for my help.

Two weeks after what became known as the Battle of Mogadishu, President Bill Clinton announced that he was ordering the cessation of all military actions against Mohammed Aidid, except those that required self-defense, and ordered the withdrawal of all US forces. For those of us who wanted to avenge the loss of our brothers, this added to our distress. However policymakers in Washington spun it, the battle had been an ignominious defeat.

I was extremely upset. Some of us blamed President Clinton; others felt Admiral Howe and General Garrison were responsible.

It was hard enough to get over friends dying. But how could the powerful United States let some savage warlord in a lawless country treat us like this and get away with it? Didn't that send a negative message to the rest of the world? Weren't we the good guys who had come to save the starving Somali people?

It was an indecorous ending to an unsound mission. Today, twenty-three years later, sounds and images from the Battle of Mogadishu still haunt me.

I needed a break. My commanders in 3rd Group realized that, and, when I returned to Fort Campbell in November '93, gave me orders in the form of a PCS to report to Defense Language

Institute Foreign Language Center in Monterey, California, to study Arabic.

Not only was I close to my family, I happened to be located in one of the most beautiful places on earth. In gentle Monterey, which was often shrouded in a fine mist, I started to slowly heal psychologically from the horrors of Mogadishu.

Halfway through the sixty-four-week course, I received orders to return to Fort Bragg and join ODA 326. Now a senior E7, I was named assistant operations sergeant with duties that included studying intel on places we were about to deploy and briefing the rest of the team.

It was the end of August '94 and ODA 326 was given seventy-two hours to prepare for Operation Uphold Democracy, which was designed to remove the military regime that had deposed Haitian president Jean-Bertrand Aristide in 1991, thereby paving the way for his return to Haiti.

Aristide, a former Roman Catholic priest and populist leader, had been elected president of Haiti at the end of 1990 with 67 percent of the vote in what was considered the most honest election in Haitian history. Eight months into his presidency he was deposed by a group of military leaders led by army commander General Raoul Cédras, whom Aristide had recently promoted to commander-in-chief. Aristide's enemies accused the president of violating the constitution and threatening mob rule.

Exiled first to Venezuela and then the US, Aristide didn't take his ouster lying down. Instead, he campaigned to organize international support to return him to power in Haiti. Part of his effort included a public relations drive that focused on human rights abuses carried out by the military junta that replaced him.

His efforts got a huge boost when Bill Clinton was elected president in 1992. One of President Clinton's first declarations after his inauguration in January '93 was to renew his campaign pledge to return Aristide to Haiti. When diplomatic efforts stalled, Clinton, at the urging of members of the Congressional Black Caucus, lobbied the UN Security Council for the passage of Resolution 940, which was adopted on July 31, 1994.

Two days later, all of us in 3rd Group Special Forces were flown to Guantánamo Naval Base in Cuba. There, we were joined by the Ranger 2nd Battalion and a fleet of ten CH-53 Sea Stallion helicopters.

While we were being briefed on plans for an airborne assault of the international airport in Haitian capital Port-au-Prince, the takedown of the Haitian military command, and detention of General Cédras, ex-president Jimmy Carter, Senator Sam Nunn, and retired chairman of the Joint Chiefs of Staff General Colin Powell launched a last-minute diplomatic mission to try to settle the crisis peacefully.

As we cooled our heels in Cuba, Carter, Nunn, and Powell spent two days in Haiti negotiating with General Cédras, who initially refused to concede to the legitimacy of the democratic elections. With a deadline from President Clinton nearing, the delegation showed Cédras a video of the 82nd Airborne Division loading into C-130s and explained that they were the lead elements of the 15,000-paratrooper-strong airborne assault force launching from Fort Bragg, North Carolina. Within minutes of watching this, General Cédras capitulated and our mission was changed from a combat operation to a peacekeeping one.

To my mind the abrupt cancellation was fraught with questions. Would the Haitian people greet us as liberators or resent us for meddling in their internal affairs? Would local gangs and even elements of the Haitian military turn on us as had occurred in Somalia?

Our commanding officers had few answers, and had us prepare for a hostile environment and proceed with caution. Lieutenant General Hugh Shelton, in charge of the entire military operation, directed us to present ourselves as both imposing and reassuring. Instead of defeating the 7,000-man Haitian armed forces (the FAdH in its French acronym), we were now going to work with them to police the country once its leadership stepped down. We'd find out how we were going to achieve that when we got there.

It was a weird situation to find myself in, especially on the heels of Somalia. And it happened to be the first time in history that the United States restored the deposed leader of another country to power. Clearly, the role of the US military was quickly evolving now that the Cold War was over. As a soldier it wasn't my job to question or debate policy. I was ready to do what I was told.

Early morning the following day, September 19, Rangers from 2nd Battalion landed in Port-au-Prince to secure the airport. They met no resistance. All of us in 3rd Group Special Forces touched down at the airport at 4 P.M. that afternoon fully loaded with M16s, Glocks, shotguns, combat vests, and helmets.

We were greeted by hot, steamy tropical air, 2nd Battalion group commander Colonel Mark Boyett, and SF battalion commander Colonel Kay, whom I'd served under in Okinawa. Our command sergeant was Sergeant Major Mike Moore.

We immediately spread out and established an armed perimeter around the fenced-in airport. Once Sergeant Major Moore announced "Area secure!" we started setting up big twenty-four-man tents on a grassy area near the runway.

Hundreds of locals started to gather outside the fence to see what we were doing. Some waved; others asked for food. We handed out MREs and tried to establish a friendly rapport despite the language barrier. The local people spoke a particular variety of French Creole that even the few French speakers among us didn't understand.

Living conditions at the airport weren't ideal. Latrines and fresh water were in short supply. Also, because the rainy season was under way and the airport runways were sloped to drain into the fields around them, we lived in a virtual swamp. Add to that the oppressive heat and omnipresent spiders and mice, and we weren't happy campers.

Thankfully, on day two, ODA 326 and ODA 324 were ordered to find a safe house in Port-au-Prince to use as our base of operations as we cooperated with FAdH units and maintained order in the city. So far, US troops had been met with little hostility, aside from some confusion on the part of locals about why we were acting friendly toward former human rights abusers in the FAdH, rather than arresting them and throwing them in prison.

On the recommendation of someone at the US Embassy

we found a dwelling owned by an American nurse who was married to a Haitian. It was located on a hill with a spectacular view of the Caribbean, and seemed large enough to accommodate two dozen men. The problem was that only the first floor had been finished. So after renting the house for $2,000 a month, we borrowed a 2.5 ton truck, loaded it up with sheets of plywood and nails, which we got from US military HQ downtown, and, with guidance from our two engineers, quickly finished the second floor.

The nurse who owned the place hired three maids to wash clothes and cook for us. All of us slept on cots with mosquito nets. The house had no air-conditioning.

While some of us readied our safe house, others patrolled the city, which in some ways was even more shocking than Mogadishu. Port-au-Prince hadn't suffered through five years of civil war, yet it was a rotting, fetid mess. We encountered throngs of desperately poor people everywhere begging for food. According to the World Bank, half of the country's 6.5 million inhabitants lived in extreme poverty and most families earned less than one dollar a day. That ranked it as one of the poorest countries in the world—even poorer than Somalia, and the poorest in the Western Hemisphere—with a per capita GNP of a mere $380 a year.

A third of Haiti's population lived in Port-au-Prince, many of them packed in slums like Cité Soleil, which was built on a landfill near the harbor's edge. There, some 150,000 Haitians lived in primitive shelters patched together out of adobe, abandoned sheet metal, and cardboard. Swollen-bellied children picked through mounds of garbage for something to eat and played in open sewage. I never imagined I would see human beings living like this.

It was especially startling because, as I learned, before its independence in 1804, Haiti had been one of the most productive and prosperous colonies in the world, generating two-thirds of France's overseas trade. In the year 1879 alone, exports of coffee, indigo, cacao, hides, and sugar filled the holds of over 4,000 ships.

Over two hundred years later it was an ecological disaster of staggering proportions. According to UN estimates only 39 percent of the population had access to safe drinking water and 27 percent to sanitation.

We saw evidence of ecological devastation in the hills around where we lived, which had been completely stripped of trees that had been cut down for making charcoal.

Travelers to Haiti in the early nineteenth century praised it for its never-ending verdure and forests of redwood, mahogany, and pine. Now experts contend that up to 97 percent of the country has been deforested.

Charcoal remained the main source of fuel for tens of thousands in Port-au-Prince. Two-wheeled wooden carts known as *brouettes* piled high with hemp bags distribute charcoal throughout the city. Once burned it shrouds the slums in brown smoke.

We didn't have to travel far to see the gap between rich and poor, which was reputedly among the highest in the world. In the hills around our safe house lived what foreign journalists called the "morally repugnant elites," their spotless houses surrounded by high security walls covered with colorful tropical foliage and bougainvillea. Most featured satellite dishes.

As we patrolled the city in Humvees handing out whatever spare MREs and food we could find, I wondered how Haiti had devolved into the sad state it was in now. The country had achieved its independence from France after the only successful slave revolt in history and was the second free republic established in the Western Hemisphere after the US. Since its independence on January 1, 1804, it had seen thirty-five changes of government, many of them military uprisings, including the bizarre fourteen-year dictatorship of Papa Doc Duvalier.

I quickly learned that while most Haitians were poor, they were also immensely proud. They were happy to see the backs of General Cédras and the leaders of the military junta, excited about the return of President Aristide, but wary of their US occupiers.

With reason, as I found out. The United States had invaded Haiti once before, in 1915, to quell political unrest and prevent Germany and France from seizing control of the unstable and heavily indebted country. But we overplayed our hand in terms of extending political and economic influence, and by the time we left in 1934 we were extremely unpopular.

Also, historically, the US hadn't been welcoming to the former slave colony, refusing to recognize the new country or allow its merchants to trade with the US until 1868, after the trauma of the American Civil War.

So I understood why even the friendliest of Haitians viewed us skeptically. As in Somalia, the women worked hard, while the men mostly lounged around waiting for something to happen. Despite the miserable conditions, the Haitians seemed like vibrant, upbeat people. One expression of their natural exuberance was the densely packed, psychedelically painted buses called *tap-taps* that careened through the streets. They sported English-language names like "Peace and Love Machine" and "Baby Love All Night."

We were alerted to keep an eye on gangs of right-wing junta supporters and pro-Aristide zealots. Poor sanitation and the mosquitoes spawned in puddles produced by daily rainstorms presented a more serious challenge. Back in 1801, a third of the 25,000 soldiers Napoleon sent to Haiti to put down a slave rebellion had been wiped out by yellow fever.

Week three, I contracted dengue fever from an infected Aedes mosquito and became so weak and sick I was convinced I was going to suffer a fate similar to that of Napoleon's troops. In my fevered state I kept reminding myself of the irony that an enemy bullet hadn't felled me, but a tiny flying bug had. As I sweated through fever nightmares of Mogadishu and endured severe headaches and pain in every bone in my body, our team medic arrived to tell me there was no medication to treat a dengue infection.

He gave me aspirin and acetaminophen and told me to drink lots of fluids. Our maids took over and slowly nursed me back to health. Bless their hearts. Ten days later and fifteen pounds lighter, I was back on my feet, and ready to resume patrols.

Most of what we encountered on the streets and slums of Port-au-Prince were disputes over food or money. Sometimes locals would come to us with some bruised individual they had taken into custody and claimed was a henchman of the former military regime. Unfortunately we couldn't do much except turn this person over to the FAdH, since they remained the only functioning government institution in the country.

Our most challenging assignments came whenever an LCU (landing craft utility) arrived at the port with new supplies. The sight of one approaching day or night always attracted a huge crowd, which local police and military guards, despite our instruction and training, seemed unprepared for. Inevitably, there would be pushing and shoving, then fights would break out and thugs from one of the local political gangs would fire shots in the air.

We'd move in quickly, contain the crowd, and arrest anyone who brandished a weapon. Sometimes locals would grow angry and shout that they wanted two things: food and for us to leave.

In the back of my mind, I was waiting for the situation to escalate as it had in Mogadishu, but so far so good. In the case of Haiti, the people had hope, which came in the form of returning President Aristide. As the day of his October 15 arrival approached, poor people swept potholed streets and painted walls with murals. One of them depicted US soldiers standing beside tanks and helicopters as a beatific Aristide (known affectionately as Titid) descended from a white cloud.

The morning of October 15, we got up early to patrol the streets around the newly whitewashed National Palace, then stood guard outside the fence covered with red and blue bunting as crowds gathered, waving branches and singing accompanied by a marching band, "He's above, he's coming!"

President Aristide arrived by US Army helicopter to ecstatic cheers, then, from behind bulletproof glass, delivered a victory speech peppered with folk sayings that included, "Many hands lightened the burden" and "You can't eat okra with just one finger." He also repeated over and over, "No to violence, no to vengeance, yes to reconciliation!"

Singing and dancing continued into the night as the country celebrated the end of a long legacy of oppression by unaccountable armed thugs, including the dreaded Tontons Macoutes, who dated back to the Duvalier dictatorship of the 1950s.

Now that order had been restored, our job was to fan out into the countryside and disarm as many of these former henchmen as we could. So we handed over our patrols of Port-au-Prince to a contingent of policemen who arrived from Australia (with plentiful supplies of Foster's beer), and then we drove six miles over mountainous dirt roads to the seaport of Les Cayes near the tip of Haiti's southern peninsula.

Picturesque Les Cayes boasted pristine white sand beaches and the birthplace of American naturalist and painter John James Audubon, who was born there in 1785 and went on to document all types of American birds in his color-plate book *Birds of America*. The sleepy port of 85,000 was also the world's supplier of a fragrant grass called vetiver, an ingredient in many cosmetics and perfumes.

When barefooted local kids saw us approaching in two Humvees, they ran out to greet us. But the local FAdH commander, Lieutenant Colonel Evens Gedeon, wasn't as welcoming and instructed his troops to defend their barracks. When we assured him that we hadn't come to disarm his men, he relaxed and started to cooperate.

As a base of operations we chose a four-room house in an alley near the port with a big backyard. After hiring a maid, cook, and translator, we started patrolling the city. With the help of intel we bought from informers, we inspected houses where people were hiding weapons. On a good day, we'd confiscate as many as 200.

In addition to disarming the populace, we also tried to win hearts and minds. So while we went house to house looking for weapons, our medics would dispense medical care to the sick and elderly. As we gained trust, some locals mustered the courage to tell us about gang members, police officers, and even soldiers who had committed abuses.

We made arrests and assisted the three-man police force in others, trying to maintain the balance between imposing and reassuring that General Shelton had set as our goal. "Peace Corps with guns," we called ourselves, as we helped repair generators, tended to the sick, and tried to settle domestic disputes. Sometimes I felt like a deputy in the Wild West administering a kind of rough-hewn frontier justice. We saved several people from being lynched or hacked to death with machetes.

We'd explain to people, "No, you can't beat up this lady just because her husband was a member of the FRAPH," Front for the Advancement and Progress of Haiti in its English translation, a paramilitary group.

Over time, the Haitians started to understand our role,

which was to create a safe environment and help maintain order. Members of the FAdH who had left their posts and loyalists to the former military were the bad guys, and required constant vigilance on our part. Even in relatively calm Les Cayes we maintained guard duty every night from 11 P.M. to 6 A.M., trading one-hour shifts on the roof.

Except for a big deployment of US troops in the capital and a smaller contingent in the southern city of Cap-Haïtien, Special Forces A-teams were the sole representatives of the American Army in much of Haiti. This made it necessary for us to travel to other towns and cities once we had established order in Les Cayes.

One night, three months into our nine-month stay, we were stationed in the city of Gonaïves farther north. It was here that Jean-Jacques Dessalines, a former slave, had declared Haiti independent from France.

One hot, sticky afternoon our intel Sergeant First Class Greg Cardott decided to go out and inspect toll booths that had been set up to collect a road tax imposed by the local government.

"Bad idea," I warned him. "Let the locals take care of it. That's none of our business."

"I'm not asking your advice, Changiz," Cardott answered.

"It's still dicey for foreigners like us," I explained.

He went anyway, accompanied by Sergeant First Class Tommy Davis, also of Special Forces 3rd Group.

According to Davis, the two were stationed in a Humvee near one of the toll booths when a car blew through without paying the toll. They proceeded to stop the vehicle and

Cardott went over to talk to the driver. Davis, meanwhile, ordered the male passenger to get out of the car. The passenger refused.

When Davis tried to pull the unruly passenger out, the Haitian reached for a pistol under the seat.

"He's armed!" Davis shouted. "Look out."

Instead of firing his M16 and escalating the situation, Cardott chose to hit him with a blast of pepper spray. While the Haitian covered his eyes and screamed, Davis went for the man's gun.

As the two men struggled over the pistol, the Haitian managed to squeeze off a shot that tore through Davis's arm and threw him against the backseat of the car. A second shot whizzed past Davis's head. A third hit Cardott in the chest and went straight through his heart. He never recovered consciousness and died two hours later.

The news of Greg Cardott's death hit us hard. We learned later that the two Haitians were members of the FAdH-sponsored paramilitary group FRAPH.

Sergeant Cardott's death turned out to be one of the few dark spots on an otherwise successful mission. Order had been restored and a peaceful transition back to democracy was under way.

Sometime in February 1995, someone from the Red Cross called our administrative branch at 3rd Group HQ, Fort Bragg, to inform them that my mother had been hospitalized in California. The news was relayed to 3rd Group commander Colonel Boyett in Haiti, who passed it on to me.

"Your mom's pretty sick," he said. "She's in a hospital in Santa Clara."

I tried contacting my brother Jon but couldn't get through. After being granted emergency leave, I packed my gear and caught a C-141 to Fort Bragg. From Bragg I reached Jon, who told me that her kidneys had failed, causing her body to bloat with liquid, which was now putting pressure on her heart.

"I'm on my way," I told him, praying that I would make it there in time.

From nearby Charlotte I caught a commercial flight to Santa Clara.

I knew my mother had a weak heart. She'd been wheelchair bound since 1991. Throughout my life and career, she'd been a constant source of spiritual support and encouragement. The thought of losing her was terrifying.

I entered the Santa Clara Valley Medical Center with trepidation. There I saw my mother lying in bed breathing through a respirator. My brother Jon and youngest sister, Lida, rose to greet me. They explained the situation: Doctors were trying to drain the fluid out of her body to relieve the pressure on her heart.

For the next three weeks, my brother and I traded shifts and stayed with her in the hospital day and night. We did this in part because my mother's English wasn't good, which made it hard for her to communicate with the nurses and doctors.

Once her condition improved, I returned to Bragg. There I rejoined ODA 326, which was back from Haiti, and we handed in our M16s and had them replaced with new M4s with Pac4 scopes. Then we humped over to the firing range and familiarized ourselves with the new weapon. The M4 was six inches shorter and three-quarters of a pound lighter, which made it easier to maneuver in tight quarters, fired the same 5.56×45mm standard NATO cartridge, and fired both semiautomatic and in three-round bursts. Both guns were extremely accurate at 300 meters.

The drawback of both in my opinion was the gas-operated rotating bolt action, which blows hot gases, carbon residue, and unburned powder back into the weapon's receiver. This required frequent cleaning and lubrication. In desert environments like Somalia or Iraq, the lubricant attracted dust, causing dangerous stoppages.

In late March we were informed that ODA 326 and ODA 322 would be deploying to Senegal. Third Group, which had been deactivated after the Vietnam War, was re-formed in July 1990 with a new motto: "We Do Bad Things to Bad People."

Its new area of operations (AO) was western Africa and the Caribbean basin. We were going to Senegal to help launch the African Crisis Response Initiative, which involved the training of African military units to respond quickly to regional humanitarian disasters and conflicts. This was a response to recent crises in Somalia and Rwanda.

With the fall of the Soviet Union and dissolution of the Warsaw Pact, the US faced new military and political challenges across the globe stemming from civil wars, famine, and other internal conflicts. In order to address these problems

quickly and efficiently we needed to develop regional partners who could help us negotiate the gaps of language and
culture.

Twenty-four of us flew to the Senegalese capital of Dakar,
which faced the Atlantic Ocean. There we were briefed by the
US military attaché, who informed us that the former French
colony of 12.5 million had experienced one of the most successful transitions to democratic government in all of Africa.
In the late 1980s and early 1990s, however, its economy had
shrunk by 40 percent due to the government's stringent price
and export control on products like rice, in addition to mis-
management.

It was a country with limited natural resources and ex-
ported mostly fish, phosphates, groundnuts, and other agricultural products. The people spoke French and Arabic and
the majority worshipped a Sufi form of Islam. Its 12,000-man
army was poorly trained and equipped, but eager to improve.

The next day we drove six and half hours north through
sandy plains to an army base outside the city of Saint-Louis
called Military Zone 2. There we spent two months training
Senegalese infantry officers in close-quarter battle drills, battlefield medical treatment, and mission planning and movement.

We lived in open barracks and slept under mosquito netting. Every night after training, we walked 200 meters outside
the base to a Lebanese restaurant where we feasted on rice,
kebabs, and hummus. Our workweek ended at 3 P.M. on Thurs-
day. Friday was a day of prayer.

I made friends with a number of officers. Several of them
invited me to their homes, where they would spread a table-

cloth on the floor and I would join members of the family and eat with our hands from communal plates placed on round brass trays.

Somehow, I never got sick.

11

SPAIN

Days after I returned to Fort Bragg I received a special assignment to go to Spain to work for the US Drug Enforcement Agency (DEA). *Spain,* I thought. *Another country on my bucket list. Sangria, flamenco, and beautiful dark-haired women. But what's the job?*

Third Group SF command sergeant explained that the request had come through the State Department for Farsi and Kurdish speakers to assist the DEA and the drug squad of the Spanish National Police—known as Unidad de Droga y Crimen Organizado or UDYCO—in their investigations of international trafficking.

"The Spanish have a serious drug trade problem," he said. "They're overwhelmed and need our help."

"Happy to assist in any way I can," I responded.

"The problem's so pervasive that our DEA is running out of resources. That's why they've turned to us."

"If nothing else it will give me a chance to get to know Spain."

According to a recent report by the European Union's Drug Observatory, three-quarters of all European seizures of cocaine and heroin were now taking place in Spain and Portugal. The same report estimated that enforcement agencies in those countries were stopping less than 10 percent of the illegal trafficking of both drugs.

I also learned that following the death in 1975 of military dictator General Francisco Franco, Spanish legislators had taken a highly tolerant approach to drug use. Considering it a personal liberty, they decriminalized the use of cannabis, cocaine, and heroin. As a result, demand soared, particularly for heroin, and international organized crime moved in to provide supplies, despite the fact that the distribution of drugs in Spain remained illegal.

In 1988 alone Spanish police seized over 4,000 kilos of heroin, far exceeding the amount confiscated in the rest of Europe. A portion of the drugs entering Spain went to domestic consumption, but most of it was transshipped to Northern Europe.

Previously, the Dutch cities of Amsterdam and Rotterdam had been the primary transfer point for drugs entering Europe. After Dutch officials cracked down hard, traffickers changed routes and started using Spain.

Language and cultural links to Latin America, where many of the drugs were coming from, made it relatively easy for Latin distributors to operate in Spain. In addition, that country's thousands of miles of unguarded or poorly patrolled coastline provided easy access. And Spain received more than 50 million tourists and visitors a year.

Under pressure from the European Union and Washington,

and in the face of one of the fastest growing AIDS rates in Europe—due almost entirely to needle sharing among heroin users—the newly installed Socialist government of Spain had recently passed laws making it a crime to consume controlled substances, including cannabis, cocaine, and heroin, in public places. It remained legal to consume them at home.

In the summer of '95, when I received my orders, the new Spanish laws and increased supply were putting enormous pressure on the understaffed local customs and police forces. So me and three other guys from SF and a Hispanic Army officer were going to Spain to assist the UDYCO. We'd learn our specific duties when we arrived.

A few days after Independence Day, July 1995, I packed my bags for a commercial flight to California for five days of leave before deploying. Having just purchased a Taurus 911 9mm handgun, I planned to take it with me and leave it at my mother's house in Santa Clara. This special model made of stainless steel with a gold trigger and accents usually retailed for over $900. I bought it from a friend in SF at a bargain price of $250.

Knowing the law for traveling with a concealed weapon, I cleared the pistol and stored it in a box in my suitcase. Since I had arrived at Charlotte Airport a day early, I decided to check my suitcase and carry a change of clothes and toiletries in my backpack, which I took with me to a nearby hotel. When I informed the clerk that one of my bags had a pistol in it, she marked it with a special tag.

The next morning as I went through security with the

suitcase with the gun in it and my backpack, I was pulled aside by cops, two male and one female.

The woman said, "Step aside, sir."

I asked, "What's wrong?"

She cut me off abruptly. "Keep your mouth shut. Kneel down over there and face the wall."

"Ma'am, if it's about the weapon, I cleared it earlier—"

"Kneel down, I said!"

"For what reason?"

"Do it and shut up!"

Police officers shoved me hard against the wall and handcuffed my wrists. Then with dozens of passengers watching, they zipped open my suitcase and tore through my things, throwing clean shirts and underwear on the floor. They removed the box with the pistol and, with my suitcase and clothes remaining on the floor, escorted me downstairs.

"Where are we going?" I asked as politely as I could manage under the circumstances.

"Don't talk!"

Downstairs, I was locked in a metal cage. After twenty minutes two men in plainclothes arrived, removed the handcuffs, and escorted me to a windowless interrogation room.

"Stand facing the wall," one of the men ordered.

"I'm with Special Forces. I've been standing for a while. Can I sit?"

"No!"

"Why are you carrying a weapon?" the second man asked.

I explained how I had checked the suitcase the night before and according to regulations had cleared the pistol and hadn't stowed it in my carry-on bag. I didn't realize that my mistake had been to try to take the bag with the gun inside it with me through security. I should have checked it instead.

"I didn't ask you what you did," the plainclothes cop responded. "I asked you why you were carrying a weapon."

As I turned to answer, he shouted, "Shut up! Don't say anything. Keep your nose against the wall."

I obeyed. Another fifteen minutes passed before the two policemen arrived and started to pepper me with questions.

"What kind of name is Lahidji? Where are you from? Why are you carrying a weapon? What were you planning to do with it?"

As calmly as I could, I explained that I was an American citizen and a member of US Army Special Forces. I was on my way to California to spend five days of leave with my family before deploying to Spain.

"Spain?" the female cop asked.

"Yes, Spain."

"Are you on an A-team?"

"Yes, I am. I've been in A-teams for nineteen years."

"Really?" she asked. "Are you sure? I don't believe you."

"Of course I'm sure. Check my military ID card," I answered. "It's in my wallet."

They found the card, called Fort Bragg, and confirmed that I was telling the truth. But instead of releasing me or telling me what was going on, they locked me back in the cage. I waited there, pissed off that I had missed my flight, and wondering when this situation was going to end.

Seventeen years earlier I had gone through a similar experience in Las Vegas. I kept reminding myself that there were ignorant people everywhere and tried not to take it personally.

Three hours passed before a man named Captain McNamara from the Metropolitan Police entered.

He walked over to me and said, "Don't worry, son. I'll get you out of here. What were you trying to do?"

I explained everything again and waited another three hours for the paperwork to be completed and signed. Finally, I was released. Captain McNamara stood waiting for me in the hall.

I said, "Sir, I hope this doesn't go on my record, sir."

"Don't worry about it," he answered as he patted me on the shoulder.

"The thing that annoys me is that the police officers, particularly the woman, showed me no respect."

He said, "Forget about it."

Upstairs past the security gate, my clothes and suitcase were still in a pile on the floor. I packed everything, but couldn't find my pistol. Looking up at the male police officer standing over me, I said, "Excuse me. But I need my weapon."

He answered coldly, "Come back tomorrow."

"I'm leaving early in the morning and need it tonight."

"Okay then. . . . Come back in an hour."

An hour later, Captain McNamara arrived carrying the box with the pistol. As he handed it to me, the box opened and all the rounds fell out and scattered across the floor. I retrieved them, packed the pistol in my backpack, grabbed my suitcase, and walked back to the hotel.

In the morning, I made sure to check my suitcase at the

check-in counter and inform the clerk that there was a registered pistol inside. She tagged the bag. With great trepidation, I went through security again.

No problem. Safely through, I found the nearest bar and ordered a beer.

Six days later, I arrived in Spain, minus the Taurus 911, which I had left at my mother's house in Santa Clara. In Madrid I was put up in a downtown hotel. A day later, my three colleagues arrived and our team leader, Kip from Special Forces, drove us to the US Embassy where we were briefed by two guys from DEA.

They informed us that we were going to spend the next seven months helping the UDYCO unit analyze surveillance tapes of suspects talking in Farsi, Kurdish, and Spanish.

Every morning we drove to National Police Corps (CNP in its Spanish acronym) headquarters, where we drank beer and coffee for breakfast, and then we went up to our cubicles on the third floor to spend the next four hours listening to tapes. Every evening, we'd report anything suspicious we'd heard on them to Kip.

The more I listened, the better I got at deciphering the oftentimes mundane code the drug traffickers used and was able to identify which conversations were important. Sometimes it had to do with a nervous tremor in someone's voice, or the very serious manner in which individuals discussed rugs or a trip to the beach.

One day in my third week, I heard a guy speaking Farsi on a wiretapped phone say, "I got the offer. One point two million. Where should I get the purses?"

"I got the purses," a guy on the other end answered. "They're made of the finest leather."

"Can you sell them?"

"Of course. Of course."

"They're good quality?"

"Very good. You can inspect them yourself."

"When?"

"I can't show them today. I'll call you."

"When?"

"Soon. Don't worry."

Over the course of several more calls, I pinpointed a house north of Madrid and the time when the exchange was going to take place. I reported everything to Kip, who passed it on to officials in the UDYCO. A raid was quickly organized. Kip and I were told that we could witness the operation but weren't allowed to participate.

"Fair enough."

That night we dressed in black and followed six Spanish police and drug enforcement officials to the site—a two-story stucco house on a quiet suburban street. Spanish officials displayed their plastic-encased IDs outside their civilian clothes and were armed with shotguns and pistols.

On a signal from their leader, they smashed in the front door and entered. Fifteen minutes later, they emerged with five suspects—three men and two women—all in handcuffs. One woman looked Iranian and spoke Farsi. The others were Spanish.

UDYCO officers found three big garbage bags full of cocaine in one of the closets and a suitcase packed with hundred-dollar bills. They brought the evidence back to HQ, and officials from the Interior Ministry arrived to stand beside it and have their pictures taken.

Very late that night our UDYCO counterparts took us out for a celebratory dinner with lots of vino rosado and sangria. The next day, we returned to listening to phone intercepts and developing new cases.

Over the course of seven months, our work resulted in fifteen more raids by the Spanish police. I accompanied them each time, observing the op from a distance and feeling left out. The suspects were Iranians, Kurds, Spaniards, or Latin Americans, and the drugs seized most often were heroin, hashish, or cocaine from the Middle East on its way to the US.

It was a different experience for an action junkie like me, developing cases instead of busting down doors and chasing suspects. But Spain more than compensated with its other charms, including history, art, food, wine, and lovely women.

One weekend every other month, the four of us on the drug detail would borrow two cars from the US Embassy carpool and drive six hours to Barcelona. On our way back to Madrid, we'd take a detour south and stop at US Naval Station Rota just north of Cádiz. At the PX we'd stock up on supplies—mostly snacks, drinks, videos, and chocolate.

When I passed through Charlotte Airport in February '96 on my way to Fort Bragg, I asked to see police Captain McNamara.

"Sergeant Lahidji, welcome back," Captain McNamara said as he bounded out of his office and wrapped me in a bear hug. "How'd it go in Spain?"

"Excellent, sir."

"Good to hear. No more problems getting through airport security?"

"None at all, sir. I got you this," I said handing him a beer stein I had bought in Spain.

"It's beautiful, Sergeant, but I can't take it."

"You must, sir. I insist."

He refused in the end, citing police department regulations forbidding the acceptance of gifts.

A month later, I got a PCS to return to Fort Lewis, Washington, and rejoin 1st Group. I was assigned to ODA 176—a special seven-man team led by a broad-chested captain who was big into weightlifting.

Our first assignment was to fly to Laos to provide assistance as part of a comprehensive Ordnance Removal and Community Awareness training program that had been approved by President Clinton. Our job was essentially to train a select group of local trainers in demining.

Laos had the unenviable distinction of being the most bombed country on the planet according to statistics kept by the Mines Advisory Group. One tragic consequence of the Vietnam War was that approximately 2 million metric tons of unexploded ordnance (UXO) had been dropped on Laos's northern provinces of Houaphan and Xieng Khouang and along the border with Vietnam. Included in this figure are 270 million submunitions—or bomblets dispersed by cluster munitions, known in Laos as *bombies*.

An estimated 80 million—or 30 percent—of these submunitions had failed to detonate. Some had been dropped at such a low altitude that the fuses didn't have time to arm. Others simply malfunctioned.

As a result of extensive ground fighting during the war, parts of Laos were also contaminated with unexploded artillery shells, antitank rockets, mortar rounds, and land mine grenades. In fact, UXO contamination was so widespread that it denied the use of agricultural land and hindered economic development.

From 1973 through 1976, the number of UXO victims in Laos had averaged 1,100 per year. Since then the number of dead and injured had dropped but remained in the hundreds. Sadly, a large percentage of the victims were children.

Children were attracted to the bombies, which were the size and shape of tennis balls, and often painted bright yellow. Other accidents occurred as people were going about their everyday work—for example, a farmer who hit an UXO beneath the soil's surface while digging. Other causes included lighting fires over hidden UXOs or deliberately breaking UXOs open in order to sell the scrap metal or explosives inside.

Sent to address this problem, we landed in the capital Vientiane, along the country's southern border, then loaded our gear and ten duffels of equipment onto jeeps and drove several hours north to a camp that had been set up by the UN called Nam Souang. We were in the Vientiane Valley, which was some of the most fertile land in the country and dotted with picturesque rice paddies. Most of landlocked Laos was mountainous and not arable, which explained why its 5.5 million people were among the poorest in East Asia.

At Nam Souang we taught classes of students selected by

the Ministry of Social Welfare on how to spread community awareness, mine and UXO clearance techniques, medical training, and leadership development. In the morning, we did classroom work, working through translators and showing slides to male and female students of what to do and what to avoid. We'd tell them that the only way to disassemble a mine and other types of UXOs was to deactivate them one by one.

Afternoons were reserved for hands-on instruction. We'd bus students into the field and show them the slow, methodical process of UXO detection. It would start with clearing strips of land three feet apart with a metal detector, then marking them with furrows. Then we'd run the metal detector over a ten-foot swath between the furrows.

If the detector remained silent, meaning it hadn't found any UXOs in the area, we'd mark that patch of land with stakes on all sides. If the detector beeped, the person holding it would back away, and I would move into position with a long stick and probe the ground for the location of the UXO. Once I found it, I'd dig around it very carefully with my hands.

If I discovered a mine, I'd use pliers to cut the detonator wire and remove the blasting caps. Some types of unexploded ordnance could be defused and others had to be detonated in place once the area was cleared of livestock and people.

It was dirty, dangerous, tedious work, but the Laotians picked up the concepts quickly. The ninety-day course was designed to turn these Laotians into trainers to instruct subsequent teams.

In October 1999 when the US technical assistance program ended, over 1,000 Laotians had graduated with a variety of UXO action skills, over 104,000 UXOs had been identified and cleared, and more than 700 villages had been visited with comprehensive UXO risk messages—especially the three Rs: recognize, retreat, report.

After a week break, we flew to Phnom Penh, Cambodia, to provide protection a US-led construction crew repairing a road called Route 4. This important highway ran from the capital city of Phnom Penh south to the port of Sihanoukville— named after King Norodom Sihanouk, who had returned to power in 1993 after the deadly eighteen-year reign of the Khmer Rouge. It spanned 500 kilometers through flatlands, jungle, several mountain passes, and remaining Khmer Rouge strongholds.

The $23 million US-funded project had been delayed because of local bureaucratic delays and security problems. A year earlier a Thai road worker had been shot and killed while traveling in a truck convoy. The shooting was blamed on rogue Royal Cambodian Armed Forces (RCAF) soldiers manning a toll checkpoint.

Some people reported that local RCAF commanders had a problem with Thai workers dominating a Cambodian con- struction project. Others blamed corruption in the RCAF and the new Cambodian government.

A month before we were called, another construction crew was attacked by Khmer Rouge rebels near Sihanoukville. Apparently, the dark shadow the Khmer Rouge regime had cast over the country hadn't completely lifted. Led by "Brother Number One," General Pol Pot, the Marxist-nationalist movement had seized power in 1975 with the help of the North Vietnamese army and Vietcong.

Once in control of the country, it launched a radical program of closing all schools, hospitals, and factories; abolishing banking, finance, and money; outlawing all religions; and confiscating all personal property. Teachers, merchants, bankers, professionals, ethnic Thais, Vietnamese, and Chinese, and all intellectual elites were executed to make way for an agrarian form of communism. What came to be known as the Cambodian genocide resulted in between 1.2 million and 2.2 million deaths out of a population of roughly 7 million.

There was real reason to fear remnants of the Khmer Rouge, who were still active in the south. USAID, which was running the road project, didn't feel they could count on the RCAF to provide security. So we were tapped to oversee local security guards and guard construction crews.

From our hotel in Phnom Penh, we left early each morning fully armed in jeeps. Cambodian and Thai workers along Route 4 were happy to see us, as were the USAID supervisors who watched the oft-delayed project progress. The biggest problems we encountered were the heat and the bugs.

Three weeks in, I came down with a high fever and started experiencing severe headaches and muscle pain and yellowing of the skin. Our medic concluded I had yellow fever—a viral infection transmitted by a bite from an infected mosquito. It had the potential to cause liver damage and in some cases could be fatal.

Since there were no good medical facilities in Phnom Penh at the time, I was given money and put on a boat that took me to Pattaya, Thailand. At the International Hospital there, the Thai doctors and nurses treated me, and three days later I felt well enough to return to Cambodia to finish the project, which lasted another two weeks.

At the end of 1997, I was promoted to E8 (Master Sergeant) and sent to 1st Group in Okinawa, where I was assigned as operations sergeant to Alpha Company. My responsibilities included running five teams, scheduling activities for all the teams, and communicating assignments from battalion command.

Our team sergeant was Sergeant Major Butch Young. While Butch returned to the States for a month and a half of R&R, I took his place.

Apparently I didn't screw up too bad because when he returned, he awarded me with my team to command, ODA 113. In certain ways, it was a dream come true—a final confirmation that I was valued and accepted. In another sense, it felt long overdue as I'd watched scores of others who'd done a hell of a lot less than I had get promoted ahead of me.

One of our first assignments in ODA 113 was to deploy to South Korea to do intel gathering along the DMZ—a 2.5 mile buffer zone that had been created as a result of the Armistice Agreement of July 1953 that had ended the Korean War. It runs 160 miles along the 38th Parallel and is considered the most heavily fortified border in the world, because of continued animosity and ideological differences between North and South Korea.

Sporadic fighting and North Korean incursions since the

armistice had resulted in over 500 South Korean casualties, at least 250 from the northern Democratic People's Republic, and the deaths of fifty US soldiers.

The Democratic People's Republic of Korea (DPRK) to the north was ruled by a hereditary dictatorship led at that time by maniacal Kim Jong-il, who spent hundreds of millions of dollars on maintaining the largest military in the world (over 9 million active, reserve, and paramilitary personnel out of a population of 23 million). He was also hell-bent on developing nuclear weapons, while hundreds of thousands of his people starved and 200,000 were locked away in political prisons. According to Human Rights Watch, the DPRK had (and still has) one of the worst human rights records in the world.

For this mission, we split up into three four-man teams and hiked into the heavily forested mountains on the southern side. At 10,000 feet we built primitive hootches out of wood and tarps, and recorded the comings and goings at the North Korean military base to the east, which we could make out clearly through high-powered binoculars.

Rain poured down on us ten out of the fifteen days we stayed there, and it was cold as hell. As I lay in my sleeping bag at night, freezing my ass off and with the wind howling outside, I reminded myself how lucky I was to be living in a country like the United States where I didn't have to live according to the whims of a maniacal dictator.

Toward the end of our mission, Battalion Sergeant Major Mike Moore trekked into the mountains with a four-man inspection team to visit us. But we were so well hidden they couldn't find our location.

From my hideout up in a tree, I spotted them and made a noise.

They looked up but still couldn't see me.

So I said. "Hey, Sergeant Major. It's Changiz. What are you doing here?"

"Why the fuck are you up in that tree?" Sergeant Moore asked back.

"It's a hide sight, isn't it? I'm hiding."

I climbed down as he and his men cracked up. Then I signaled the rest of the guys on my team to come out of their hides.

A few days later, we broke camp and passed through a village on our way down to Camp Casey—a US military base forty miles north of Seoul—and one of several US bases near the DMZ. Tom, Chris, Jason, and I were standing at a local bus stop, soaking wet, waiting to get picked up, when a man came out of his house and invited us inside. We removed our wet clothes and dried them before a fire, and the old man served us a dinner of soup, fish stew, kimchi, and rice.

The rain continued to come down in sheets for two days, and our host insisted on sheltering and feeding us. When the clouds finally parted, we wanted to find a way to thank him. I knew that South Korean men loved US uniforms, so I asked the guys on my team to pitch in anything they could spare. We left him uniforms, knives, flashlights, and MREs, then called for a truck from Camp Casey to pick us up.

More training assignments took ODA 113 to Thailand. By January 2001, I'd served in Special Forces for twenty-three years. I felt like it was time to step aside and welcome in the Pepsi generation. So I put in for retirement and was honored with the highest award in Special Forces—the Legion of Merit.

Three of my longtime SF buddies, Ken, John, and Dave, were retiring at the same time, so the three of us pooled our money and hosted a three-day, two-night bash on Torii Beach in Okinawa. Wives, girlfriends, and friends danced and partied. We went out in style!

12

AFGHANISTAN

I'm not the kind of guy to kick back and play golf. Yes, I had retired from Special Forces, but I immediately started looking for something else to do besides ride my Harley up and down the Pacific Coast Highway.

Since I'd moved back in with my family in Santa Clara, I started looking for work in Northern California.

In February 2001, Lockheed Martin hired me as a security coordinator responsible for checking credentials and supervising other security personnel. Early in the morning of September 11, 2001, I had just completed my rounds as security duty captain at a plant in Sunnyvale, California, when one of the four off-duty guards inside the day room pointed to a TV screen and said, "Changiz, you've got to see this."

"What?" I asked, feeling a sense of déjà vu from 1979.

"Some planes have crashed into some buildings in New York!"

Instead of rioting Islamic students on the screen, I saw

black smoke and flames pouring from the two huge build-ings. "That's the World Trade Center! How the hell did that happen?"

We watched in horror as the towers burned and collapsed to the ground. I felt a sick feeling rise from the pit of my stomach. Obviously, this wasn't an accident. Then a news commentator announced that a third plane had crashed into the Pentagon.

"We're under attack!"

My instinct was to grab my gear and prepare to deploy. But I was no longer in the service. The four guards and I linked hands and prayed for the victims of the attack and for the future of our country.

Throughout the day, more news trickled in about the number of brave firefighters who were missing and the fact that some of the hijackers had been identified and linked to the terrorist group Al Qaeda.

I was bursting at the seams to go after Osama bin Laden and his followers and kick their asses. I was also pissed that our government had dropped the ball. Not only was our bor-der security seriously flawed, but we had also failed to destroy Al Qaeda after they had bombed our embassies in Kenya and Tanzania in August 1998 and attacked the USS *Cole* on October 12, 2000, in Yemen.

While our government was focused on impeaching a president who had lied about a sexual indiscretion, we had allowed a small group of Sunni radicals to plan and deliver a shockingly devious and damaging blow on American soil. And it could have been worse. I learned later that in mid-August 2001 bin Laden and his deputy Ayman al-Zawahiri sat down with two Pakistani nuclear scientists in a mud-walled compound in southern Afghanistan and discussed the possibility of Al Qaeda obtaining a nuclear weapon. Bin Laden left that meeting abruptly, telling the Pakistanis that something momentous was going to happen soon.

Throughout the rest of that grim day in September 2001, I kept reminding myself that we should have seen it coming. I'd come very close to brushing shoulders with bin Laden and his Al Qaeda followers in Pakistan and the Panjshir Valley of Afghanistan in 1981 when I was training mujahedeen and first heard his name. I'd also heard bin Laden discussed during my undercover visits of mosques in Brooklyn and Queens while on assignment to the FBI in '92. More recently, some members of Al Qaeda had aided Somalia militiamen during the Battle of Mogadishu.

Shaken and angry, I called a friend at FBI headquarters in New York and asked, "Is there anything I can do to help?"

He said, "We're completely overwhelmed now, Changiz, but thanks for calling. I'll keep you in mind."

"I'll do anything," I said. "You know my language skills and familiarity with the region. I'm in California now, but I can be in New York or DC tomorrow. Send me to Afghanistan to go after the bastards. I'll do whatever you need."

"Okay. Thanks. As soon as I see what our needs are, I'll let you know."

I was too upset to sleep. The next morning, I called a former commander from 5th Group Special Forces named Colonel Jack Hook, who was now working as a military contractor for a firm called Military Professional Resources Inc. (MPRI) based in Alexandria, Virginia. MPRI hired me immediately. A week later I was on a plane to Germany to do "red cell" testing—or security penetration testing—of US bases.

Investigators looking into the 9/11 attacks learned that a number of the Al Qaeda terrorists, including leader Mohamed el-Amir Awad el-Sayed Atta, had previously been part of a secret cell living in Hamburg, Germany. Knowing that Al Qaeda had a strong presence in Germany, the Pentagon was concerned about the security of the more than a dozen military bases and the 100,000 Army, Navy, and Air Force personnel we had there.

Working with a small team of former SF and SEAL operators, I broke into bases in Heidelberg, Berlin, Frankfurt, and Stuttgart, gained access to top secret areas, and even stole equipment. Then we wrote detailed reports on these breaches so they could be corrected.

On a rainy night in October 2002, I was in my hotel room in Stuttgart getting ready for bed when the phone rang. It was Mike Smith, a friend and former colleague from 5th Group.

He asked, "Changiz, what the hell are you doing?"

"I'm on a contract with MPRI doing red cell work overseas."

"How do you like it?"

"It's fine. Why?"

"You still have your top secret clearance?"

"Yeah. Of course."

"What is MPRI paying you?" he asked.

I gave him a figure, which was twice what I had earned in Special Forces.

"How would you like to make even more?" Mike asked.

"I wouldn't complain."

"You'd have to go to Afghanistan."

"No problem," I answered. I'd been longing to go to Afghanistan, which was where the action was.

After it had been established that Al Qaeda leadership had planned and directed the 9/11 attacks from training camps in that country, President George W. Bush had given the Taliban regime an ultimatum: Hand over the Al Qaeda terrorists and stop giving them sanctuary in Afghanistan or suffer the consequences.

When the Taliban refused to comply, the US responded with air strikes against terrorist and military targets. President Bush also authorized sending in small teams of CIA officers and Special Forces operators to work with Northern Alliance opposition militiamen (commanded by my old friend Ahmad Shah Massoud, before his death at the hands of Al Qaeda assassins on September 9, 2001) to topple the regime.

The combination of air strikes and CIA/SF teams coordinating with Northern Alliance units worked better than anyone had expected. By the end of December 2001, the Taliban had been pushed out of Kabul and most major cities, and bin Laden and his remaining followers were fleeing the country.

A week after Mike called, I met him at United States Information Service (USIS) headquarters in Tysons Corner, Virginia—just outside DC.

A government official explained that they were putting together a team to train a personal security detail for the newly installed president of Afghanistan.

Back in December 2001, twenty-five Afghan political leaders met in Bonn, Germany, in a conference organized by the UN to form a transition government in Afghanistan. As a result of what became known as the Bonn Agreement, signed on December 5, Hamid Karzai, a longtime critic of the Taliban regime who fought with the Northern Alliance and US Special Forces teams, was named chairman of the Interim Administration. Six months later, he was appointed interim president of Afghanistan until presidential elections could be organized in 2004.

With Taliban units still roaming the country and no real Afghan army to count on, US Navy SEALs and other special operators had been charged with protecting President Karzai. In July 2002, Afghan vice president Abdul Qadir and his driver had been shot to death by two gunmen with automatic weapons as their vehicle left a ministry compound in downtown Kabul. A month later President Karzai barely escaped an assassination attempt.

Soon after that attack, the State Department announced that members of their Diplomatic Security Service would replace US troops and begin training a local security force to protect the Afghan leader. According to a senior Afghan government official, "the important thing to remember is that the ultimate aim is to have Afghans providing security for our head of state, not Americans."

Because of my extensive Special Forces experience I

was considered a perfect candidate. Officials at USIS supplied me with a black passport—which carried the protection of diplomatic immunity—and an airplane ticket to Tashkent, Uzbekistan. I arrived there two days later, and spent several very cold days in a hotel waiting for a CIA flight to Afghanistan.

The view of the Hindu Kush Mountains as we descended through the clouds was breathtaking. Twenty years after my last visit, I was back in Kabul. Greeting me at Bagram Air Base were two officials from the US Embassy, who drove me to Camp Watan, a small secret State Department facility close to the US Army's Camp Phoenix and four miles from the US Embassy. Across the street sat a huge NATO-led International Security Assistance Force (ISAF) compound that housed soldiers from Holland, New Zealand, Turkey, Spain, Australia, the UK, and other Coalition partners.

Inside a barbed-wire perimeter heavily fortified with machine gun nests, bunkers, and guard towers was the football-field-sized camp with mobile homes for sixteen instructors, two big barracks for the Afghan recruits, a generator to provide electricity, a lunchroom, gym, and lounge. Adjoining the camp was a huge junkyard filled with rusting tanks, helicopters, trucks, and cars discarded by the Soviets when they fled Afghanistan.

The next day we met 120 handpicked Afghans—a motley crew that spoke no English, had no birth certificates, and were largely illiterate. Out of that group only seventy-six managed to pass a basic test and join our first class. I communicated with them in their local Dari. The other trainers depended on seven translators, known as *terps,* fluent in both Dari and Pashto.

My primary responsibility was firearms instructor, and I also taught the recruits how to line up for inspection, march, drive a dune buggy, make a bed, take a shit in a latrine, and wipe their asses. I'm not kidding.

The course lasted nine weeks, with our days starting at 0530 hours when all the recruits went on a five-mile hike in all weather conditions, including pouring rain and snow. While they ran, I packed a Humvee with M4s, Glocks, 6,000 rounds of ammo, food, and water. After breakfast half of the recruits would march off for classroom work, while my SF buddy John and I loaded the remaining thirty-eight into four trucks and escorted them to a firing range about forty-five minutes away. It consisted of a field with a 2,000-foot hill on the right, topped with a French flag.

We taught them how to care, clear, reload, and fire M4s and Glocks. Then we'd return to Camp Watan in the afternoon and take out the second group. Friday—a day of rest in Afghanistan—was our only day off.

After dinner, I'd sit with the Afghan recruits and tell stories about living in the States, and my adventures in the SF. One night, one of the Afghan guards assigned to man the base watchtowers was in the room next to ours cleaning his AK. Apparently, he hadn't cleared the chamber first. When I heard the gun discharge, I hurried in to find him slumped to the floor with a bullet entry wound under his chin. I ripped off my shirt, wrapped it around his head, and shouted to the Afghans to fetch a truck.

Once loaded in the vehicle, I drove him to the field hospital contained in the ISAF compound across the street. The Canadian doctors there declared him dead.

Most days when we approached the firing range, kids would run out of nearby huts to greet us. I always carried a bag of candy, which I'd hand out to them. One morning when we reached the range, an old man hobbled over to tell me that a six-year-old boy had fallen into an oven and was badly burned. I ran to the hut and found the boy's family huddled around the unconscious six-year-old and praying. A medic was summoned and the two of us cooled the boy's burns with water and then wrapped him in oil gauze.

The burns were so extensive I thought he'd die. Every time I went to the range, I'd stop in to look in on the kid, bring him medicine, and give MREs to him and his family. Slowly he recovered. After five months the boy was healed enough to stand and give me a hug. It touched my heart.

Two months before graduation, we hired a local tailor to measure the thirty-five students (out of seventy-six) who had passed. All of them were given three suits, shirts, and three pairs of shoes, socks, and underwear. I showed them how to march and stand at attention for the ceremony. US ambassador Robert Finn came with thirty other US and Afghan VIPs. President Karzai was expected but didn't show.

All of us instructors took a ten-day break and then started to train a second class of recruits. Meanwhile, the first class served as the outer ring of security around President Karzai and supplied logistical support to the State Department inner detail.

One of the biggest pleasures of working in Afghanistan was making friends with local military and intelligence officials. During the months I spent at Camp Watan, I grew close to two high-ranking Afghan police and intelligence officials—Zacur and Abdullah. Both were Pashtuns; Abdullah's father was a high-ranking military officer.

One afternoon, while the three of us were drinking tea and talking, I asked if they had any idea where Osama bin Laden was hiding. At the time, bin Laden's location was a big topic of conjecture in both the US and Afghanistan.

Everyone knew that he had managed to slip across the Pakistani border in December 2001. Most experts thought he was living somewhere in the lawless Federally Administered Tribal Areas of western Pakistan where the Taliban leadership was based. But no one knew for sure.

What had been widely announced was that the United States had put a $25 million bounty on his head. The size of the reward attracted a wide variety of fortune seekers, from Afghans in the city of Jalalabad (near the Pakistani border), to a private investigator from Texas who was arrested on his way to Syria, to a construction worker from Colorado who was detained by Pakistani authorities in a forest near the northwestern tribal area of Chitral carrying a samurai sword and loaded pistol.

At my next meeting with Zacur and Abdullah, they informed me that Afghan intel sources had told them that bin Laden was back in Afghanistan living in a valley in the mountainous Tora Bora region near the border with Pakistan. That made sense because he had maintained a camp and private residence in that very remote area since the war against the Soviets.

In December 2001, he and several thousand of his followers had been discovered there by a handful of Special Forces and CIA operatives. For the next fourteen days, US officials called in air strikes. They had cornered bin Laden and a large concentration of Al Qaeda fighters in some of the most forbidding terrain on earth.

The air strikes were so devastating that bin Laden expected to die. In his last will and testament, written on December 14, 2001, he wrote, "Allah commended to us that when death approaches any of us that we make a bequest to parents and next of kin and to Muslims as a whole. Allah bears witness to the love of jihad and death in the cause of Allah that has dominated my whole life."

But appeals to General Tommy Franks for 800 Rangers to block bin Laden's escape were rejected. And on December 16 bin Laden and a group of his bodyguards crossed the border into Pakistan.

His location had remained a mystery since. In September 2003, I asked Zacur and Abdullah if they could take me into Tora Bora so I could see bin Laden with my own eyes. They agreed and recruited another of their Afghan intel colleagues to escort us.

We dressed like local farmers with Pashtun-style hats, baggy pants, vests, and robes. With my long graying beard and dark eyes, I blended in.

On an overcast morning, the four of us climbed into a white extended-cab Toyota pickup—the kind favored by local warlords and farmers—and set off north on the asphalt Jalalabad–Kabul highway, which *The New York Times* had recently described as the most dangerous road in the world. Taliban and IED (improvised explosive device) attacks on ISAF convoys occurred daily. Under my robes I carried a Glock and four mags.

Abdullah, at the wheel, turned off the paved road before we reached the Darunta Dam and continued on a dirt road east into the mountains. The scenery was spectacular, a big lake and valley to our left, sharp peaks of the White Mountains to the right. After passing the village of Azizkhan we turned right again onto a smaller, rougher path and climbed for another two hours until we reached the Melva Valley.

It was immediately obvious to me why bin Laden had used this area as a hideout for so many years. First of all, it was extremely remote and populated by only a handful of farmers and their families. Secondly, access was so difficult that it was easy to stop anyone coming up the steep narrow paths. Finally, the terrain offered hundreds of hidden gorges, natural caves, and valleys to hide in.

The road ended at a little gathering of huts. A couple of battered pickups rested nearby. Abdullah parked, and we followed him to a crest of a hill dotted with tall pine trees. From there we looked down into a valley.

I saw furrowed fields and steep, winding paths, but no people.

Then, I felt a hand on my shoulder. It belonged to Abdullah, who whispered in Dari, "Above."

As I looked up, a chill shot up my spine. "Where?"

About sixty feet above stood another flat ridge. Just beyond it rested four trucks. Sitting and crouching around them were two dozen men holding automatic weapons. On their right periphery four men stood talking. One of them was six or seven inches taller than the others.

"That's him," Abdullah whispered. "The Sheikh."

The tall man wore a Pashtun cap and had an AK slung over his shoulder. When he turned, I saw a face I'd seen many times on magazine covers and posters—Osama bin Laden.

"Holy shit!"

I was so excited I felt an impulse to climb up to the ridge and attack him. But there were more than twenty of them and four of us, and they were armed with AK-47s and we only had a few pistols. We would have been quickly wiped out.

So I followed Abdullah and the other Afghans back to our pickup, where I drew a rough map of the path we had traveled and our location. We spent the remainder of the day with Abdullah's uncle, who lived nearby in a small gathering of huts, never mentioning the reason for our visit.

We returned to Kabul that night. The following day, I drove downtown and parked near Freedom Circle, which was lined with stores selling everything from fruit to shoes. From there I walked several blocks to the US Embassy. After identifying myself and entering the building, I asked to speak to an intel officer.

I was told to wait in a room on the third floor. Twenty minutes later a middle-aged man entered and identified himself as a military attaché. I related the account of my trip into Tora Bora and what I'd seen.

He left and returned a few minutes later with three young intel officers.

I showed them the primitive map I'd drawn and told them who I'd seen.

"Are you sure it was him?" one of them asked.

"Absolutely. He's taller than most people here and stands out."

"What was he wearing?"

I described everything from boots to cap.

"How far away were you standing?"

"Not far. No more than sixty feet. Maybe seventy."

"And you're sure it was him?"

"Absolutely sure. I have three witnesses. Three Afghan intel officers went with me. I can bring them here, if you like."

"That won't be necessary."

The three US intel officers seemed excited by my news. They asked if they could keep the map.

"Of course," I answered.

"We need to show this to some people."

"I understand. If you want me to escort a team of special operators to the area, I'm happy to do so. I would suggest it be a small team and they all disguise themselves as locals. We'll need to infiltrate the area at night. Drive up to a certain altitude then complete the rest on foot wearing NVGs."

"Yes."

"It won't be easy, but it can be done with trained operators."

The three men nodded.

"I can draw up some plans if you want."

"Thanks," they said, rising from their chairs. "Go ahead and do that. We'll be in touch."

Days passed and I never heard from them. Thinking that maybe they had sent a team into Tora Bora without telling me, I followed the daily military action reports carefully. But I didn't see any mention of any military engagement in Tora Bora.

Curious as to why the intel officers hadn't responded, I returned to the US Embassy a week later. But this time no one wanted to speak to me. Disappointed, I returned to Camp Watan, where I ran into a Delta operator I knew and trusted. I told him what I had seen in Tora Bora and how the US intel officers I spoke to had reacted.

My Delta buddy shrugged his shoulders and said, "Maybe the guys running the show don't want to catch him."

"What do you mean?"

"Or they don't want to catch bin Laden yet."

"Who are talking about?" I asked.

"The big shots in DC," he answered. "Think about it. They're so deeply invested in the war on terrorism. We're in Afghanistan and we've invaded Iraq. We're committed to rebuilding both countries. If the president announced tomorrow that we'd killed bin Laden, how is he going to justify staying in Afghanistan and Iraq?"

"Good point."

I remained in Afghanistan and trained several more classes of recruits for President Karzai's personal protection detail. At the end of 2003 we got a new team leader. In the past I had always handed out ammunition to the students for their M4s and pistols after we arrived at the firing range. Our new leader wanted the recruits to load their weapons before we left Camp Watan.

I considered this unwise and explained that arming the students before they reached the range would put them at unnecessary risk. He insisted we follow his protocol.

Feeling I couldn't do that in good conscience, I submitted my resignation. Three other SF trainers did the same. A few weeks later, the four of us were hired to go to Pakistan and train members of their new antiterrorism unit. Spurred by the influx of vanquished Al Qaeda and Taliban fighters from Afghanistan, Pakistan was experiencing its own upswing in terrorism and the government of General Pervez Musharraf was determined to stop it.

Meanwhile, military contracting firms I'd never heard of before were contacting me on a weekly basis. What I was witnessing was a virtual explosion in the private military contracting sector. Unable to fill all the needs associated with running and supporting the war on terrorism and rebuilding Afghanistan and Iraq, the Pentagon and State Department were handing out huge contracts to private firms. The USG—US government—was outsourcing everything from military training, to supplying food to base dining facilities, to maintaining air assets.

Starting in late 2001, even jobs like intel gathering and quick reaction forces that had once been the exclusive purview of the Army were now being transferred to private contractors. The contracts awarded by the USG were enormous—$1.5 billion to Triple Canopy to provide security teams in Iraq, and $293 million to Aegis Defense Services to support and protect the USG's restructuring of Iraq. Firms based in DC, London, and Stockholm like G4S, MPRI, Securitas AB, and others were becoming billion-dollar operations overnight.

According to the DOD, by 2011, they had hired more contractor personnel in Afghanistan and Iraq (155,000) than uniformed personnel (145,000). This meant that the need of private contracting companies to hire qualified people was massive.

I saw this with my own eyes in Afghanistan in late 2003. While I was completing my training assignment in Pakistan, a contracting firm I had never heard of used my résumé and those of some of my former SF colleagues to win a $60 million contract to train guards to protect the US Embassy in Kabul.

When we arrived in Kabul in late 2003, my colleagues and I quickly realized that the firm didn't have the staff or resources in place to run the project. Everything had been slapped together at the last minute. Managers were ineffective and quarreled over responsibilities. Rather than renting a house to accommodate a dozen trainers, the contracting firm put us up at an expensive hotel.

Shocked by the amount the hotel was charging, we took it upon ourselves to locate a four-bedroom house a few blocks behind the embassy. A few days later we met the recruits the firm wanted us to train only to learn that they were Peruvian and could barely speak English. Things went from bad to worse, and a year later the State Department terminated the firm's contract citing inadequate personnel.

Sadly, it was only one example of poor staffing by private contractors. To my mind it was a result of a failure of policy. In both Afghanistan and Iraq we had taken on the burden of trying to heal fractured societies and rebuild institutions. It was an impossible task. How were we going to fix other countries' problems when we couldn't solve the long-standing issues in dysfunctional, crime-ridden neighborhoods of our own?

13

DARFUR

March 2004 wasn't the best time to be in Baghdad, but that's where I chose to be, in the action and living in the heavily fortified Green Zone. Signing my paycheck was the military contractor DynCorp. DynCorp was based in Reston, Virginia, and one of the federal government's top twenty-five contractors with billings of over $1 billion a year. Prior to 9/11, DynCorp provided aircraft and helicopter maintenance crews to support the US military during the First Gulf War. Its pilots and planes flew defoliation missions in Colombia. It managed border posts between Mexico and the US, made up the core of the police force in Bosnia, and serviced the fleet of Air Force One presidential planes and Marine One helicopters.

Since 9/11, DynCorp had expanded its operations to fill the needs of the USG in Afghanistan and Iraq and grab part of the $18 billion the US Congress had recently appropriated to rebuild Iraqi schools, factories, and oil facilities. Additionally, the USG was forced to allocate additional resources to deal with the deteriorating security situation in the country.

One year after the start of Operation Iraqi Freedom—aka the invasion of Iraq—the peaceful transition from the authoritarian rule of Saddam Hussein to a representative form of government wasn't happening. From my perspective on the ground, I saw a constant escalation of attacks by Sunni extremist groups against Coalition forces, Shiites, and Kurds in an effort to provoke civil conflict.

The invasion launched by the US and Coalition partners Great Britain, Australia, and Poland on March 19, 2003, had shocked and awed Iraq's army and forced Saddam Hussein into hiding. On May 1, 2003, President Bush stood on the deck of the aircraft carrier USS *Abraham Lincoln* and, with a huge MISSION ACCOMPLISHED banner behind him, announced the end of major combat operations.

No doubt military planning and execution of the war had been highly effective. But postwar planning . . . not so much. When the Saddam government imploded, Iraqi police and military abandoned their posts, leaving a security vacuum in much of the country. With an insufficient number of Coalition troops to police a population of 26 million, mobs looted museums, banks, hospitals, government facilities, and businesses. Thousands of ancient artifacts were stolen, along with cached weapons, and hundreds of thousands of tons of explosives.

In this unstable political atmosphere, US special envoy Paul Bremer and the Bush administration made two decisions that destabilized the situation further and set a perilous course for the country's future. One was to disband Iraq's army and replace it with a brand-new one built from the ground up. The second was to bar senior members of Iraq's secularist and nationalistic Baath Party, which had ruled the country since 1968, from holding positions in the new government.

Both decisions were made counter to the advice of CIA, State Department, and Pentagon officials. In the political uncertainty that followed, suspicion and hostility exploded between Sunnis, Shiites, and Kurds that the secular government of Saddam Hussein had managed to keep in check.

Sunni extremists who felt disenfranchised by the US decision to curtail the Baath Party started to unleash violence on Coalition and Shiite targets. Every day saw more IED attacks on military convoys, bombings of soft civilian targets, kidnappings, and assassinations. Shiite-led militia groups responded. Militia leaders on both sides gained influence through intimidation and by offering protection, undermining efforts of the US to organize a new Iraqi government.

I saw the stepped-up hostility every time I left the Green Zone to escort convoys of supplies to Coalition bases in various parts of Iraq—gangs of armed men roaming the streets, mosques destroyed by car bombs, and groups of civilians shouting obscenities and throwing rocks at passing convoys. There was no respite within the Green Zone either, where rockets and mortars rained down on us nightly, despite the massive concrete walls, checkpoints of sandbags and iron gates, and squads of heavily armed US troops. Again, as in the latter months of our engagement in Somalia, I wondered what the hell we were doing here and what we were trying to accomplish.

Midday March 31, 2004, I set out in a heavily armored

Land Cruiser, my M4 locked and loaded, to lead a convoy of seven trucks filled with supplies for a US Marine base a few miles west of the city of Fallujah. Though the temperature hovered in the comfortable mid-70s, I sweated under my armored vest. Part of that had to do with my state of anxiety. That morning five US Marines had been killed outside Fallujah by a roadside bomb. Fifteen Iraqis had been seriously wounded when a car bomb intended for an Iraqi police convoy exploded in the city of Baqubah.

The four of us in the armored Land Cruiser were on high alert. I sat in the backseat, and a colleague manning a .240-cal machine gun sat beside me. Our team leader (TL) rode in the passenger seat beside the driver. Providing security at the end of the convoy were four military contractors from Blackwater riding in two unarmored Mitsubishi SUVs. One of them was a friendly former Navy SEAL and workout fanatic named Scotty Helvenston, who had been featured on the reality TV show *Man vs. Beast*.

The rubble-strewn road we were on served as Fallujah's main highway and cut through the center of what was known as the Sunni Triangle—a densely populated region northwest of Baghdad where Saddam Hussein had strong support. Locals referred to Fallujah as "the city of mosques." We followed the ancient Euphrates River and passed the drab concrete walls of Abu Ghraib prison, which was being used by the CIA and US Army to house Iraqi detainees.

Few people outside Iraq knew its name at this point. A month later it would gain worldwide notoriety following a story detailing prisoner abuse on the TV show *60 Minutes*.

Ahead stood a narrow metal bridge that would take us over the river and into the city. Blocking our approach stood a crowd of angry locals, some of whom carried handmade signs.

"Looks like we've got ourselves a welcome party," our driver announced.

They were mostly young men and numbered around fifty. I wondered who had alerted them and if any of them were armed.

"What do we do now?" the contractor beside me asked.

"Keep moving," our TL responded. "We're going to try to push through."

"What happens if they're insurgents?" the driver suggested.

"Keep moving. Don't engage unless they fire first!" Through his headset, the TL told the four guys in the SUVs at the back of the convoy to wait.

"For what purpose?" someone in the rear Mitsubishi asked.

"So you can clear the bridge in case we have to turn back."

"Maybe we should call for backup," I suggested.

"Guns up!" said our TL. "Keep pushing forward."

I readied my M4 and focused on the hands outside to see if anyone was carrying a weapon. The protesters screamed in broken English and Arabic, "Death to America! Death to President Bush! *Allah Akhbar!* Fallujah will be free!" They parted just enough for us to squeeze through, our hearts in our throats while the Iraqis outside slapped, punched, kicked, and spat at our Land Rover.

"Nasty motherfuckers!" the gunner beside me groaned.

Stealing glances to our rear, I saw the first truck make it

through, then the second, third, and fourth, and reported everything to the rest of the team. As the fifth truck emerged from the crowd, I heard a peal of automatic weapons fire.

"What the fuck was that?"

"Must be the guys from Blackwater."

More shots followed as our TL tried to make radio contact with Scotty Helvenston and the others.

"All vehicles report," he shouted into the radio.

I couldn't hear anything outside over the roar of the engine. Peering through the dust behind me, I tried but couldn't make out the two Mitsubishis.

"Boss," I said. "I don't think they made it."

"Maybe they turned around," he responded.

"You want me to go back?" the driver asked.

"Hell, no," someone barked. "Haul ass to the base."

The ordeal had lasted no more than three minutes, but felt like hours. When we reached the Marine camp we were greeted with the terrible news that the four Blackwater guys had been killed by the mob.

I was shocked and horrified. Later, I watched the video of their burned bodies being desecrated, dragged through the streets, and hung from the bridge.

I felt sick for weeks afterward. Maybe we could have saved the four contractors by turning back. Maybe the mob would have overwhelmed our SUV and killed us, too.

Angry and distressed, I quit my job at DynCorp and went to Jordan to try to get my head together. A two-hour swim in the Dead Sea helped. After that, I flew home to Santa Clara to spend time with my family.

Three months later, I was back in Iraq, this time working as the base manager at a place called Camp Taji, on the outskirts of Baghdad. Out of five mobile homes guarded by Iraqis, I ran armored security teams that escorted VIPs from the airport to the Green Zone and back—on a road known to the Iraqis as "Death Street" and to the Americans as "IED Alley." My unit consisted of twenty Lebanese soldiers, four South African army vets, and five Americans. Despite the tall barricades and tight security, our base was frequently hit by mortars and rockets.

The attacks became so frequent that we started to take them for granted. One night I had just flopped down on my bed and fired up my laptop when Katyusha rockets started to rain down on us with their distinct whistling sound.

A few seconds later my door flew open and a Lebanese guy on my team named Hassan flew in.

"Changiz," he exclaimed, "are you coming to the bunker?"

"Not this time," I replied. "I think I'll watch a movie."

Thereupon, I clicked on a link to *Mission: Impossible* and the credits started rolling. Hassan shrugged, pulled up a chair, and we watched the movie together as Katyushas fell around us.

The six-lane expressway my team and I traveled daily, from what was once known as Saddam Hussein International Airport to central Baghdad, was ten miles of concrete hell flanked by Sunni neighborhoods populated with Hussein loyalists. These neighborhoods, which were once designed to protect the military strongman from possible assassins, were now insurgent hideouts.

Driving the highway was a mobile form of Russian rou-
lette. You never knew when an insurgent car might drive up
beside you at high speed, lower its window, and hit you with
a burst of machine gun fire. Or when a truck laden with explosives would fly down one of the on-ramps straight into your
convoy. Or when a daisy-chain of artillery shells buried under
the roadway might be set off by a cell phone.

It was so dangerous that death was a common occurrence,
and local cab drivers demanded $2,000 per person for a one-
way trip. Over a dozen Westerners lost their lives on the road
while I was there, and several of my men were seriously
injured.

The contracting work in Iraq was plentiful, but the atmosphere
poisonous and bleak. Everywhere you went people were angry at the US, because their families were dying and their
homes, mosques, and businesses were being destroyed. Day by
day, hope seemed to get buried under more levels of hatred,
debris, and dust. Conditions were going from bad to worse.

Determined to escape the cycle of death, I started shopping for opportunities elsewhere. In January 2006, an old
friend named David Stroop called. He said he was working for
PAE International—an engineering firm that had been founded
in the 1950s during the effort to rebuild Japan, which later
diversified to provide support to US military bases and State
Department facilities overseas. It had recently been purchased
by Lockheed Martin.

Dave asked, "How would you like to go to Darfur?"

"Darfur, Sudan?"

"Yes."

"To do what?"

"Serve as a cease-fire monitor for the African Union."

"A cease-fire monitor? What does that entail?"

"It's pretty straightforward. I'll explain everything when you get to DC."

"Okay, Dave. Should I bring my combat gear, or a weapon?"

"Negative on both," Dave answered. "Any kind of uniform or insignia you get will be provided by the AU."

I bought an old pair of Army desert fatigues, packed them in a duffel, and flew to Dulles Airport for a flight to Khartoum. Waiting in line to board the flight were two guys wearing green berets. I recognized one as my former SF colleague Richard Rodriguez and slapped the beret off his head.

Richard turned to see who it was and recognized my smiling face. "Changiz, you son of a bitch," he said. "What the fuck you doing here?"

"They hired me to keep your ass in line," I joked.

"More likely the other way around."

The other guy was another former SF colleague, Serafin "Serf" Tellez.

We traded war stories all the way to Khartoum. Outside the sleek-looking airport we were met my two locals driving a beat-up SUV. They drove us to a PAE International safe house in the urban center where the Blue and White Niles meet. I had expected a cleaner, less run-down version of Mogadishu. But the city I saw out the window was boisterous and modern with a surprising number of tall glass business towers. The locals gave off a friendly vibe.

That positive impression lasted the three days we waited in Khartoum for a twin-engine plane to ferry us west to Darfur—which means "Land of the Fur People," who were seventeenth-century immigrants from Central Africa. The land itself consisted of mostly semiarid plains in an area roughly the size of Spain. Nothing about it shouted agricultural productivity, or economic development.

I learned that the crisis in Darfur, which had been termed "genocide" by the first Bush administration and International Criminal Court, had its roots in the long-term economic and political marginalization of non-Arabs in Africa's largest country, Sudan. This problem was exacerbated by a series of droughts that began in 1972 and intensified the desertification of the country and led to disputes over land between non-Arab sedentary farmers from the Fur, Zaghawa, and Masalit tribes and Arab nomads.

In the mid-1980s, when a Libyan-sponsored Arab supremacist movement spread into neighboring Sudan, many non-Arab Darfuri farmers felt that their interests were marginalized further. The wedge between the tribes of Darfur and the Arab-dominated national government widened even more in 1989 when General Omar Hassan Ahmad al-Bashir seized power in a bloodless coup. Declaring himself president, Bashir disbanded rival political parties and institutionalized Sharia law throughout northern Sudan.

Over the next two decades, President Bashir adopted a policy of segregating non-Arabs and dividing Darfur into three separate regions in order to weaken tribal unity. This led to armed rebellion on the part of some tribesmen, which began in February 2003 when two separate African rebel groups—the Justice and Equality Movement (JEM) and Sudan Liberation Army (SLA) took up arms against the Arab-led government. The rebels contended that the Sudanese government had ignored the Darfur region, leaving it underdeveloped and stripping it of political power.

In response, the Bashir government bombed villages to force the rebels out. It also armed an Arab militia known as the Janjaweed (or "Devils on Horseback")—characterized as a militantly racist and pan-Arabist organization recruited from Sudanese Arab tribes. Mounted on camels and riding in helicopters, the heavily armed Janjaweed militias stormed through villages, pillaging, raping, and otherwise brutalizing terrified tribespeople. They specifically targeted members of the Fur, Zaghawa, and Masalit tribes. An estimated 1.4 million of them fled from farms and villages and sought shelter in hastily organized refugee camps. The crisis eventually spread into neighboring Chad as 100,000 refugees fled into that desperately poor country pursued by Janjaweed militiamen.

The UN, US, and other members of the international community condemned the Sudanese government's scorched-earth tactics. Complicating the situation in Darfur was the appearance of splinter rebel groups that kidnapped humanitarian workers and seized food supplies. Amnesty International and other groups accused China and Russia of supplying arms to the Bashir government in violation of a UN arms embargo.

As the Bashir government and rebel groups traded accusations, an eclectic coalition of religious leaders, NGOs, college students, human rights groups, and Hollywood celebrities spread awareness of the large-scale humanitarian disaster. World powers were reluctant to intervene. Some called the crisis genocide, others termed it a civil war that had gotten out of control.

No one argued that the consequences were catastrophic. A 2005 British parliamentary report estimated that over 300,000 Darfuri had died and countless others were injured— some by fighting and many more by disease and malnutrition brought on by the conflict.

Most international efforts centered on negotiating a cease-fire to end the fighting. Many observers accused the Sudanese government of purposely drawing out these talks in order to complete its ethnic cleansing of Darfur. Between 2003 and early 2006, when I arrived, numerous cease-fires had been signed and broken.

Richard, Serf, and I joined a force of eighty-some African Union cease-fire monitors protected by roughly 800 troops from Rwanda, Nigeria, Algeria, and South Africa. The AU assigned me the rank of major and sent me to a base outside the town of Al-Fashir—the capital of North Darfur and a traditional caravan post. My job was to report any movement of JEM rebels against Sudanese government forces and vice versa.

The contrast between Khartoum and Al-Fashir was startling. While the former presented itself as a bustling city filled with confident, well-dressed people, Al-Fashir was a collection of tin-roofed huts on a parched plain. Its several thousand residents lived in constant fear of attack.

Every morning, my fellow monitors and I would attend a briefing led by a South African colonel, who served as base commander. We'd hear reports of what had occurred in the field the day before. Most of them were horrific—a half-dozen villagers burned to death in such and such sector; a food convoy attacked on the way to such and such refugee camp; residents of another camp beaten with sticks; a third camp raided and eighteen residents held captive and ordered to pay a *diya*—also known as blood money.

In most cases we received conflicting reports about who was responsible. Oftentimes the inciting event was some sort of personal vendetta or tribal dispute. The victims were usually from among over a million refugees housed in camps run by the UN and other organizations. A night didn't pass when either Janjaweed militiamen or JEM or SLA rebels attacked a camp or village.

Two or three times a week, I'd help guard convoys of trucks that went to resupply these camps. I wasn't supposed to be armed, but I carried an AK-47 with three full mags, which I'd hide under the front seat. I always stationed myself in the lead Toyota extended-cab pickup with a Senegalese driver and two Algerian soldiers behind me.

There were no roads to speak of, so we'd bounce over flat, parched terrain and stop at different camps, which were scattered across the plain and made up of primitive tents enclosed with a barbed wire fence. There were over 200 of these camps scattered throughout Darfur. Some were run by NGOs like CARE International Switzerland and World Vision and were guarded by local police officers trained by the AU-UN mission or Rwandan soldiers. Many had no protection.

The camps had names like Kass, Chad, and Zam Zam.

One of the biggest, Kalma, boasted over 70,000 refugees—predominantly women and children. Overcrowding and poor sanitation were endemic.

Families used to abundant vegetables and fruit now lived on a watery stew made out of wheat, beans, oil, salt, and protein powder. The women carried water, gathered firewood, did the cooking, and cared for the children, while men and boys in dust-covered jeans and robes, who had previously worked on small farms, sat around with nothing to do.

Daily temperatures shot up to 120 degrees Fahrenheit and makeshift shelters offered little respite from the sun. The June–September rainy season brought some relief. But because of a lack of proper drainage, once the rain started, shelters and latrines flooded, and there were outbreaks of dysentery and cholera. Medical assistance from organizations like Doctors Without Borders and the Red Cross couldn't meet the needs of thousands, and children died daily.

As peacekeeping monitors we had no resources of our own, but I tried to help any way I could, handing out whatever candy, cookies, sweets, medicine, or food I could get my hands on. I did a lot of listening, introducing myself as Mohammed and addressing the locals in Arabic. Everyone had a point of view, the refugees, the tribal leaders, the police, the foreign troops, and even locals loyal to the JEM.

I collected all their cell phone numbers, kept in touch, tried to mediate conflicts, and reported on needs. Progress was painfully slow and the resources of the AU-UN mission were woefully inadequate.

At night I returned to our AU mission house in Al-Fashir,

which was luxurious by Darfur standards but would have been considered primitive in the States. In town I got a chance to see livestock and something that approached normal life. Every morning women passed outside our barbed wire fence transporting bundles of twigs and branches. As they rode by seated sidesaddle they'd point to their mouths, indicating they wanted something to eat.

The flip side of outside assistance was dependence. Everywhere I went I met locals looking for the international community to solve their problems. The truth was that although the Darfuri didn't have much, they were resourceful people.

One morning a cow grazing on the street got caught in the barbed wire fence surrounding our house. I ran inside to get a pair of wire cutters. By the time I returned, local men had already slashed the animal's neck and were cutting away chunks of meat to take to market.

Nigerian General Martin Agwai, who commanded the AU force of 600–800, complained to anyone who would listen of the minimal support he was getting from the international community. His soldiers, mostly from Rwanda and Algeria, were poorly trained and lacked basic equipment, including weapons. They also lacked the helicopters they needed to help relieve camps under attack.

One night the main AU camp at Haskanita was raided by a large force of rebels, thought to be a splinter group of the SLA. The battle raged until 0400, when the AU force ran out of ammunition and was overrun, suffering over two dozen casualties. The rebels escaped with money, vehicles, fuel, and weapons. UN relief helicopters weren't permitted to land until after the fight was over, constrained by a policy that prevented them from getting involved in combat.

When I reached Commander Ibrahim Abdullah Al "Hello," who controlled the northern Darfur town of En Siro for one branch of the SLA, to ask what had happened, he claimed that he didn't know who was responsible for the attack.

Instead he expressed distrust for the AU force. "All the soldiers of the rebel movement are ashamed now to cooperate with the African Union," Commander Hello said. "The AU came to look after the cease-fire and report to the international community but they have been unable to stop the big incidents carried out by the government and the Janjaweed."

"And your men have had no hand in the attacks?" I asked.

"It's very easy for the government to push the AU around and that makes us view them as the enemy," he responded.

Commander Hello might not have been educated at a Western university, but he had mastered spin and double-talk as well as any sophisticated politician. Nobody on any side of the conflict ever took responsibility. The government and Janjaweed blamed the SLA and JEM rebels, and the rebels pointed the finger at the Sudanese government and international community.

Meanwhile, the raids continued and the plight of the refugees worsened. As cease-fire monitors we weren't allowed to involve ourselves in any form of combat. One night, we received a radio alert that my buddy Serf Tellez's camp was under attack. I said, "Fuck the policy," grabbed my AK and ammo, and organized a relief convoy. It took us three hours to get to the camp. By the time we arrived, everything had been burned to the ground—guard towers, medical huts, tents. The rebels had left six dead and disappeared into the night. My buddy Serf was uninjured, but so badly shaken that he returned with me to the AU mission house in Al-Fashir.

The next day, I started training a battalion of Rwandan soldiers to act as a QRF. I even built a firing range at the edge of town. The Rwandans expressed their deep appreciation, but without helicopters, which we didn't have and couldn't get, their effectiveness was limited.

Without question, the overall AU, UN, and international community effort left a lot to be desired. Everyone's hopes rose with the announcement that a group of Nelson Mandela–organized "Elders" would visit in October. The group was to include Nobel Peace Prize winners Archbishop Desmond Tutu and former US president Jimmy Carter.

When the visit was announced, Archbishop Tutu told the press, "We want community leaders in Darfur to feel that they have been heard from us. We want the suffering to end, and we want to contribute to that."

Members of the Secret Service arrived in Al-Fashir ahead of the delegation and asked me if I would drive the Elders to some of the local camps.

"It would be an honor," I answered.

They handed me a Glock. At 0600 hours the morning after the arrival of the Elders, I used a flashlight to carefully check the Toyota SUV I would be driving for hidden explosives. A half hour later, freshly showered, shaved, and dressed in the best clothes I had, I arrived at the State Department house where they were staying. Lined up outside were hundreds of locals, hoping to see the Elders.

An hour later, I set out for the nearby Abu Shouk refugee camp with President Carter, Archbishop Tutu, Nelson Mandela's wife, Graça Machel, and two Secret Service agents—one male and one female. My colleague Richard drove the SUV behind me, containing billionaire Richard Branson, two more Secret Service agents, and two support staff. Guarding our convoy were a half-dozen jeeps filled with AU soldiers.

As we drove south, President Carter, who was seated behind me, asked me about my name and background.

"Changiz Lahidji," I answered. "I was born in Iran and served twenty-five years in the US Special Forces."

"It's a pleasure to meet you, Changiz," he said. "And thank you for your service."

"The pleasure is mine, Mr. President. You probably don't remember, but during the early days of the Iran Hostage Crisis, I wrote you a letter offering to volunteer to go into Tehran."

He frowned. "I'm sorry that didn't go well, Changiz."

"No need to apologize, Mr. President. Not to me. The important thing is that the hostages returned home alive."

"Eventually, yes."

I had clearly brought up a bad memory. Hoping to change the subject, I said, "I respect what you're trying to do here in Darfur, sir, in a very difficult situation."

He said, "Thank you, Changiz. And thank you for your enthusiasm."

When we reached Abu Shouk, which housed 40,000 refugees living on food supplied from the World Food Program,

President Carter asked men, women, and children what they needed and what he could do to help, and patiently listened to their answers. Their wants were simple: peace, food to feed their children, a job, a new home.

Pro-government Janjaweed militiamen blocked the Elders from entering a camp in the North Darfur town of Kabkabiya, claiming it wasn't on the schedule that had been approved by President Bashir. Some refugees managed to slip notes through the fence. One of them written in Arabic read, "We are still suffering from the war as our girls are being raped on a daily basis."

Inspired by President Carter and the Elders, I arranged a meeting between JEM leaders, the AU base commander, and officers from the Sudanese army. Nothing like it had ever been attempted before. The South African officer who ran our base, Colonel Strum, grudgingly agreed to attend.

Everyone thought we were taking a huge risk, because we were traveling into JEM-controlled territory. But the JEM intermediaries I spoke to assured me that they would welcome us in peace.

I was nervous myself as we boarded a huge Russian Mi-27 helicopter, entered an area that was considered a JEM rebel stronghold, and landed at a designated site near the town of Deesa. On the other side of the field where we had touched down, I saw fifteen chairs that had been set up near a collection of huts. But no people.

"Where the bloody hell are they?" Colonel Strum asked.

"Wait here, Colonel. I'll find out."

I reached the seating area and waited. A man came out of one of the nearby huts and offered me tea and water.

"What the bloody hell is going on?" the colonel shouted. "Are the buggers coming or not?"

"I believe they are, sir," I said, glancing at my watch. The rebels were already twenty minutes late. Then I heard a roar of engines. Beyond the huts rose a cloud of yellow dust.

A column of battered trucks entered the area, their cabs and beds stuffed with armed rebels wearing an assortment of masks, bandannas, and turbans. Many wore bandoliers of bullets across their chests.

They were a fearsome-looking group, all armed with Chinese weapons.

I raised my arms over my head and said, "I am an AU peacekeeping monitor. My name is Mohammed. *Salam alla-com!*" (Peace be with you.)

Their leader stepped forward, wearing a Sudanese turban and a mask over his face, and presented me with a necklace of beads.

I bowed and thanked him. He removed the mask to reveal a very serious and dark face and a light-colored beard. He offered his hand. Then we hugged.

He said in a local Arab dialect, "Welcome."

"Thank you for coming here," I responded. "We need to talk."

The mayor of the village appeared with helpers, who unrolled a carpet. We were shown to our places. I was seated facing the rebel commander, and a Sudanese army major and two captains sat on either side of me. Next to the major were the South African colonel and his translator.

Our fifteen guards stood behind us. Standing behind the rebel leaders were 100 very fierce-looking fighters.

The mayor's aides served chai tea, dates, and cookies. All the principals introduced themselves, and then the meeting started. It was tense at first. The two sides hadn't talked like this in twenty years.

The rebels explained that they attacked refugee camps, food convoys, and AU outposts because they lacked food, gasoline, and money. Their tone was friendly and respectful.

The Sudanese army major, who happened to be from the same tribe as the rebel leader, said, "If you need something, we can help you. Tell us what you need, but don't attack us."

The rebel leader replied, "If you give us gas, food, and money, we won't attack the camps or convoys."

After an hour of talking back and forth, a deal was struck and the leaders of both sides shook hands.

14

COMBINED JOINT
TASK FORCE PALADIN

My tenure as a cease-fire observer ended at the close of 2007, when I got a call from Bruce Parkman, who was working for the contracting company NEK Advanced Securities Group, based in Albuquerque, New Mexico. He asked me if I was interested in working as an IED expert in Afghanistan. Bruce and I had served in Special Forces together at Fort Bragg and Okinawa.

"Sure," I answered. "But I know almost nothing about IEDs except that they're a real nasty problem."

"We're seeing a big spike in IED attacks and expect that number to keep climbing. They accounted for seventy-five percent of all Coalition casualties in '07, up from fifty percent in '06."

"Where are they coming from?"

"Everywhere," Bruce answered. "They're planted by the Taliban. Goddamn things complicate our entire mission. Primitive roads and difficult terrain make IEDs a powerful deterrent to everything we do. Every time we move supplies or personnel, we're vulnerable to attack."

"How can I help?"

"How close do you follow the news?" Bruce asked.

"Close enough to know that things aren't going well in Afghanistan."

"August 2007 the House passed RH 3222, which allocated $500 million over the next two years to the Joint IED Defeat Fund."

"That's a lot of cash!"

"It means they're taking this threat seriously and want to defeat it," explained Bruce. "Come aboard and we'll train and equip you and send you in the field, ASAP. You'll be coming in as a GS-15 so the pay is sweet."

"That was going to be my next question."

"You'll be making 10K a month."

The pay sounded good and I was ready for a new adventure. "How long is the assignment?" I asked.

"One year. You start the end of the month."

"I'm in."

I spent some time with my family in California, then flew to DC for a couple weeks of training at Fort Meade, Maryland. There I met the rest of the guys in my class—one former SEAL, the others all SF. A lecturer from military intelligence covered the basics, namely that IEDs were very easy and cheap to build and gave insurgents the potential to engage an enemy with a much larger and more sophisticated military.

That's exactly what was happening in Afghanistan, where

Taliban insurgents were taking advantage of their superior knowledge of the roads and terrain to hit Coalition troops and convoys with IEDs, either detonated remotely or equipped with a trigger device. Increasingly, the Taliban followed up IED attacks with ambushes to inflict more damage on a vulnerable opponent. Once a Coalition truck or Humvee was disabled, they'd move in quickly, usually in technicals with .50 cal machine guns mounted in the beds.

In 2007, when American troops were losing limbs from blasts about every other day on average, the word IED—a military acronym for "improvised explosive device"—became so widely used it formally entered the American lexicon, accepted into Merriam-Webster's *Collegiate Dictionary*. These primitive devices ranging in size from a soda can to a tractor-trailer had dramatically affected how the American military deployed in the war zone, creating a heavy reliance on helicopters and other aircraft in order to avoid roads.

At Meade, we learned that instructions for assembling IEDs could be easily downloaded from the internet or transmitted via USB thumb drive or CD-ROM. The materials required weren't expensive and included explosives, a detonator, and some sort of power source. The aim of the bomb maker was to combine blast, fragmentation, and armor penetration to maximum effect.

IEDs fell into three basic categories:

Package-type IEDs
Vehicle-born IEDs (also known as VBIED or truck bombs)
Person-born IEDs (sometimes called suicide vests)

They were generally activated in three ways:

Victim operated IED (VOIED)—by pressure plate or switch (in the case of suicide vests).
Radio controlled IED (RCIED)—usually set off by a signal from a cell phone or garage door opener.
Command wire IED (CWIED)—uses an electric firing cable.

Package-type IEDs—the most common—could be buried, disguised, or hidden in practically anything, including the body of a dead animal left alongside a road. While Iraqi IEDs typically used military-grade explosives, the Afghan variety was generally much cruder, using commonly available potassium chlorate and ammonium nitrate fertilizers as accelerants. But that didn't mean the enemy wasn't clever. When the US Army added more armor to their vehicles, the Taliban responded with bigger bombs buried deep under dirt roads and capable of delivering huge underbelly blasts.

And when the US and their Coalition partners began using metal detectors to uncover buried IEDs, the Taliban eliminated metal triggers and packed bombs with rocks instead of metal shrapnel.

We were engaged in a cat-and-mouse struggle to save limbs and lives.

At the end of February 2008, we flew to Kuwait's Ali Al Salem Air Base. As I passed through Customs, Kuwaiti officials pulled me aside and detained me.

The reason, they explained, was that I had an Iranian name.

"Yes," I said in Arabic, "and I also have a US passport. Why? Because I'm a US citizen."

They seemed perplexed and started to take me away to be interrogated.

I said, "I helped liberate your country in 1991, and now you're going to give me a hard time. I don't believe it."

I was released only after US Embassy officials arrived to vouch for me. It sucked to go through airports and look Middle Eastern.

At the US base, the guys on the team and I were outfitted with binos, toaster-sized IED-detection devices, tools, body armor, and CAC (common access) Uniformed Services ID cards, which gave us access to military service benefits and privileges—especially free meals at DFACs—dining facilities—and the use of base gyms, cinemas, gaming rooms, and PXs.

From Kuwait it was a relatively short hop to Bagram Air Base, Afghanistan, where we were attached to a JSOC demolition team from Fort Lewis, Washington, as part of Combined Joint Task Force Paladin (CJTF Paladin)—defined as an International Security Assistance Force command responsible for counter-IED efforts and Explosive Ordnance Disposal (EOD).

We were bused to a wooden hootch and went through three days of processing, during which we were kitted out with M4s, Sig Sauer handguns, level-4 body armor, and protective glasses.

The afternoon of day three, four of us had to go to nearby Camp Phoenix to be briefed by an SF demolition team based there. Even in relatively secure Kabul, we traveled fully loaded—meaning weapons ready and wearing body armor.

As I sat in the passenger seat of the Humvee waiting to exit the base, I felt a funny feeling at the pit of my stomach. It was as if someone was telling me not to go. When the Marines opened the gate, we turned left and saw two Humvees hurrying toward us. I took a breath and BOOM! The second Humvee hit an IED.

The explosion lifted the vehicle three feet in the air and pushed it five feet to the right and against the wall of the base, causing it to turn over and land on its side.

We drove around it and parked on the dirt shoulder. Then, with our M4s cocked and ready, we formed a perimeter around the injured vehicle. The Humvee's windshield was shattered and there were five soldiers inside. The guy in the passenger seat was covered with blood. Another soldier in back had been wounded in the leg.

While my colleagues called for medics, I stuck my head in the Humvee and tried to calm the wounded soldiers: "Medics are coming. Everything will be okay."

They were young kids, and couldn't hear me because their eardrums were messed up. Instead, they stared back in shock. We were literally seventy meters from the entrance to the base, which was manned 24/7 by over a dozen armed soldiers.

The young guys in the Humvee couldn't be moved before being checked to make sure they hadn't sustained any damage to their spines. So I carefully unstrapped their helmets and fed them sips of water.

One of my colleagues poked his head in and said, "They put it in a goddamn watermelon."

"What are you talking about?" I asked.

"The IED."

It was broad daylight. Usually the insurgents set their IEDs at night. When the emergency medical team arrived, we donned gloves and started to gather every piece of evidence we could find—shards of metal, inch-long pieces of wire, even chunks of watermelon—and put it all in plastic evidence bags.

When we finished, I turned to our TL and asked, "Should we go or not?"

"Go where?"

"Camp Phoenix."

One of my colleagues said, "Fuck it!"

Our TL looked shaken up.

"Yes or no?" I asked.

"Uh . . . no."

We were still in training and had already experienced our first exposure to a real IED attack. Back at Bagram, we briefed the base commander, then I said a "thank you" to God, and thanked my mother for constantly praying for my safety. The evidence we had gathered was sent to an FBI lab in DC.

A week later, we received our assignments. I was headed to FOB Salerno, located in the southeastern province of Khost, thirty miles south of Tora Bora and twelve miles west of the Pakistan border. Nicknamed "Rocket City" because of nightly Taliban rocket attacks, it had been established in 2002 and quickly grew to house nearly 5,000 US troops, civilians, and contractors.

When I landed there and took a look around and saw the 5,000-foot runway and what appeared to be a small city, including a combat support hospital, large gymnasium, post

exchange, chapel, large chow hall, aviation hangars, maintenance facilities, and billets, I thought the United States had
lost its mind. *Are we planning to stay here for 100 years?* I
asked myself.

Given FOB Salerno's geographic isolation with high
mountains on the Afghan side and the Federally Administered
Tribal Areas of Pakistan on the other, it seemed like a crazy
waste of taxpayer money. I soon learned that most of the military contractors and support troops assigned there never left
the base and never experienced combat. Instead, I'd see them
lining up at one of the chow halls for freshly grilled steaks or at
one of the gyms lifting weights. (Five years later on November 1, 2013, US forces withdrew from FOB Salerno and transferred control of the installation to the Afghan National Army.)

Not only was the base highly vulnerable to insurgents
who slipped across the border from Pakistan, but supplies had
to be airlifted into the base when the roads became impass-
able. I worked with a forensic specialist from the FBI and five
other IED specialists. We even had our own little lab.

Every time there was an IED attack or IEDs had been discovered in the area, we'd go out as a team and inspect the site.
Our team consisted of four men: two IED experts (also known
as Weapons Intelligence Specialists), including myself; one Ammunition Technical Officer (ATO), or bomb disposal operator, whose job it was to defuse the bomb; and an Electronic
Countermeasure (ECM) operator (aka the Bleep), whose job
was to jam any radio signals that could detonate a radio-
controlled IED. I was the only contractor. The others were
Army guys assigned to Paladin.

We always traveled with an infantry escort. If an attack had already taken place, we'd gather evidence, examine it in our lab, and file a report. If we had reason to suspect IEDs had been placed in a certain area, we'd park our APC at a distance away. While several Army snipers kept guard, we'd fire up our toaster-sized metal detectors (known as Vallons) and inspect the area.

The ongoing debate among us was whether searching for the IEDs was more dangerous than disarming them. Both were extremely tense work.

Almost all the IEDs we found were of the pressure-plate variety, built around two strips of metal that were held slightly apart. Simple household wires attached to each strip ran to a set of domestic batteries. The wires were also connected to a detonator placed in the main explosive charge, usually housed in a cooking container. Once the pressure of a soldier's foot or a vehicle's tire pressed the two plates together, a circuit would form to activate the detonator and trigger an explosion.

Once we defused a bomb, we'd take it back to our lab and get to work analyzing its components and trying to discover the signatures of specific bomb makers. All of this went into a database that served to link members of a specific IED network that included tribal chiefs, makers, planters, and those providing source materials and financing.

Two weeks into my stay at Salerno, our four-man Counter-IED Task Force team was sent out to clear the road for a convoy of food, fuel, and other supplies headed to FOB Super a hundred miles north in Paktika Province. We rode in two RG-31 mine-resistant vehicles that featured monocoque (single shell) armored V-hulls designed to deflect an upward-directed blast from an IED and thus increase crew survivability. They also sported run-flat tires and cost in the neighborhood of $600,000 without the optional cup holders.

The metal beasts weighed over seven tons and could hit 60 mph, but not on the potholed, dusty roads we traveled. I sat in the lead RG next to the driver. The second RG followed, staggering to the right behind us. We did this so that if we encountered an IED buried on the road, the lead RG would take the blast and spare the seven trucks and two Humvees traveling behind.

The dirt track wound through narrow mountain passes dotted with scrub pines and crossed verdant valleys filled with fields of poppies, which yielded opium and heroin, the sale of which helped fund the production of IEDs. At the time, 2008, poppies from Afghanistan produced 90 percent of the heroin in the world.

A whole lot of human misery came from the magical fields of white, red, and pink flowers in valleys like the ones we were passing through now. Three hours out of Salerno, we started taking gunfire to our right. The US Army captain in charge of the convoy ordered us to stop.

I rolled out the passenger door and under the RG, setting up behind the big front wheel and fixing my M4 to my shoulder.

I heard the captain shout through my earbud, "Get down! Get down! Don't fire!"

"Why the fuck not?" I asked.

"Because I have to call and get authorization to engage first."

"Are you kidding, Captain?" I asked as enemy rounds tore into the ground around me. "We're in a fucking war zone."

"I said: Hold your fire!"

I wasn't in the mood to argue, nor did I feel like being a target. Despite the captain's orders, I lined up the enemy in my sights and fired in short blasts. By the time I'd emptied the first mag the enemy had stopped shooting.

The captain stared at me like he was pissed, but said nothing. Now he was insisting that we wait thirty minutes for a Black Hawk with a QRF to arrive and inspect the area. When they did they found nothing. The enemy had run off and escaped into the rocky hills. I wasn't surprised. Usually, the Taliban didn't engage unless they had a tactical advantage.

We continued to FOB Super, dropped off the supplies, and returned to Salerno without further incident.

Three weeks later I was told to deploy to Firebase Wilderness, also known as FOB Tellier, also in Paktika Province and near the Pakistani border. Wilderness had been built to provide security along the Khost–Gardez highway, a critical road link to Kabul.

The tiny base, roughly the size of a football field, was tucked into a spectacular gorge surrounded by sharp mountains with peaks that reached over 10,000 feet. The terrain and enemy were hard and relentless. The latter attacked the firebase with rockets and mortars day and night.

The enemy in this case was the Taliban and militants from the Haqqani Network—an insurgent group and drug trafficking gang led by warlord Maulvi Jalaluddin Haqqani and his son Sirajuddin Haqqani—who shared the Taliban's goal of driving the US and other Westerners out of Afghanistan. Like the Taliban, they operated out of bases located in Pakistan's Tribal Areas. Because of that, taking our fight to the enemy wasn't really an option.

The best we could do was defend ourselves and try to destroy them when they showed their heads, which wasn't often. Their usual tactic was to fire rockets and mortars, then disappear into the mountains or slip across the border.

When I was there in 2008, Wilderness was manned by about fifty soldiers from the Army's 101st Mountain Division, five translators, fifteen members of the Afghan Counterterrorism Pursuit Teams (CTPTs), and one doctor.

I lived in a hootch with ten other guys and slept on the top bunk. I grew my hair long and wore my beard to my chest.

One day a sergeant major from the 101st walked into our hootch while I was sitting and working on my laptop. He pointed at me and asked the other guys there, "Who's the dude with the beard?"

"That's Changiz," one of the Army guys answered.

"What the fuck are you doing here?" he asked me.

I smiled and said, "Sergeant Major, I'm Sergeant Major Lahidji, formerly with Special Forces and now a contractor with DOD."

He smiled back and said, "I thought you were bin Laden's brother. Welcome, Sergeant Major. You come to get your slay on?"

"You better believe it."

Because there was only one road that ran to the base, we

had to be supplied by helicopters, which arrived three times a week. The whole setup was risky and stupid. But it was a job, and I was determined to do it to the best of my ability.

We ran roughly two missions per day, looking for caves where militants hid bomb-making materials and weapons. When we found them, they were usually stocked with new Chinese-made RPGs, AKs, and IED components. We also cleared roads around the base of IEDs and retrieved evidence from IED attacks.

If the IED was close, four of us would drive in a single RG-31 over rough mountain roads. If the IED attack had taken place more than an hour's drive away, we got there by helo.

One morning we got a report that a Humvee had been hit on the Gardez–Kabul highway and called for a Black Hawk to ferry us in. By the time we arrived the Humvee was burnt to a crisp and an Afghan policeman lay along the side of the road bleeding from a wound to his chest. Another two policemen had been blown to smithereens.

We helped retrieve pieces of their bodies and loaded the wounded man aboard the Black Hawk. Then we went about our real work, which was to gather evidence. The culprit was another pressure-plate bomb built inside a pressure cooker probably bought in a market in Pakistan for $2.

A week or so later, we received a report that a bomb had gone off in a nearby village. Because of the condition of the roads, it took us two hours to get there. We arrived at a little square with mud houses around it. Local policemen pointed to a two-story house on the right.

The four of us entered with weapons ready. A big explosion went off in one of the upstairs bedrooms, tearing out part of the roof and wall and leaving pieces of a body scattered everywhere. I remember retrieving a hand and a pair of boots filled with flesh. Apparently the house had doubled as a Taliban bomb-making factory.

After nearly two hours spent collecting evidence, local police led us to another location in town near a small stone bridge where they had found an IED. We very carefully defused it.

Then one of the policemen pointed to another suspicious house up a hill.

I told them in Dari: "You go first; we'll be right behind you."

The house was empty. By the time we finished, the sun had set over the mountains and the sky had turned dark. An eerie feeling came over me. Knowing that we would be easy targets if we attempted to travel at night, we chose to sleep in the village.

The four of us camped in a hut owned by the Afghan police and took turns keeping watch. I didn't sleep a wink. The next morning, I stood outside on the street talking to a forty-five-year-old policeman I had become friendly with. The fresh mountain air fragrant with the smell of pine was invigorating. Earlier the policeman had told me about his large family and son who was studying to become an engineer. He had just handed me a cup of green tea.

I turned to thank him, when a single shot rang out . . . *PING!* The thin sound echoed against the mountain peaks behind me. As I looked at the policeman a bullet struck him in the forehead and exploded out the back of his head.

Before I had a chance to shout, he hit the ground and rolled past me.

Fuck!

The shot had come from the direction of a house across the street. I went down to my knees half in shock, and pushed the button near my collar to activate my radio. "Shots fired! Man down!"

My voice sounded like it was coming from someone else. Two of my teammates—Anderson and Garcia—ran out of the house carrying M4s and looking alarmed.

"Changiz, we heard a shot. What happened?"

Before I had a chance to answer, they saw the policeman lying in the road under an expanding pool of blood.

"Jesus Christ . . ." Anderson groaned.

"Get down!" I shouted. "The shot came from that house, over there. He's dead."

Two Afghan policemen wandered out to see what was going on. One of them was carrying a plate of crackers.

"*Besheen! Besheen!*" (Get down! Get down!) I shouted.

They radioed their station and two trucks filled with policemen rumbled up. We covered each other as we leapfrogged up the hill across the street to the house. I kicked the door in and entered. Near a second-floor window, I found an AK. The chamber was hot, but the shooter had escaped.

The Afghans brought a black body bag from one of their trucks and loaded their colleague inside. Before they carried him away, I knelt with them and we all said a prayer together.

My heart was hurting. I wondered what was going to happen to his son and the rest of his family.

Back at Firebase Wilderness we were getting hit by rockets and mortars several times a day. The guys from the 101st would respond with machine guns and mortars.

I went out every day, climbing rocky peaks, looking for weapons stashes and visiting remote villages. It was ball-busting work, with guys slipping, falling, and cursing. I took a few good tumbles myself.

The area had served as a mujahedeen hideout during the war against the Soviets. Now it was teeming with Taliban and Haqqani Network insurgents. In my backpack, I carried candles and pencils to hand out to the kids in remote hamlets.

Often, when I asked a group of farmers about Taliban activity in the area, one of them would answer, "They come here and bother us, demanding food and other things. We don't know what to do."

I also carried a special laptop, which I'd use to register people and record their fingerprints. Few of the people I met knew their date of birth. I collected over 1,000 profiles, which I emailed to DC and were added to a special database.

One morning in early June, I sat with my gear waiting for a helicopter to ferry me to FOB Salerno. Twenty minutes later, three Black Hawks roared in from the west and landed. I loaded into one of them with an Army colonel, two majors, a guy named Andy from the FBI, and two E7s. Seven passengers total. I sat in a seat behind the pilot facing Andy and the back of the aircraft.

The helo went up about seventy feet and swooped west, when I heard a loud bang. The pilot shouted, "We've been hit! We've been hit!" Then he turned off the engine.

I thought to myself: *This is the end.*

Smoke poured from the back of the helo and we were spiraling straight down. There was not a damn thing I could do but utter a quick prayer and hold on. Seconds later we slammed into the ground hard, jarring every bone, tooth, and muscle in my body. Then the bird flipped right, and I flew and smashed my head against the side door frame.

Stars circled in my head. The helo lay on its side. Half-conscious, I braced myself against the seat and tried to yank the side door open, but it was stuck. Blood poured down my face. I wiped it away from my eyes, and kicked the door five or six times until it jarred free and I could pull it open.

Andy was unconscious. I grabbed him under my left arm and pulled him out. Then I went back for the pilot. The blade and tail of the Blackhawk had been ripped off in the crash. As I crouched on the side of the helo, trying to catch my breath, I heard a weapon discharge from a group of trees about seventy feet to my left. I pointed my M4 in that direction and returned fire. I was fucking pissed.

Blood dripped down my cheeks to my neck and chest. Rounds zinged over my head and tore into the helo beneath me. I lay on my belly and kept looking for targets and shooting. After what seemed like ten minutes, the incoming fire stopped.

The other two Black Hawks had heard the SOS from the pilot and circled back. One of them landed nearby, and soldiers jumped out with their M4s ready. My colleague Garcia was with them. He found me standing in front of the downed helo, covered with blood and with a big smile on my face.

He said, "Changiz, you okay?"

"Yeah. Yeah."

"Then why the fuck are you laughing?"

"I'm laughing, man, because I'm still alive!"

I don't know if it was the rush of adrenaline or something else, but I was so happy to be alive that I could have danced a jig, even though my right knee and foot were messed up and I was bleeding from several gashes to my head. Garcia wrapped a bandage around my skull to stanch the bleeding. Then someone snapped some photos.

The copilot and one of the majors died in the crash. One of the E7s had his ribs broken. One of the terps was badly injured. Garcia and the others loaded us into the second Black Hawk.

Over the chop of the helo blades, I heard the pilot shouting over the radio, "Casualties coming! Casualties coming!"

I fell back into a half-conscious haze but recall landing at Salerno, and some medics there helping me out of the helo. Sirens wailed around me.

I stopped and said, "Wait! I need my gun."

"Don't worry, sir," one of them responded. "You're safe here, sir. We'll get it for you."

Next thing I remember was lying on a gurney and watching some medical personnel cut my uniform off. It took twelve stitches to close the gash on my head and another five for the cut to my forehead.

Three days later in the hospital, an Army doctor came to check on me. My right knee had swollen to the size of a basketball.

He said, "Changiz, we're going to have to medevac you to Germany to have the knee drained and scanned."

"The hell with that, Doc," I responded. "It'll be fine in a couple days. I've been through worse."

He said, "I know you're a tough guy, but you have to do this."

Two days later, I was leaning on crutches on the tarmac at Bagram with a bandage wrapped around my head about to board a C-17 to Germany when two beautiful female Air Force pilots came over and asked if they could have their pictures taken with me.

"Sure. But why?" I asked.

"Because with your long beard and hair you look like such a badass."

"You read me all wrong," I replied. "I'm a lover at heart."

They smiled.

15

10TH GROUP SPECIAL FORCES

In August 2008 I was back in Afghanistan, assigned to 10th Group Special Forces Alpha Company as a Counter-IED advisor. We worked out of a special compound within Camp Phoenix, Kabul.

One advantage of being a private contractor was that I could wear anything I wanted. Sewn in the middle of my combat vest was a special patch that I had made by local tailors. It read, "Hey, Fuck face." It was my greeting to the Taliban fighters, who were known to wear mean, determined expressions on their faces.

One day I was standing outside ISAF headquarters waiting for some colleagues to drive me back to Camp Phoenix, when a two-star general walked over to me. He pointed at the patch and asked, "Are you kidding me? What the hell is this?"

"It's part of my uniform, sir," I answered.

"Your uniform? Are you regular military?"

"No, sir, I'm a contractor."

"A contractor, huh. Then watch yourself three-sixty."

"Yes, sir."

Guys from other SF A-teams often visited our compound at Camp Phoenix between assignments to more remote parts of the country.

One afternoon, I was outside talking to a couple of colleagues when a guy from one of the visiting A-teams shouted at me, "Hey, terp, come here and translate something for me."

I walked over to where he was standing with four of his colleagues and said, "Hey motherfucker, I'm no terp. I'm a retired sergeant major in SF. I have more time in A-teams than you have years."

I smiled and they laughed and apologized. Then we became friends.

In October, I was assigned to go to Tora Bora as part of Alpha Company's twelve-man B-team. The French had built an outpost high in the Uzbin Valley near the village of Garda Khazaray, which was staffed with members of their Foreign Legion and one SF A-team. The Legion's motto, painted on the roof of the base headquarters, read: LEGIO PATRIA NOSTRA (The Legion Is Our Homeland.)

The legendary group, which had been in existence for 178 years, had fought wars in Bosnia, Cambodia, Chad, Kuwait, Algeria, Vietnam, and Somalia. Its 7,500 members, drawn from eighty nationalities, were known to be ferocious fighters. Over 900 of them had died during the Franco-Prussian War of 1870–71. Around 2,000 had been killed or deserted when France invaded Mexico in 1861. More recently, they lost 1,976 men in the eight-year struggle over Algerian independence.

They were extreme warriors from all over the world, including Ecuador, the Czech Republic, and New Zealand. I fit right in.

Some had shady, even criminal pasts, which were kept secret once they joined the French Foreign Legion and were given a new name and a new lease on life. They were foreign mercenaries, distrusted by French leftists, and embraced a nihilistic attitude expressed by one veteran Legionnaire, who said, "We are dust from the stars. We are nothing at all. So fuck off with your worries about war."

Many of them didn't even speak French.

What they didn't like was sitting around with nothing to do but shoot the shit, watch videos, and listen to European techno music, which is what we did from our mountain outpost two-thirds up the Uzbin Valley. The top of the mountains were controlled by the Taliban and some remnants of bin Laden's men.

I ended up doing 135 missions with 10th Group SF over the course of ten months, saw a ton of action, and killed and captured lots of bad guys.

One night we went out on a mission in five Black Hawks to grab some HVTs (high value targets) in a small cluster of huts on top of a hill. The high-tech NVGs I wore that cost $15,000 a pop helped me see in the pitch dark. Cold wind through the open Black Hawk door stung my face. The helo I rode in came up fast over a valley and hovered over a clearing seventy meters from the cluster of shacks. It jerked up and I thought we had touched down. So I jumped.

Turns out it was still five feet off the ground. I hit it hard with my knees bent, and rolled forward past a group of shrubs and down an embankment. Blood in my mouth, my head spinning, I got up slowly and realized I'd lost my NVGs.

Other guys on the team were already on their way to the huts. I heard them communicating with one another through my comms.

"Cover left. Entering hut, center-right."

"Roger."

"Cover! Cover!"

I found the lost NVGs in the approximate place I'd come down. My knees and feet barked like hell. Thinking that at over fifty I was too old to do this shit, I hurried and caught up with my unit, assumed my position, and helped raid two of the huts. We found none of the HVTs and no weapons or bomb-making material. The intel we had taken action on wasn't right. Either that or the HVTs had been alerted somehow and escaped.

While waiting for the Black Hawks to circle back to pick us up, I saw something moving in some trees at ten o'clock.

"Possible enemy, at ten!" I exclaimed into the radio.

Our TL Larry shouted back. "Don't shoot! Don't shoot!"

We flanked the trees, found a hiding place with weapons, and detained six suspects—four men and two women, all un-armed but who appeared suspicious as hell. The TL instructed us to load them in one of the helos and take them in for questioning. I never heard whether they turned out to be Taliban or not.

On another nighttime raid north of Kabul, we landed in a

valley and had to climb up a steep 1,000-foot incline to a cluster of huts. We set a charge against the door of the hut we were targeting and blew it in. Inside we confronted two terrified men, a woman, and two young children. All of them had shit their pants. As usual, I did the talking and tried to calm them down while my colleagues searched the hut. They found a laptop and a couple of pistols.

The engagements passed in a blur—night raids, firefights, patrols. I loved the action but sensed we weren't winning the war. Back in Washington, generals were petitioning Congress for more money and more troops.

Everywhere we went, when I got a chance to talk to the locals, they expressed their displeasure with the Taliban. But they didn't trust us, either. We were foreigners, *gharibe kgahgi,* and as far as they were concerned we didn't belong in their country, especially if we were wearing uniforms and carrying weapons.

Three months later, during our return from Tora Bora, we ran into traffic on the Jalalabad Road. Seeing black smoke ahead, we hurried in our two RGs and two Humvees to see what had happened. Turned out it wasn't a run-of-the-mill fender bender but a Taliban ambush of an ISAF convoy.

Vehicles were ablaze and bodies lay scattered across the road.

Before we could attend to the wounded we had to stop the firing coming from a cluster of mud huts to the right. We took cover and readied our weapons. Drivers and passengers scurried out of the trucks and cars behind us and hid behind the opposite embankment.

Surrounded by chaos, death, and fear, our master sergeant shouted, "One o'clock!"

We unleashed on targets along the perimeter wall 150 meters away with automatic weapons fire, machine guns, and rockets. My buddy Brian tore the wall apart with the .50 cal. I saw whole clunks of it flying and enemy shooters being propelled back and hitting the ground. The whole hamlet became enveloped in a cloud of thick red dust.

A few shots kept ricocheting around us.

"Two o'clock," our MS shouted.

The enemy was moving south. I lined one up in my sights and took him down in two short bursts. The firing subsided.

While some guys in my unit ran to help the wounded, four us of us stayed back to surveil the huts to our right. Out of my left periphery, I glimpsed the barrel of an AK on the floor of a battered Nissan waiting in traffic.

I hurried over to the car with my weapons ready. The three men inside looked like typical Afghan men from the south—young with thick beards, wearing loose pants, shirts, and caps. Could have been simple farmers, opium traffickers, members of the Taliban, or all three.

"Gentlemen," I said. "I'm with the police. I'm going to ask you to exit your vehicle."

They complied without protest. As an SF colleague kept them under guard, I reached into the Nissan and recovered the AK. It was loaded. I removed the mag and stuffed it in my back pocket. Then I checked the car for more ammo and weapons.

Finding nothing, I waved the three dudes back into the

car. They remained silent and sat stoically. God knows what was going on in their heads.

It took thirty minutes before the road was cleared and traffic resumed moving. Any travel in Afghanistan, day or night, was dangerous. Even in Kabul. As members of the ISAF, we were constant targets.

Back at Camp Phoenix, I stood in line at the mess hall when I recognized a familiar figure in front of me. It was my former team leader from ODA 171, Ron Johnston. He wore silver birds on his uniform indicating he was now a full colonel.

I came up behind him and put him in a headlock. He spun me around to face him. Seeing a wild man with a beard down to his chest, he smiled.

"Changiz, goddammit. I heard you had retired."

"It's not so easy to get rid of me, sir."

"Cut the sir shit," he said. "What are you doing here?"

"I'm working with 10th Group Special Forces."

We arranged to meet a couple nights later at a Lebanese restaurant in town, where we chowed on lamb kebabs, smoked a hookah, and reminisced about old times.

Later that night when I returned to Camp Phoenix, I learned that General Michael Repass, commander of US Army Special Forces, was visiting Kabul and had requested to see me. General Repass had been my team leader when I was with SF ODA 561 thirty years earlier. I had become friendly with his wife, Linda, who was an E4 at the time working in the mailroom.

Since his days as a second lieutenant, Repass had rocketed

up the military chain of command with tours at NATO headquarters in Europe, Grenada, and Iraq.

I drove over to ISF headquarters with Ron Johnston. I had
just climbed out of our Humvee and was standing near the
gate fully loaded with my M4 pointed at the ground when a
three-vehicle convoy entered and stopped abruptly.

General Repass climbed out of an armored SUV, threw
his helmet on the seat, and hugged me.

"You son of a bitch, Changiz. It's so good to see you. I
love you."

"I love you too, General." He stood a head taller than me
at six-four and looked the epitome of the modern warrior, con-
veying strength and determination in everything he did. My
appearance was more unusual—desert cammos, long salt-and-
pepper beard to my chest, Ray-Ban wraparound sunglasses.

He said, "I can't wait to tell Linda. She'll be thrilled."

"Please send her my love, sir."

"I absolutely will."

A couple of the general's aides had gotten out of the vehicles to see what was going on. One of them turned to the
other and, nodding in my direction, asked, "Who is this guy?"

General Repass overheard him, draped his long arm over
my shoulder, and replied, "This is Changiz. He's a hero of
Desert One and a legend in Special Forces."

It was one of the proudest moments in my career.

November 2009, I was back in California, riding my Harley
up and down the coast and looking for other ways to kill the
boredom, when I got a call from a friend who was working at

CACI International—described as a professional services and information technology company headquartered in Alexandria, Virginia. Their website boasted 20,000 employees worldwide. My friend asked if I was interested in being a BETSS-C operator.

"What the hell is a BETSS-C operator?"

"You'll be working with what are called Persistent Threat Detection System (PTDS) blimps."

I'd never heard of them, but they sounded interesting.

"They've become our most trusted reconnaissance resource in the field," he explained. "You worked on Counter-IED teams before, correct? So you know how pernicious the problem is."

"Pernicious" wasn't in my vocabulary. I said, "I think so. Yes."

"Well, one of the things the PTDS blimps do is spot insurgents planting or tending to the power supplies of bombs."

"My AOR?" (area of responsibility)

"Operate all sensor systems, perform preventive maintenance, document incidents, et cetera."

Intrigued, I flew to Fort Bragg for a month of training. It was like returning home.

Soon after I arrived, I walked over to SOCOM headquarters to pay my respects to General Repass. He wasn't there, so I left a message, and a week later he called to invite me over for dinner. After dining on steaks grilled to perfection by Linda, we sat on the back patio drinking beer. The general stretched his long legs on a lounger and asked why I was at Bragg. I told him about the PTDS assignment I had signed up for.

He turned to me, nodded, and said, "Changiz, you've had a great career. Why do you need that shit?"

It was a good question, and one that I'd contemplated many times myself. "I want to help my country," I answered. I didn't tell him about my mother's hefty medical bills, and the fact that my entire military pension was going toward her support. But I did add, "Hopefully, this will be my last go-around."

A week later I deployed to Camp Holland, a combined Dutch, US, Czech, and Australian base on the outskirts of Tarin Kowt, the capital of Uruzgan Province in southern Afghanistan. The place was known to the soldiers of all nationalities as TK—a godforsaken dust bowl smack in the middle of Taliban territory and surrounded by magnificent snow-capped mountains.

Why anyone in their right mind was willing to fight over this place beat the hell out of me. All I saw inside town and out was misery, poverty, and dust. Subsistence farmers toiled on narrow strips of fertile land along the Teri Rud River. The winters were bitter cold, and the summers sizzling.

No industry; no natural resources; no schools, police, health clinics, or businesses.

Most locals lived in mud huts without electricity. The only local color was found at the central bazaar where vendors who looked like extras from the movie *Exodus* sold produce, hookahs, and handwoven rugs.

The city of 70,000 boasted a whole list of Pashtun tribes, some of which originated in the twelfth century. To the naked eye not a whole lot had changed since then—except for the airport and our base, which was surrounded by layers of reinforced cement walls topped by razor wire. Everything, including our living quarters, was heavily armored to withstand the constant Taliban rocket attacks.

TK stood sixteen kilometers from the provincial capital, but, as many put it, was 300 years away. It boasted many of the comforts of home—a Green Beans coffee shop run by two amicable Indian dudes, PXs, game rooms, gyms, a memorial to those who had lost their lives, and even a recreation center where young Filipino women gave pedicures and massages.

Even with the amenities it was often described as a shithole, and that's where I ended up, working twelve-hour shifts in a bunkerlike PTDS command module. Part of a four-man team led by a captain in the Australian army.

The PTDS was an aerostat balloon, approximately thirty-five meters in length, made from a durable multilayered fabric suitable for all environments. It was filled with lighter-than-air helium and equipped with sophisticated surveillance and communications equipment.

According to its manufacturer, Lockheed Martin, the PTDS "leverages a wide-area, secure communications backbone for the integration of threat reporting from multiple available sensors." It was moored to a 100-meter tower by a retractable tether that allowed it to ascend another 1,500 meters. From that altitude its 360-degree high-speed cameras could record images thirty miles away.

The all-weather, all-temperature, day-and-night-capable platform was armed with infrared and color video cameras and a sophisticated GPS tool that offered four modes of operation:

- Synthetic Aperture Radar: generates an earth map that's transmitted to ground stations for analysis; creates overviews and specific object images, such as buildings, fences, and stationary cars; facilitates mission planning for possible direct assault; and helps assess potential collateral damage.

- Coherent Change Detection: reveals tiny differences in maps of the same area over time, revealing disturbed earth and moved vehicles.

- Moving Target Detection: sees objects of interest up to 360 degrees around the PTDS. Data is laid over ground station maps, letting operators cue the optical sensors for positive ID, tracking, and target designation.

- Ground Moving Target Indicator: pinpoints suspect vehicles from wide terrain and tracks them from start to endpoint.

Flying like a kite with no propulsion, the aerodynamically shaped aerostat always pointed toward the wind with fins and a tail system that remained buoyant. Filled with 74,000 cubic feet of helium, it was effective even in windy conditions. We usually kept ours at max altitude to keep it out of range of small arms fire.

Because the aerostat operated on a low-pressure system even when hit, which happened once a week, it didn't pop like a party balloon. Instead the helium oozed out, giving us time to reel it in and patch it up.

Every month, we had to climb up the tower and take the camera down to clean it. Otherwise, it was monotonous work.

Especially at night when the only visible part of the aerostat was a single blinking light. We directed the camera to roads, bridges, checkpoints, and other sites where insurgents were known to plant bombs.

When our base was attacked, which happened on average three or four times a week, I'd turn on the camera to see where the fire was coming from. Then I'd pick up a phone and alert the QRF, which would hurry out to try to neutralize the insurgents.

Wanting a break in the routine, I convinced the leader of the Australian-led QRF to let me go out with them one night on patrol. Accompanying the Brisbane-based Two Platoon Alpha Company, I searched several compounds of interest four kilometers west of the city. We uncovered weapons and explosives and chased some suspected insurgents into an adjacent canal.

Trouble always loomed outside the gate in the form of IEDs, insurgents, and armed farmers who didn't want us there. A sign on the gate advised: USE OF DEADLY FORCE IS AUTHORIZED.

Most of the people who worked at TK never left the wire. They spent their free time working out or watching movies on laptops or tablets. On a daily basis I saw groups of muscular guys in gym clothes moving around the base, often applying Blistex to lips cracked by the dry wind. A form of defense-speak was generally spoken—a polyglot of acronyms that included DFAC (dining facility), ECP (enemy control point), DG (dangerous goods), DPCU (disruptive pattern camouflage uniform), LN (local national), OMF (opposing military forces), PAX (passengers), TB (Taliban), and TIC (troops in combat)—adding another strange element to an already surreal environment.

While in TK, we were told to keep body armor close at all times in case of a "situation" or the warning siren went off. When that happened, everyone would jump into action, filing into our "rocket-proof" sleeping quarters, where we were told to put on our armor and helmets until further notice. There, we'd sit silently, usually thinking of family and friends back home.

I tried to make the best of an unusual situation, keeping the boredom at bay by jogging, lifting weights, reading, and watching the news. One day during my time off, I was watching a US senator being interviewed on CNN. While he was expounding about the dangers of terrorism, he said that he believed all Muslims were terrorists, including those born and raised in the United States.

It felt as though he was talking about me. I thought: *How fucking dare you, you asshole?* I wanted to ask him if he had ever served in the military and the number of years of combat experience he had.

One night, while on duty in the PTDS command module, I saw a Black Hawk hover over three individuals on a dusty street on the outskirts of Tarin Kowt and shoot them dead. When I played back the tape, it appeared that the locals weren't armed.

I reported it to an officer in our unit and never heard another word about the incident.

But it bothered me a lot. As a member of SF, I appreciated the importance of winning the support of the local population.

Apparently, a lot of people in the USG, including high officials and some senators, didn't.

I'd been at Tarin Kowt almost a year, when in 2010 I was summoned to the office of our Australian TL.

He said, "Sorry, mate, seems like you're being called back to the States."

Immediately I thought of my mother and her precarious health.

"Why? Is something wrong?"

"It appears your security clearance has been denied," he answered.

I did a double-take. "My security clearance . . . denied for what reason?"

"All it says here," he said, pointing to the email, "is 'investigation.'"

"Investigation? Of what?"

He shrugged. "Sorry, Changiz, but as a result your contract has been suspended. You better gather your things, because you're leaving tomorrow."

"Tomorrow?"

"Yes, that's correct."

I was stunned. How had I become a security risk overnight? Why was I being forced to give up the $45,000 that was still owed me under the contract with CACI?

I racked my brain all the way back to Fort Bragg, trying to figure out what I could have done. Had someone taken revenge on me because I had reported the incident with the Black Hawk? Was this part of the fallout from another contract I had been involved in?

These questions were answered when I arrived at Bragg and learned that my security clearance had been suspended as a result of information discovered during the course of updating my background information. According to the Statement of Reasons (SOR) filed by DOD's Central Adjudication Facility (CAF), investigators had learned that I had an uncle in the Iranian Revolutionary Guards.

The charges were absurd.

My only course of action was to file a detailed written response and request an appearance before a Defense Office of Hearings and Appeals (DOHA) administrative judge. They asked for a full accounting of how I had immigrated to the US, including a copy of the visa I had obtained thirty-eight years ago. All of it was stupid and insulting, and took eight months. I spent that time teaching Arabic, Dari, and Farsi at the Defense Language Institute in Monterey, California, and racing motorcycles.

Finally, in February 2012, I appeared before the female DOHA judge who had flown to nearby San Jose for the hearing. I said, "Your Honor, I worked for the government for thirty-three years. When I was getting shot at or going behind enemy lines, no one challenged my security clearance. Now when I'm trying to support my family, they pull my clearance and claim that I have an uncle who is a member of Iran's Revolutionary Guards. First of all, my uncle has never been a member of the Revolutionary Guards. In fact, he despises them and always has. Furthermore, he's been retired for over fifteen years and is now an old man. So none of this makes sense."

The judge overturned the ruling against me and informed me that I could now apply to have my clearance restored. But I was sixty-two years old, and it seemed like a good time to finally settle down.

The Monterey Peninsula appealed to me for a number of reasons, including the spectacular setting and proximity to my family. One day as I walked through a house that was for sale near the coast, I came face-to-face with a woman I had imagined thirty-some years ago in the Philippines when I asked a local artist to draw a portrait of my dream woman. She turned out to be a beautiful Native American named Linda.

I ended up buying the house from her and soon after that we started dating. Two years later, she moved in with me. The portrait of her hangs in our living room. We've lived together ever since.

Life is good!

EPILOGUE

Hearts and Minds

Because of my background as an Iranian-American, I often see at least two sides of any situation. During my career, that usually meant the objectives of the US military and the perspective of the people I encountered in the countries I was stationed. Sometimes we were in those places as friends; sometimes we were fighting enemies. One of the many things I admire most about US Special Forces is the emphasis it places on winning hearts and minds. It's one of the reasons I succeeded in Special Forces and it suited me so well.

When Brigadier General Robert McClure helped found the Green Berets in 1952, he understood that winning a war requires more than weapons, supplies, and troops. Successfully achieving military goals in any country is contingent on the support (or at least compliance) of the local population. General McClure realized that the help of local populations in Europe and elsewhere was a key to the Allied success in World War II.

Because of this, General McClure not only was a strong proponent of bringing the psychology of winning the hearts and minds into the realm of military science but also making it one of the cornerstones of the Green Berets. Since the inception of Special Forces, every recruit, including myself, has received instruction in Psychological Operations (PSYOPS) at the Psychological Warfare Training Center at Fort Bragg. Recruits are also trained in languages, cultural sensitivity, and the study of particular areas of operation (AOs).

To my mind, it's this aspect of Special Forces that makes them "special"—namely, the importance placed on establishing cultural and personal rapport with other peoples. Today, after my many years of service, it's something I believe in even more strongly. I'm encouraged that other elements of the US Special Operations Command—including the Operation Detachment Delta and the US Naval Special Warfare Development Group, commonly known as DEVGRU or SEAL Team 6—are following the SF example.

I grew up in a country in the throes of political turmoil and saw how it impacted my friends and family. I thank God that most of my fellow US citizens have never had to experience violent, abrupt political change. But I've observed that because many people here don't understand what it's like to have their political system uprooted, they lack sympathy for those who do and forget that living under a stable, representative government is a rare privilege that needs to be nurtured and protected.

Our government was designed by enlightened people who realized that individuals are happiest and most productive when they can live under a set of laws that protect their ability to choose what they believe in. Freedom of religion and freedom of speech are unknown in most parts of the world. Kids growing up in many countries in Africa and the Middle East have a set of political and religious beliefs drilled into their heads from birth. Because they aren't taught how to read or write, they have little ability to learn anything else. They're told to distrust Westerners and are highly suspicious of people different from them.

I don't pretend to be a strategist or a political philosopher. Most of what I've learned is based on experience and observation. I believe we as a people and a country face a fundamental choice. We can either make friends around the world, or we can make enemies.

The first step toward making friends is to realize that a huge majority of the people in other parts of the world want the same things we do: peace, prosperity, and happiness. They want a better life for their children. There are more similarities between individuals in Santa Clara, California, and Islamabad, Pakistan, or Tehran, Iran, than there are differences.

It's ignorance, fear, and distrust, often exacerbated by differences in religious beliefs, that underline our differences. It's ignorance, fear, and distrust on our part that could cause us to lose the war on terrorism.

I love the United States and our country's core values, and I've dedicated a large part of my life to defending them. Instead of putting so much emphasis on dropping bombs, launching rockets from drones, and, as an unintended consequence, killing innocent civilians, I believe we should be investing more in helping poor people in the Middle East and North Africa and disseminating our message of tolerance for all people and respect for personal freedom.

Don't get me wrong—there are bad people out there spreading terror, death, and hatred, like the followers of ISIS and Al Qaeda, who need to be captured and destroyed. But in doing so, we have to stop blaming entire religious and national groups. It's wrong and counterproductive.

So far I've visited and worked in fifty-three countries. I've observed over and over that most people everywhere want peace, and a good, healthy, happy life for themselves and their families.

If we help and encourage them in achieving those goals, we will prevail.

ACKNOWLEDGMENTS

Changiz would like to extend special thanks to his Special Forces teammates 1st Sgt. IMA Fenny, 5th SFGA CSM Lopage, Jack Joblen, Paul Pool, members of his first A Team ODA 561: Team Sgt. Phil Quinn, Team leader Mike Repass, and all the rest of the guys who supported me at the beginning; ODA 134 Team Sgt. Larry and all the rest; blood brother and team leader Bernie O'Rorke, who almost killed me; "Black Frog" Charlie Sammon, who can swim like a fish; Sgt. Major Carlo Farnquet, Colonel Boyet; and all my other SF brothers who have fought beside me in combat: Doug Watson, Ron Johnson, Dave Hutchenson, Tom Mude, and Carlo Eshinder. I love you all and would do it all again! God bless America!

And he expresses his eternal love to Linda and his family.

Ralph expresses his deep appreciation to Eric Lupfer, Marc Resnick, Jaime Coyne, and all the copy editors, proofreaders, designers, and marketing and publicity people at SMP. To his dear friends, Changiz and Linda, and especially to his family: John, Michael, Francesca, Alessandra, and Jessie.